PEL

THE PYRAMIDS OF EGYPT

Dr I.E.S. Edwards was born in London in 1909. He was educated at Merchant Taylors' School and Gonville and Caius College, Cambridge, where he was a scholar of the College and a student, scholar, and prizeman of the University. In 1934 he was appointed to the British Museum, became Keeper of Egyptian Antiquities in 1955 and retired in 1974. He has excavated with the Egypt Exploration Society in Egypt and the Sudan and is now a Vice-President of the Society. In 1948 he was awarded the T.E. Peet Travelling Prize by Liverpool University. He was Visiting Professor of Egyptology at Brown University, Providence, Rhode Island, from 1953 to 1954. From 1973 to 1980 he was a member of the Committee of Archaeologists appointed by Unesco to supervise the removal of the temples of Philae. His other publications deal chiefly with the Egyptian language, and he is joint editor of the *Cambridge Ancient History* (Third Edition). He pioneered and chose the objects for the Tutankhamun Exhibition at the British Museum in 1972 and wrote the exhibition catalogue. Dr Edwards, who was elected a Fellow of the British Academy in 1962, was appointed C.B.E. in 1968 and C.M.G. in 1973. He is married and has one daughter.

I. E. S. EDWARDS

THE PYRAMIDS
OF EGYPT

PENGUIN BOOKS

Penguin Books Ltd, Harmondsworth, Middlesex, England
Viking Penguin Inc., 40 West 23rd Street, New York, New York 10010, U.S.A.
Penguin Books Australia Ltd, Ringwood, Victoria, Australia
Penguin Books Canada Ltd, 2801 John Street, Markham, Ontario, Canada L3R 1B4
Penguin Books (N.Z.) Ltd, 182–190 Wairau Road, Auckland 10, New Zealand

First published 1947
Reprinted 1949, 1952, 1954, 1955
Revised edition 1961
Reprinted 1964, 1965, 1967, 1970
Reprinted with revised Bibliography 1972
Reprinted 1975
Reprinted with minor revisions 1976
Reprinted 1977, 1978, 1979
Reprinted with minor revisions 1980
Reprinted 1982
Revised edition 1985

Made and printed in Great Britain by
Hazell Watson & Viney Limited,
Member of the BPCC Group,
Aylesbury, Bucks

CONTENTS

CONTENTS

LIST OF BLACK AND WHITE PLATES

1. Tutankhamun as the sun-god emerging from a lotus growing from the primeval mound. (*Photograph Griffith Institute, Oxford*)

2. Model heads of cattle on the terrace of a Ist Dynasty mastaba. Saqqara. (*Photograph Egypt Exploration Society*)

3. Subsidiary brick mastaba of the Ist Dynasty. Saqqara. (*Photograph Egypt Exploration Society*)

4. Stepped mound in a Ist Dynasty brick mastaba. Saqqara. (*Photograph Service des Antiquités, Cairo*)

5. Mereruka represented emerging from the false door in his tomb-chapel. Saqqara. (*Photograph Gallimard – L'Univers des Formes, Paris*)

6. Wall-relief from the tomb of Mereruka. Above: a fish seized by an otter; below: forepart of a crocodile and a harpooned fish. Saqqara. (*Photograph Gallimard – L'Univers des Formes, Paris*)

7. Reserve head of Seneferu-senb. Cairo Museum. (*Photograph Museum of Fine Arts, Boston, Mass.*)

8. Gateway to the Step Pyramid enclosure. Saqqara. (*Photograph A. Burges and B. Sandkühler*)

9. Limestone relief of Zoser performing a religious ceremony. Step Pyramid, Saqqara. (*Photograph Service des Antiquités, Cairo*)

10. Limestone statue of Zoser. Cairo Museum. (*Photograph Cairo Museum*)

11. Papyrus-stem engaged columns. Saqqara. (*Photograph A. Burges and B. Sandkühler*)

12. Entrance colonnade of the Step Pyramid – a reconstruction by J.-P. Lauer. (*Photograph Service des Antiquités, Cairo*)

13. Tiled panelling in the South Mastaba of Zoser – a reconstruction by Mrs C.M. Firth. (*Photograph Service des Antiquités, Cairo*)

14. The Layer Pyramid. View from the north. Zawiyet el-Aryan. (*Photograph Museum of Fine Arts, Boston, Mass.*)

15. The Layer Pyramid – accretion coatings. Zawiyet el-Aryan. (*Photograph Museum of Fine Arts, Boston, Mass.*)

16. Pyramid of Seila. East side. (*Photograph L.H. Lesko*)

17. Pyramid of Meidum. View from the east. (*Photograph University Museum, Philadelphia*)

18. Seneferu's pyramids at Dahshur. View from the north-west. (*Photograph A. Burges and B. Sandkühler*)

19. Upper corridor of the Bent Pyramid. Dahshur. (*Photograph Service des Antiquités, Cairo*)

20. Upper part of a stela of Seneferu. Dahshur. (*Photograph Service des Antiquités, Cairo*)

21. Cedarwood framework in the upper chamber of the Bent Pyramid. Dahshur. (*Photograph Service des Antiquités, Cairo*)

22. Female offering-bearers personifying Seneferu's estates. Dahshur. (*Photograph Service des Antiquités, Cairo*)

23. Ivory figure of Cheops. Cairo Museum. (*Photograph A. Burges and B. Sandkühler*)

24. The pyramids of Cheops and Chephren. In the foreground are the tomb of Queen Khentkaues and the head of the Sphinx. Giza. Lithograph of drawing by David Roberts, c. 1838. (*Photograph Carol Andrews*)

25. The pyramids of Giza. (*Photograph G. W. Allan*)

26. Entrance to the Great Pyramid. Drawing by E. W. Lane, c. 1826. (*Photograph Griffith Institute, Oxford*)

27. Underground chamber in the Great Pyramid. Giza. Drawing by E. W. Lane, c. 1826. (*Photograph Griffith Institute, Oxford*)

28. Granite plug-blocks in the Ascending Corridor of the Great Pyramid. Giza. Drawing by E. W. Lane, c. 1826. (*Photograph Griffith Institute, Oxford*)

29. Boat of Cheops. Giza. (*Photograph John Ross*)

30. Gilded canopy and furniture of Hetepheres. Cairo Museum. (*Photograph Museum of Fine Arts, Boston, Mass.*)

31. The Giant Sphinx of Chephren. Giza. (*Photograph A. Burges and B. Sandkühler*)

32. The Giant Sphinx of Chephren largely engulfed in sand. Giza. Drawing by E. W. Lane, c. 1826. (*Photograph Griffith Institute, Oxford*)

33. The valley building of Chephren. Giza. (*Photograph A. Burges and B. Sandkühler*)

34. Diorite statue of Chephren. Cairo Museum. (*Photograph John Ross*)

35. Pyramid and mortuary temple of Chephren. Giza. (*Photograph A. Burges and B. Sandkühler*)

36. Schist triad: Mycerinus, Hathor and the goddess of the jackal-*nome*. Cairo Museum. (*Photograph A. Burges and B. Sandkühler*)

37. Schist group-statue of Mycerinus and Queen Khamerernebty II. Boston Museum. (*Photograph Museum of Fine Arts, Boston, Mass.*)

38. Quartzite head of Djedefrē. Louvre Museum. (*Photograph Louvre Museum*)

39. Podium of obelisk and alabaster altar in the sun-temple of Niuserrē. Abu Gurab. (*Photograph A. Burges and B. Sandkühler*)

40. Schist head from the sun-temple of Userkaf. Abu Gurab. (*Photograph H. Ricke*)

41. Head of a colossal granite statue of Userkaf. Cairo Museum. (*Photograph A. Burges and B. Sandkühler*)

42. The pyramid of Neferirkarē showing the inner stepped formation. View from the north-north-east. In the foreground is part of the mortuary temple of Sahurē. Abu Sir. (*Photograph Andreas Brodbeck*)

43. Causeway of the pyramid of Unas. Saqqara. (*Annales du Service des Antiquités, Vol. 38, Plate XCIV*)

44. Burial-chamber of Merenrē, showing Pyramid Texts, and his granite sarcophagus and Canopic chest. Saqqara. (*Photograph Gallimard – L'Univers des Formes, Paris*)

45. Alabaster figure of Pepi II as a child. Cairo Museum. (*Photograph A. Burges and B. Sandkühler*)

46. Ruined funerary temple of Neb-hepet-Rē Mentuhotep. Deir el-Bahri, Thebes. (*Photograph A. J. Arkell*)

47. Limestone statue of Sesostris I. Cairo Museum. (*Photograph Cairo Museum*)

48. Limestone panel inscribed with the name of Sesostris I. Metropolitan Museum of Art. (*Photograph Metropolitan Museum of Art, New York*)

49a. Gold cloisonné tie and Hathor-pendant of a necklace inlaid with lapis lazuli, feldspar and carnelian from the tomb of Sat-Hathor at Dahshur. Cairo Museum. (*Photograph A. Burges and B. Sandkühler*)

49b. Gold cloisonné clasp of a bracelet inlaid with lapis lazuli, feldspar and carnelian from the tomb of Sat-Hathor at Dahshur. Cairo Museum. (*Photograph A. Burges and B. Sandkühler*)

49c. Gold cloisonné pectoral with the name of Sesostris II and inlaid with lapis lazuli, feldspar and carnelian from the tomb of Sat-Hathor at Dahshur. Cairo Museum. (*Photograph A. Burges and B. Sandkühler*)

50a, b. Gold cloisonné pectorals with the names of Sesostris III and Ammenemes II and inlaid with lapis lazuli, carnelian and feldspar from the tomb of Merit at Dahshur. Cairo Museum. (*Photograph A. Burges and B. Sandkühler*)

51. The pyramid of Ammenemes III. In the foreground are the remains of brick residences of priests on the north side of the causeway. Dahshur. (*Photograph Dieter Arnold*)

52. Tomb-chamber and sarcophagus of Ammenemes III. Dahshur. (*Photograph Dieter Arnold*)

53. Upper part of a granite statuette of Khendjer. Cairo Museum. (*Photograph A. Burges and B. Sandkühler*)

54. Natural pyramid dominating the Valley of the Kings, Luxor. In the foreground is a modern wall protecting the approach to the tomb of Tutankhamun. (*Photograph Carol Andrews*)

55. The pyramid of Tirhaqa. Nuri. (*Photograph Museum of Fine Arts, Boston, Mass.*)

56. Pyramids in the northern cemetery. Meroe. (*Photograph Museum of Fine Arts, Boston, Mass.*)

57. Trenches cut in the rock for levelling. Giza. (*Photograph Jean Battersby*)

58. Copper implements of the Ist Dynasty. Cairo Museum. (*Photograph Service des Antiquités, Cairo*)

59. Quarrymen's wedge-slots. Aswan.

60. Limestone model of a step pyramid. Petrie Museum. (*Photograph University College, London*)

61. Limestone model of the Hawara pyramid. Petrie Museum. (*Photograph University College, London*)

62. Relics of brick retaining walls of a building-ramp at the First Pylon of the temple of Karnak. (*Photograph Robert Edwards*)

63. Tomb-chapel of Tia, a sister of Ramesses II, and her husband (also named Tia). The lower part of a pyramid can be seen in the foreground. Saqqara. (*Photograph G. T. Martin*)

LIST OF FIGURES

PREFACE
TO THE FIRST EDITION

The following chapters are, in the first place, an attempt to describe some of the principal features of a number of pyramids, nearly all of which were built over a period of about a thousand years. Only those pyramids which illustrate most clearly the evolution and subsequent decline of that class of tomb are discussed in any detail, the remainder being merely mentioned in passing. The last chapter gives some account of the methods employed in construction and of the motives which prompted the Egyptian kings to adopt the pyramid form.

Although I have visited, either before or during the war, most of the pyramids described and have made use of notes which I recorded on their sites, a considerable part of the factual matter is, of necessity, taken from the published reports of the various archaeologists who have surveyed or excavated these monuments in the course of the past century. My debt to these archaeologists and to the publishers of their reports will be apparent to every reader. Many of the interpretations given are also based on the works of previous writers; in some cases, however, I have ventured to offer explanations of my own.

I must here express my gratitude to the friends who have helped me in different ways when writing the book and, in particular, to John Cruikshank Rose, whose line-drawings are an indispensable adjunct to the text. Some of the drawings have been adapted in points of detail by Mr Rose, either because direct reproductions from the publications in which they first appeared would have been unsuitable for the purpose of this book or because subsequent archaeological discoveries have necessitated small adjustments. The authors of the books or articles from which the drawings were made are listed at the beginning of the book. For the opportunity of consulting these works while in the Middle East, I am greatly indebted to Mr Bernhard Grdseloff, Librarian of the Egyptological Institute of the late Dr Ludwig Borchardt in Cairo; to Dr I. Ben-Dor, Librarian of the Palestine Archaeological Museum in Jerusalem; to Dr Nelson Glueck, Director of the American School of Oriental Research in Jerusalem; and to Mr Seton Lloyd,

Technical Adviser to the Directorate of Antiquities in Baghdad. Mr ‑Guy Brunton, of the Cairo Museum, kindly enabled me to obtain the photographs of objects in that museum which are included among the Plates. For similar assistance in securing a photograph of the group-statue reproduced in Plate 37, my thanks are due to Mr Dows Dunham of the Museum of Fine Arts, Boston. The authorities of the Metropolitan Museum have shown great generosity in allowing me to include fig. 44 before the final report of the excavation has been published. My visits to the various pyramid sites were greatly facilitated by Dr Étienne Drioton, Director-General of the Service des Antiquités, and by local officials of the Service.

In forming my conclusions on several problems touched upon in the course of the book, I have received valuable help from discussion with Lieut.‑Colonel W.B. Emery, to whose excavations references appear in the text; with Professor J. Černý of London University; with Mr Bernhard Grdseloff; with Mr H.W. Fairman, Director of the Egypt Exploration Society's excavations in the two years before the war, and with Lieut.‑Colonel R.D.H. Jones of the Royal Engineers. My special thanks are due to Professor A.M. Blackman of Liverpool University, and to Professor S.R.K. Glanville of Cambridge University, both of whom read my entire typescript before it went to press and whose suggestions have resulted in the introduction of several improvements; also to Dr Sidney Smith, Keeper of the Department of Egyptian and Assyrian Antiquities in the British Museum, who read the last chapter and contributed many helpful comments. Finally, I owe a particular debt of gratitude to my wife, who not only typed the whole of my manuscript, but helped to improve the wording of many passages in the text.

I. E. S. EDWARDS
London, 1946

PREFACE
TO THE REVISED EDITION

Since 1947, when the first edition of this book appeared, discoveries of the highest importance for tracing the early history of the pyramids have been made, chiefly by the Antiquities' Department of the Egyptian Government, at Saqqara and Dahshur. Excavations by the Egypt Exploration Society at the early dynastic cemetery of North Saqqara have yielded evidence which seems to supply a vital link in the chain of development from the simple tomb of the predynastic period to the Step Pyramid of Zoser. Notable additions to knowledge have resulted from surveys by J.-P. Lauer of the mortuary temples of the Great Pyramid and of the pyramid of Userkaf. Many useful details have also emerged from the investigations of the Fondation Égyptologique Reine Élisabeth at the pyramid of El-Kulah and from the work of the Swiss and the German Institutes of Archaeology in Cairo at the sun-temple of Userkaf.

No less striking than the discoveries made in the field has been the number of books and articles on subjects dealing directly or indirectly with pyramids which have appeared since 1947. More than a quarter of all the publications included in the Bibliography fall into this category.

In order to take into account the additional information now available, it has been necessary to expand the text of the present edition in comparison with its predecessor. Discussions which time had rendered out of date have been revised and some fresh problems have been mentioned. Advantage has been taken of the opportunity now offered to augment very considerably the number of illustrations. Once again I am indebted to Mr John Rose, who devoted to the preparation of the drawings many hours of his leave from his duties in the service of the Government of the West Indies. For the additional photographic illustrations I am especially grateful to Herr A. Burges and Herr B. Sandkühler, who have generously allowed me to include no fewer than seventeen photographs from their private collection. Other friends who have kindly provided photographs are Mr G.W. Allan, Professor R. Anthes, Professor W.B. Emery, Dr Ahmed Fakhry, Dr W.C. Hayes,

Dr W.S. Smith, Dr H. Ricke, and Monsieur J. Vandier. Dr R.A. Caminos, Dr Ricke, and Monsieur J.-P. Lauer have kindly assisted me by answering queries. To my wife I owe a particular debt of gratitude for again typing the whole manuscript and for her help in keeping a watchful eye on details of presentation.

I. E. S. EDWARDS
London, 1961

PREFACE

No branch of Egyptology has received, in recent years, more attention from scholars than the study of pyramids. Since the last major revision of this book appeared, more than twenty years ago, additional pyramids have been discovered, scientific excavations have been conducted at pyramid sites which had previously been examined only rather superficially, and written documents of the highest importance for understanding how pyramids and the temples associated with them were maintained and administered have been studied and published. The resultant advances in knowledge, which have necessitated a substantial increase in the length of the text, have been achieved by archaeologists of many nationalities, notably Egyptian, French, German, Czechoslovak, Italian and British. Between 1965 and 1977 some twenty pyramid complexes were surveyed by two Italians, V. Maragioglio and C.A. Rinaldi, both of whom died before completing their project, but the six volumes of reports and observations which they were able to finish constitute a work of reference of inestimable value to those who wish to study the geometry and measurements of pyramids.

Wherever possible I have mentioned, either in the text or in the Bibliography, the names of those archaeologists who were mainly responsible for the exploration of the monuments described. I am conscious of my indebtedness to all of them, and to none more than the French architect and archaeologist J.-P. Lauer, whose unremitting efforts over nearly sixty years have done so much to bring to our knowledge the architectural marvels of Zoser's Step Pyramid and its surrounding buildings, as well as to reveal and record what have survived of later pyramids at Saqqara. Another archaeologist who has made an outstanding contribution to pyramid studies is Dieter Arnold. As a result of his excavations at Thebes and his reinterpretation of the surviving evidence, our conception of the design of the royal tombs of the XIth Dynasty has undergone some radical changes.

In order to obtain information about current or recent excavations,

I have consulted the heads of the missions responsible for them, and in particular the following: Dr Miroslav Verner, director of the Prague University excavations at Abu Sir, Dr Rainer Stadelmann, director of the excavations of the German Archaeological Institute in Cairo at the northern pyramid of Dahshur, Dr Nabil Swelim, who discovered a small pyramid at Abydos, and Dr G.T. Martin, director of the Egypt Exploration Society's excavations at the New Kingdom necropolis at Saqqara. Dr Gerhard Haeny, Director of the Swiss Institute in Cairo, Dr Manfred Bietak, Director of the Austrian Institute in Cairo, Professor and Mrs L.H. Lesko, of Brown University, Providence, and Dr Jaromir Málek, of the Griffith Institute, Oxford, have very kindly replied in detail to questions which I addressed to them. I have also profited greatly from discussions with members of my former department in the British Museum.

Besides the archaeologists, to whom I owe so much for providing the basic material necessary for explaining the significance of the two kinds of pyramid, I am also indebted to a number of other helpers, especially to my wife, who has again given me secretarial assistance and advice on presentation, to Sir Irvine Goulding, whose help I sought on a mathematical problem, to Mr C.F.J. Lisle, a civil engineer, Professor Rushdi Said, a geologist, and Professor Magdi Wahba, an Arabic philologist and lexicographer. Sources of the illustrations are noted in the lists of plates and drawings. The entries are intended to serve two purposes: as acknowledgements of my gratitude to those who supplied the illustrations and, where appropriate, as references to the original sources in books and articles from which the illustrations were obtained. In this connection, I have to record with sadness that John Cruikshank Rose, who produced all those drawings which first appeared in the previous editions and are repeated here, died in the West Indies in 1971. Alterations rendered necessary by further knowledge, together with a small number of additional drawings, have been made by the staff of the publishers. I am very grateful to them, and particularly to Catriona Luckhurst, for all the friendly cooperation I have received while carrying out this revision.

I. E. S. EDWARDS
Deddington, Oxford, 1985

INTRODUCTION

One of the first questions which occur to the mind of anyone looking at an ancient monument is its date. In the case of Egyptian monuments it is often difficult, and sometimes impossible, to answer the question in terms of years before the beginning of the Christian era, because our knowledge of Egyptian chronology, especially in the early periods, is still very incomplete. We know the main sequence of events and frequently their relationship to one another, but, except in rare instances, an exact chronology will not be possible until the discovery of material of a different and more precisely datable character than anything found hitherto.

Partly for the sake of convenience and partly because a century of study has demonstrated that it is fundamentally sound, the method of grouping the kings of Egypt into thirty-one dynasties, which is first known to us from Manetho's *History of Egypt*, has been universally adopted by modern historians as a substitute for closer dating. Since the end of a dynasty did not always entail any very marked political or artistic changes, it has also been found convenient to group the dynasties into periods roughly corresponding with the most important of these changes. There are nine main periods, to which the following names and approximate dates may be given:

I–II Dynasties	Early Dynastic Period, 3100–2686 B.C.
III–VI Dynasties	Old Kingdom, 2686–2181 B.C.
VII–X Dynasties	First Intermediate Period, 2181–2133 B.C.
XI–XII Dynasties	Middle Kingdom, 2133–1786 B.C.
XIII–XVII Dynasties	Second Intermediate Period, 1786–1567 B.C.
XVIII–XX Dynasties	New Kingdom, 1567–1080 B.C.

I

XXI–XXV Dynasties	Late New Kingdom, 1080–664 B.C.
XXVI Dynasty	Saite Period, 664–525 B.C.
XXVII–XXXI Dynasties	Late Period, 525–332 B.C.

The Pyramid Age, *par excellence*, covers the second of these groups – the period beginning with the IIIrd Dynasty and ending with the VIth Dynasty. During this time the kings, with few exceptions, and many of their queens were buried in tombs having superstructures in pyramidal form. Pyramids were also built for several kings and queens of the subsequent dynasties, but they were in the nature of archaisms, lacking not only much of the architectural splendour of their predecessors, but also some of their religious significance. The total number at present known in Egypt is about ninety; many of them, it is true, are reduced to little more than sand and rubble, but they are still recognizable to the archaeologist as having once been pyramids.

Those pyramids which belong to the Pyramid Age were, in almost every instance, built on the fringe of the desert west of the Nile in the neighbourhood of Memphis, between Meidum in the south and Abu Roash in the north. If later tradition is to be believed, Memphis was built on ground which had been reclaimed by Menes, the first dynastic ruler of Egypt, by dyking the Nile so that it flowed through a channel to the east of its original course. Whether or not this tradition is true in detail, there can be little doubt that it was Menes who founded Memphis, for the archaeological remains in its immediate vicinity dating from the time of the Ist Dynasty are plentiful, whereas nothing has yet been found there which can be ascribed to an earlier period. The discovery of a considerable number of predynastic settlements near the Mukattam hills, on the opposite bank of the river, only emphasizes the complete absence of any corresponding settlements at Memphis itself.

Hitherto, it has not been possible to determine with certainty whether Memphis was designed by Menes to be the capital of Egypt or whether it was originally built simply as a fortress-city and became the seat of government at some later date, perhaps at the beginning of the IIIrd Dynasty. The circumstances surrounding the accession of Menes to the throne would undoubtedly favour the choice of just such a place for his capital. Before his reign, Egypt was composed of two

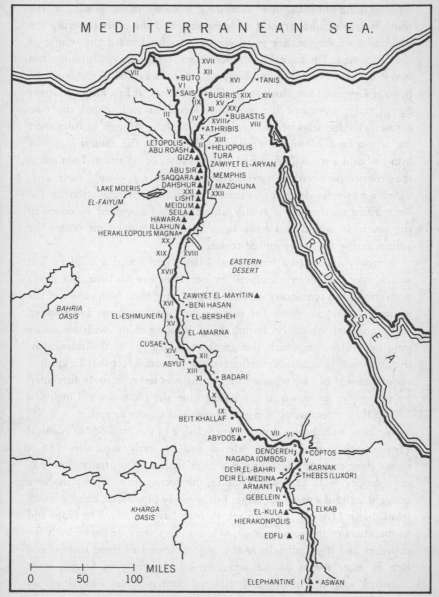

M E D I T E R R A N E A N   S E A.

XVII
XII
VII   • BUTO   XVI   • TANIS
VI
V   • SAIS   • BUSIRIS XIX   XIV
IX   XV   XX
XI   • BUBASTIS
III   IV   XVIII/
• ATHRIBIS   VIII
X   XIII
LETOPOLIS •   II   • HELIOPOLIS
ABU ROASH ▲   TURA
GIZA ▲   ZAWIYET EL-ARYAN
ABU SIR ▲   MEMPHIS
SAQQARA ▲▲   MAZGHUNA
LAKE MOERIS   DAHSHUR ▲   XXI ▲
EL-FAIYUM   LISHT ▲   XXII
MEIDUM ▲
SEILA ▲
HAWARA ▲
ILLAHUN ▲
HERAKLEOPOLIS MAGNA •
XX
XIX   XVIII
EASTERN
XVII   DESERT

BAHRIA   XVI   ZAWIYET EL-MAYITIN ▲
OASIS   • BENI HASAN
EL-ESHMUNEIN ○   • EL-BERSHEH
XV
○ EL-AMARNA
CUSAE ○
XIV   XII
ASYUT •
XIII
XI   • BADARI
X
IX
BEIT KHALLAF •
VIII   VII VI
ABYDOS ▲ ○
DENDEREH •   ○ COPTOS
NAGADA (OMBOS) ▲   V
DEIR EL-BAHRI ○   KARNAK
DEIR EL-MEDINA •   THEBES (LUXOR)
ARMANT IV
GEBELEIN ○
KHARGA   EL-KULA ▲   ○ ELKAB
OASIS   HIERAKONPOLIS •
EDFU ▲   II

MILES
0   50   100

ELEPHANTINE I ▲ ○ ASWAN

Figure 1. Sketch-map of Egypt

3

separate kingdoms: the one extending possibly from Aswan, in the south, to the neighbourhood of Memphis, and the other covering the remainder of the country northwards, which included the whole of the Delta area. The capital of the southern (Upper Egyptian) kingdom was situated at Nekhen (Hierakonpolis) and the capital of the northern (Lower Egyptian) kingdom at Pe (Buto). Menes, at first king of Upper Egypt only, overcame the northern kingdom and united the two former kingdoms under one crown, establishing himself as ruler over the whole land. Memphis would thus have been the natural place for him to build a strongly fortified city because, being situated almost at the frontier between the two former kingdoms, it would have provided a powerful deterrent against any attempts at retaliation by the vanquished northerners if at any time they had suspected weakness in the south. It would also have been the most convenient centre for administering the newly united country.

By unifying the two kingdoms, Menes performed a military feat which may have been attempted by others before his time, but never with more than temporary success. Menes, however, both achieved the military victory necessary for uniting the two kingdoms and ensured that its effects would be lasting by following it up with an astute political policy, on which the greatness of Egypt in the subsequent dynasties was founded. Nevertheless, the historical fact that Egypt had once consisted of two separate kingdoms was never entirely forgotten by its people, for down to the latest times the pharaohs still included among their titles that of 'King of Upper and Lower Egypt'.

We have scarcely any detailed knowledge of the methods of political administration employed by Menes and his early successors, but it seems clear that they introduced a high degree of centralization. Excavations by W.B. Emery at Saqqara, the necropolis of Memphis, have brought to light a group of large, but severely plundered, tombs dating from the Ist Dynasty, some of which may have belonged to kings and to members of the royal family, while others were certainly built for courtiers and high officials. Many objects found in these tombs, and also in other tombs of the same period elsewhere in Egypt, were inscribed with the names and titles of contemporary officials, from which it is possible to deduce that the king was surrounded by a large body of counsellors and executives; a complete lack of biographical detail, however, precludes any reconstruction of their personal history.

Even before the reign of Menes, Egypt was divided into districts, which we generally call *nomes* after their Greek name. Their number had probably varied from time to time, as the more powerful had absorbed the weaker or the larger had decayed internally and had disintegrated; eventually there were forty-two, twenty-two in Upper Egypt and twenty in Lower Egypt, but the number in the time of Menes is not known. Menes allowed the *nomes* to continue as separate units, but placed at the head of each a governor, who was responsible for directing its social and religious affairs. At first these governors, or nomarchs as they are generally called, held office for only a limited period, but by degrees the office became the hereditary right of certain families. Thus there grew up a provincial ruling class which gradually threatened the authority of the king until, at the end of the VIth Dynasty, it played an important part in the collapse of the monarchy.

We know little about the political constitution of the *nomes* or their relations with the capital – though doubtless each *nome* was required to contribute to the royal exchequer – but it seems clear that they were permitted a very high degree of religious independence. Every *nome* possessed its own local deity or deities, usually represented in animal form or in human form with an animal head: Wepwawet, the wolf-god of the Asyut *nome*, Bastet, the cat-goddess of Bubastis, and Harsaphes, the ram-headed god of Herakleopolis, are examples. Some local gods, however, were always represented entirely anthropomorphically, Ptah of Memphis, Min of Coptos, and Osiris being three of the best known.

Within a single *nome* many different deities might be worshipped, their relative importance naturally varying according to the number of their adherents and the wealth of their temples. In the Memphite *nome*, for example, there were, besides the principal god Ptah, also Sakhmet, a lioness-headed goddess, Nefertem, an anthropomorphic god with a lotus-flower head-dress, and Sokar, a falcon-headed god who dwelt in the desert west of Memphis. Each of these deities originally possessed an independent sanctuary, but, in the course of time, Ptah, Sakhmet, and Nefertem came to be considered as a single family and were worshipped in one sanctuary. There were similar triads elsewhere – Osiris, Isis, and Horus forming the most famous.

In permitting complete religious independence to the different *nomes*, the early kings can hardly be accused of having allowed their conduct of affairs to be dictated by reasons of political expediency; in an age when polytheism was the universally accepted philosophy, no alteration in the established religious order would have seemed to them either necessary or desirable. With the possible exception of a few gods connected with the elements, who appear to have gained wider recognition at a very early date, most of the deities were regarded as having authority mainly within fixed geographical limits. It is certainly useless to speculate on the effect which a less liberal policy would have had on the subsequent development of Egyptian religion. But it is of importance to realize that the different elements which determined the character of that religion, as it is known to us, were chiefly local in origin. Herein lies the reason for many of the divergent, and sometimes even contradictory, beliefs held by the Egyptians in dynastic times.

The development of an official religion began in the Pyramid Age. It was derived from the cult of a temple with a powerful priesthood, situated a little to the north of Memphis at the city which the Greeks later called Heliopolis, known to the ancient Egyptians as On and so named in the Book of Genesis, where Potipherah is described as a priest of On. In very ancient times the cult of this temple was represented by a fetish in the form of a pillar, but by the beginning of the IVth Dynasty it had become the centre of the sun religion. The most sacred object within the temple was the *benben*, probably a conically shaped stone which was thought to symbolize the first phenomenon in the creation of this earth.

One of the most popular myths concerning the creation portrayed the earth as a mound which rose from Nun, the personification of the primordial ocean. A lotus grew on the mound and from it emerged the sun-god, thus bringing life into existence. This myth is well illustrated in a painted wooden model from the tomb of Tutankhamun, which represents the young king as the sun-god with his head and neck projecting from the flower (Plate 1). When they conceived these ideas the Egyptians must have been influenced by the reappearance of patches of high ground as the flood-waters of the Nile began to subside each year after the inundation. The similarity was enhanced by the growth of vegetation on the high ground and the seemingly autogenic appearance of the lotus on the primeval mound. The lotus itself added to the force of the image, not only because it was an aquatic plant, but because it reacted to the light of the sun by opening its petals. In a variant version of the myth, the sun-god was alleged to have revealed himself on the primeval mound as a bird, which the Egyptians of later times represented as a heron and the Greeks identified as their phoenix. This image too was prompted by nature and the common sight of wading birds alighting on the turtlebacks left by the flood-waters.

Early in their history the priests of Heliopolis evolved a cosmogony which affirmed that Rē-Atum, the sun-god, had generated himself out of Nun. Rē-Atum's offspring were Shu, the god of the air, and Tefnut, goddess of moisture, who in turn had given birth to Geb, the earth-god, and Nut, the sky-goddess. From Geb and Nut had sprung Osiris, Isis, Seth, and Nephthys. These nine deities were known as the Great Ennead of Heliopolis. There was also a Little Ennead, composed of a group of lesser gods under the leadership of Horus.

Rē-Atum was not, however, the only form in which the sun-god was worshipped at Heliopolis: Harakhte - meaning Horus of the horizon - and Khepri, in the form of a scarab, were also venerated there. Some attempt was made by the Heliopolitan priesthood to differentiate between these forms, Khepri being regarded as the morning sun and Rē-Atum as the evening sun, but the distinction was never very strictly observed. The Egyptians of the Pyramid Age clearly found little difficulty in regarding their sun-god not as a single indivisible being but rather as a composite deity whose various attributes were derived from local solar deities, originally separate and subsequently united, without proper co-ordination, with Rē of Heliopolis. Some of the constituent deities can be identified by their special functions or by their epithets. One, for instance, was the sun-god with whom the king became integrated after his death. Others, whose epithets are known, are 'Rē in the *senut*-house', 'Rē in the sanctuary of Upper Egypt' and 'Rē on the roof' (of the temple of Heliopolis). In these circumstances it is not surprising that the sun-cult contains many inconsistencies as it is presented in the earliest body of religious texts in our possession, namely the texts carved on the walls of the chambers and corridors of pyramids in the late Vth and the VIth Dynasties.

In order to illustrate the divergent beliefs which might exist simultaneously, it is only necessary to cite the various explanations offered to account for the daily passage of the sun across the earth. According to the view most commonly accepted, Rē, accompanied by his retinue, traversed the sky each day in a boat. The moon and the stars were likewise believed to journey across the sky in ships. No method of transport would seem more natural to the ancient Egyptian than a ship, for both he and his ancestors from time immemorial had used the Nile to travel from place to place, and it was only logical that the heavenly bodies should be conveyed on their celestial journey by similar means.

According to another school of thought, the sun was carried through the firmament on wings, like a bird. This belief was particularly associated with the sun-god in the form of Harakhte, who, since the earliest times, had been regarded as a falcon. Inasmuch as no visible object could support itself for long in the air unless it had wings, it must have seemed only reasonable that the sun should be subject to the same fundamental laws as other bodies. The falcon was chosen because it excelled all other birds known to the Egyptians in its ability to fly at a very great height.

Possibly the most picturesque of all the different ideas concerning the passage of the sun across the sky was that which ascribed to the sun-god the form of a scarab-beetle; this conception was especially connected with him in his name of Khepri. The ancient Egyptian was familiar with the spectacle of the scarab-beetle pushing a ball of dung along the ground until it found a suitable crevice in which to deposit it. From this ball, he believed, the young scarab, by a process of self-generation, subsequently emerged. In view of an imagined resemblance between the sun, regarded as the source of all life, and the ball of dung from which the young scarab was thought to emerge, it is not surprising that the force which propelled the sun across the sky, namely the sun-god, should have been pictured as an enormous beetle, which pushed the sun as its earthly counterpart pushed the ball of dung. In this connection it is immaterial that modern entomologists have shown that the ball of dung rolled along by the beetle is simply a reserve food-supply, while the one which contains the egg is not spherical but pear-shaped, and is kept in a hole by the mother-insect until the egg has hatched.

The nocturnal course of the sun also gave rise to different theories. There was the natural explanation that it spent the hours of darkness passing by ship through the underworld, called the Det (commonly known as the Duat), before reappearing above ground each day at sunrise. A more fanciful solution, however, postulated that the sky was formed by the body of the goddess Nut, spanning the earth like an enormous arch, with her head on a level with the western horizon, her groin on the eastern horizon, and her arms and legs extended beneath the horizons. The sun was consumed by this goddess every evening at sunset and traversed her body during the night, to be reborn at sunrise. It was an explanation which never lost its appeal to the Egyptians and which, until the latest times, continued side by side with that of the sun's nocturnal passage through the Det.

The solar cult of Heliopolis, while exercising a predominant influence on the religion of the pyramid builders, was compelled to recognize, and in time to incorporate within its theology, a cult which was certainly not solar in origin, namely that of the god Osiris. This cult, in the form in which we know it, suffers from almost as many inconsistencies as that of the sun, and from a similar necessity to embody beliefs derived from originally unrelated local gods into the cult of the principal god with whom they had become assimilated.

In remote antiquity, before the union of Upper and Lower Egypt under Menes, Osiris had been probably first the king and then the local god of the ninth Lower Egyptian *nome* with its capital at Busiris. Subsequently his influence spread until he became the chief god of a group of *nomes* in the eastern Delta. At some time during this development he was identified with a local god named Andjeti and assumed his insignia – the shepherd's crook and the flail. Horus, later regarded as the son of Osiris, was at this time a completely independent god, ruling a group of *nomes* in the western Delta. Isis, who figures in pyramid times as the wife of Osiris, seems also to have been a Delta goddess, but nothing is known with certainty about her origin.

After the cult of Osiris had become linked with that of Horus, its influence began to extend southwards until, by pyramid times, Osiris had become identified with Sokar, the god of the Memphite necropolis, Wepwawet, the wolf-god of Asyut, Khentiamentiu, the jackal-god of Abydos, and possibly others. The most important of these associations was undoubtedly that with Khentiamentiu, for, with the advance of time, Osiris came to be connected primarily with Abydos, while Busiris, his original home, gradually lost its significance.

Egyptian religious texts, though containing innumerable references to the legend on which the cult of Osiris was based, nowhere give a full and connected account of it. The reason for this omission is not far to seek, for the legend must have been so well known in ancient times that a detailed record was unnecessary. The earliest complete version known at present is that of Plutarch in his work *De Iside et Osiride*, which, though differing in detail, agrees in all important respects with the allusions in the Egyptian texts and must therefore represent substantially the standard account of all time. The following are the main features of the narrative as preserved in Plutarch and the Egyptian texts:

Osiris, the elder son of the earth-god Geb and the sky-goddess Nut, ruled as a just and benevolent king over the whole earth, instructing mankind in the various arts and crafts and converting them from barbarism to a state of civilization. In time, however, his brother Seth, prompted by jealousy, murdered him. Plutarch states that the murder was committed by a cunningly conceived trick: Seth, having prepared a banquet ostensibly in honour of his brother's return to Egypt from a foreign land, invited seventy-two of his friends to attend as guests. In the course of the meal a chest of clever workmanship was carried into the room and offered by Seth as a present to anyone who, when lying down inside it, fitted it exactly. By a prearranged plan, a number of the other guests first tried the chest, but were not of the right size. Osiris then entered it and, owing to his unusual dimensions, exactly fitted it. While he was still inside the chest, however, some of the accomplices closed it and carried it to the Nile. After ferrying it downstream to the Tanite mouth, they cast it adrift in the sea, which at length washed it ashore at Byblos.

Isis, when she discovered that Osiris had been murdered, set out on a long and eventful search for his corpse, which she ultimately found and brought back to Egypt from Byblos. For a time she remained at Khemmis, in the marshes of the Delta, keeping watch over the coffin of Osiris and awaiting the birth of her child Horus, who appears to have been conceived after his father's death. Seth, however, when out hunting, discovered the coffin and removed the body, which he cut up into fourteen or sixteen pieces, scattering them over different parts of Egypt. Isis again went in search of the body, and buried each piece in the place where she found it – the head at Abydos, the neck at Heliopolis, the left thigh at Bigeh, and other parts elsewhere. The only part missing was the virile member, which had been thrown by Seth into the river and devoured by the fish of Oxyrhynchus.

Another version of the story states that, after Isis had found the body, Rē ordered Anubis to embalm it; Isis then fluttered her wings over it and restored it to life. It is an important variant, because the process of embalmment, as we know it from the Egyptian mummies, was certainly connected closely with the Osirian legend. After being restored to life, Osiris became king of the region of the dead and thus assumed the role in which he figures throughout historical times.

The remainder of this legend, which is recorded on an excellently preserved papyrus from the New Kingdom, concerns the long and furious struggle between Seth and Horus, who resolved to slay his uncle and thus avenge his father's death. In the course of the struggle Seth plucked out one of his nephew's eyes, but Horus triumphed in the end and succeeded to the throne of Osiris. His missing eye was restored by the god Thoth and his title to his father's throne was endorsed by the verdict of a tribunal of the gods of Heliopolis. As a result of this episode, Horus became for all time a model of filial devotion, while the eye which he lost in the struggle was henceforth regarded as a symbol for every form of sacrifice.

The sun-cult and the cult of Osiris were certainly not connected either in origin or in their main theological conception. Rē was primarily a god of the living, with whom certain privileged persons might be associated after death, while Osiris was essentially the god of the blessed dead and of the region of the dead. Both gods, however, shared one most important feature in common: they provided a divine example of survival after death. Osiris, though murdered by Seth, had been restored to life by the magic of Isis, and Rē, whose daily disappearance beneath the western horizon was considered as his death, was reborn each morning at sunrise. In the experiences of these gods, the ancient Egyptian found reason to hope for his own survival. But a continuance of life after physical death did not follow as a normal and natural consequence: it was something which could only be assured by observing the proper ritual and by supplying the dead with all the material assistance which had been required by the gods for their own survival. Herein lay the need for providing the dead with a tomb, whether pyramid or otherwise, and with a burial which would conform in all the essential elements with an accepted pattern.

In spite of their meticulous attention to detail in practical matters, the Egyptians of the Pyramid Age never evolved a clear and precise conception of the after-life. That conservatism so noticeable in Egyptian art is even more emphasized in matters of religion; elements which had once been admitted into the canon continued side by side with later innovations, even though they were logically superfluous and sometimes irreconcilable. It will be seen that, in a comparable fashion, architectural features were sometimes retained in tombs long after their original purpose had ceased to exist or had been largely superseded. The impression made on the modern mind is that of a people searching in the dark for a key to truth and, having found not one but many keys resembling the pattern of the lock, retaining all lest perchance the appropriate one should be discarded.

Even in very early times, before the Osirian and solar cults had gained any considerable following, the Egyptians believed that man was composed of body and spirit. They also believed that the spirit could remain alive after physical death if the body were preserved and provided with the necessary sustenance. Where the after-life of the spirit was thought to take place is not known, but it may have been in a kind of underworld to which access was gained through the pit of the tomb.

This simple conception of an after-life closely associated with the tomb and dependent on the preservation of the body was never entirely supplanted by other ideas, with the result that, in later times, we find Egyptian tombs provided with every imaginable article for the use of the dead. The tomb of Tutankhamun with its magnificent equipment, which included even chariots and regal accoutrements, is but a single instance of the persistence of this creed in a highly developed form more than two thousand years after its earliest appearance.

A more advanced conception of a blissful after-life gained as a reward for virtue may have been entertained by adherents to the Osirian cult from remote antiquity, but the absence of any contemporary evidence of its beliefs and tenets renders any attempt to reconstruct the creed in its primitive form very hazardous. Even in early times, however, the Osirian hereafter was probably regarded as a kind of idealized version of this world, situated below the western horizon and presided over by Osiris. This region, called by the Egyptians the Fields of Reeds and subsequently known to the Greeks as the Elysian Fields, was represented in later times as a group of isles reached by a magic boat, where those who had been accepted by the god could dwell in perpetual spring. As was only fitting to the kingdom of the god of fertility, the ground yielded fabulous harvests, with corn growing to a height of nine cubits. The cultivation of these crops provided the fortunate dwellers of the Elysian Fields with their main occupation.

Abydos assumed a position of unique importance in the Osirian creed, and early supplanted Busiris as the chief centre of the cult. Temples equal in magnificence to any in Egypt were built there and dedicated to the god. It was at Abydos, according to one tradition, that Isis had found and buried the head of Osiris; another tradition alleged that she had buried there the whole of the body with the exception of the virile member. Every year it was the scene of a solemn festival, including a Passion Play in which the principal events in the life and death of Osiris were re-enacted. The thousands of potsherds still lying on the ground testify to the number of offerings presented to the god by pilgrims.

It was inconceivable to the ancient Egyptians, who regarded the after-life as a kind of mirror of this world, that an event of such importance in his earthly life as the annual festival at Abydos should not have its counterpart in the life to come. From the end of the Old Kingdom, therefore, many tombs were equipped with boats to enable their owners to make the journey to Abydos. By the Middle Kingdom, and possibly very much earlier, those who could afford the cost of a second tomb might even build a cenotaph at Abydos; their spirits could thus dwell at will near Osiris and participate in his annual festival, while still maintaining through their real tombs the link with their native towns. For instance, Sesostris III, one of the greatest kings of the Middle Kingdom, caused a rock cenotaph to be hewn for himself at Abydos, while his body was buried in his pyramid at Dahshur. Those who could not afford a cenotaph would often set up, near the supposed shrine of Osiris, a stone slab carved with figures in relief and bearing an inscription, generally of a formal character, in order to ensure that their names would remain perpetually in the presence of the god.

In all matters concerning their religion, the Egyptians placed considerable reliance on the magic power of the written word. They believed that, by using the correct formulas, they could impose their will upon the gods. The spells carved on the walls of the chambers and corridors of the late Vth and the VIth Dynasty pyramids are the best example of this form of magic in the Pyramid Age. A remarkable instance, however, is also provided by the Osirian practice of placing the name of Osiris as a title before the name of the dead, with the object of transforming him into the god himself. The explanation of this universal deification may be that it was an extension of a privilege originally intended for the king alone. During his earthly life he was considered as the embodiment of Horus, the son of Osiris; it was only natural, therefore, that he should be regarded as Osiris when he had died and his son, the next embodiment of Horus, had succeeded him on the throne. In time, the privilege of becoming an Osiris was extended, first to other members of the royal family, then to a few chosen people not of royal blood, and finally it became a right claimed by all. We cannot actually trace these successive stages in the democratization of the Osirian cult, but comparison with the course followed by other religious and funerary practices enables its development to be conjectured with a measure of probability.

In the solar cult also the after-life was originally considered as a royal prerogative. This after-life, however, was not to be spent either in the west or in the underworld, but in a celestial region in the east. To reach it, the dead king must cross a lake, called the 'Lily Lake', which extended from the northern horizon to that of the south. An austere figure named 'He-who-looks-behind-himself' – a name resulting from the belief that he performed his duties facing backwards – ferried him across the lake, but only after he had been convinced that the king was entitled to enter the 'Fields where the gods were begotten, over which the gods rejoice on their New Year's Days', as the eastern side was called. In order to convince the ferryman, the king could resort to a number of different stratagems: he could try to persuade him that he was bringing the sun-god something which he needed; he could pretend that the sun-god required him to perform some function; or he might have recourse to magic and take with him a jar containing a substance which would render the ferryman impotent to resist his demands. If other means failed, the king could entreat the sun-god himself to instruct the ferryman to grant him a passage.

Having crossed the lake, the king arrived at the gates of the other world. Heralds were standing in readiness to announce the news of his arrival and the gods immediately gathered to greet him. One of the Pyramid Texts describes the scene in the following words: 'This king Pepi found the gods standing, wrapped in their garments, their white sandals on their feet. They cast off their white sandals to the earth; they threw off their garments. "Our heart was not glad until thy coming," they say' (Spell 518).

Once he had been admitted into this other world, how was the king to employ his time? The Egyptian texts are very inconsistent on this point. In one of the earliest Pyramid Texts it is asserted that he becomes the sun-god's secretary and his duties are thus described: 'King Unas sits before him (Rē); King Unas opens his chests (of papers); King Unas breaks open his edicts; King Unas seals his documents; King Unas dispatches his messengers who weary not; King Unas does what he (Rē) says to King Unas' (Spell 309). Yet other texts present a picture of the king ruling in all the splendour which had accompanied his earthly sovereignty: courtiers surround his throne while his subjects prostrate themselves before him and kiss the ground at his feet. He even sits in judgement and issues edicts as he used to do on earth.

Every day the king would accompany the sun-god on his voyage across the skies. Sometimes he is described as a rower in the barque, for example: 'King Pepi receives to himself his oar; he takes his seat; he sits in the bow of the ship of the Two Enneads; he rows Rē to the west' (Spell 469). Elsewhere he is promoted to the position of captain of the barque. At night the voyage would be performed in the reverse direction, through the underworld, thereby giving light to ordinary deceased mortals who were thought to dwell there.

With the advance of time, the dead king became even more closely associated with the sun-god until, by the VIth Dynasty, he had become completely identified with him. One of the texts in the pyramid of Teti expresses the relationship in the following terms: 'O Rē ... thou art Teti and Teti is thou ... make Teti sound and Teti will make thee sound' (Spell 405). An even more striking instance occurs in the Pyramid Texts of Merenrē, where the king is addressed thus: 'Thou embarkest therein (the sun's barque) like Rē; thou sittest down on the throne of Rē that thou mayest command the gods; for thou art Rē who came forth from Nut, who brings forth Rē every day' (Spell 606).

Closely connected with the problem of the location of the after-life and its occupations was the question of the form which the king would assume when entering upon it. The physical body was probably at all times thought to dwell in or near the tomb, while the immaterial element was believed to become at death a separate entity termed the *ba*. In early hieroglyphic writings the *ba* was represented by a stork with a tuft of feathers on the front of its neck; later the sign was changed to a bearded human-headed bird preceded by a lamp. Possibly the later sign was a relic of an ancient belief that the stars were simply innumerable *bas* lit up by their lamps. Although the physical and spiritual elements were thus separated, they were still interdependent; for the well-being of the *ba* could only be ensured, it was believed, if the body were preserved intact and able to receive it. Herein lay a further reason for the elaborate care taken to protect the body from disturbance and decay.

Another entity which played an important part in the fortunes of the king was his *ka*. In Egyptian symbolism the *ka* was represented sometimes as a bearded human figure with a crown composed of two upraised arms bent at the elbow, and sometimes as the two arms in the same position but without the human figure. It came into existence at the time of the king's birth and remained with him after death. Two famous groups of reliefs in the temples of Deir el-Bahri and Luxor, which date from the XVIIIth Dynasty, show the god Khnum creating at the same time both the royal child and his *ka* by moulding them on a potter's wheel.

The precise nature of the *ka* is far from clear. Many different explanations have been suggested: Gaston Maspero, one of the greatest of French Egyptologists, regarded it as a twin or double of its owner, made of the same substance and coeval with him; Adolf Erman thought it was the embodiment of the life force – that mysterious element which distinguishes the living from the dead; J.H. Breasted believed it was a protecting genius comparable with the Christian conception of a guardian angel; H. Kees detected in it the personification of those abstract qualities, such as might, prosperity, reverence, splendour, which were essential for a continuance of this life. Sir Alan Gardiner considered that it embraced the entire 'self' of a person regarded as an entity to some extent separable from that person. Modern concepts, he suggested, to which that of the *ka* occasionally corresponded were 'personality', 'soul', 'individuality', and 'temperament': the word might even mean a man's 'fortune' or 'position'.[1] All these explanations can be justified in different contexts and it seems necessary to postulate that the ancient Egyptians did not always entertain one single and immutable conception of the *ka*, but allowed their ideas to be modified, even in fundamental respects, according to their different doctrines of the human make-up.

Whatever may have been the true function of the *ka* in relation to its owner during his earthly life, it is certain that the expectation of close association with it in the next world provided him with one of his most cherished hopes of the after-life. The dead king and his *ka* are often mentioned in the Pyramid Texts as being together, sometimes in the kingdom of the sun-god where the *ka* acts as his guide, even

1. Quoted in J. Černý, *Ancient Egyptian Religion*, p. 82.

introducing him to the god or providing him with the food necessary for his subsistence, and sometimes in the tomb, where the *ka* shares its benefits with the owner. Indeed, one of the Egyptian names for a tomb was the 'house of the *ka*', and the priests responsible for its maintenance were called the 'servants of the *ka*'. It is hardly surprising therefore that the Egyptian texts occasionally refer to the dead as those 'who have gone to their *kas*', so important an element in a blissful after-life was the union considered.

CHAPTER ONE

MASTABAS AND EARLY
BURIAL CUSTOMS

By far the greater part of the rich collections of Egyptian antiquities now in the museums of Egypt, Europe and America has been obtained from tombs – a fact which is easily explained, because tombs dating from predynastic times and from nearly every period during the three thousand years of Egypt's dynastic history have been found in considerable numbers, whereas few of the houses in which the people lived or of the buildings in which they worked have survived. Even capitals of the importance and size of Memphis and Thebes have disappeared, leaving hardly any trace. Nothing remains of the palaces of those kings whose pyramids have been from ancient times among the most famous monuments in the world; it is not even known whether they were built in Memphis itself or somewhere nearer to the actual sites of the pyramids. So complete a disappearance can only be due to the nature of the materials and to the methods employed in construction. Houses and palaces were almost certainly composed mainly of mud-brick, wood, and gesso; they were built, moreover, above ground. Tombs, on the other hand, lay partly below the ground, and those elements which stood above ground were, after the early dynasties, generally either hewn out of rock or built of stone. Although the total number which has survived to the present day is large, it is but a fraction of those which once existed; successive generations inhabiting the country have drawn liberally on the edifices of their predecessors when building for their own requirements.

In a land where stone of excellent quality could be obtained in abundance, it may seem strange that the rulers and governing classes should have been content to spend their lives in buildings of inferior quality to their tombs. The ancient Egyptian, however, took a different view; his house or palace was built to last for only a limited number of years and could be renewed or replaced whenever necessary, but his tomb, which he called his 'castle of eternity', was designed to last *for ever*. Its construction was normally finished during his lifetime. In the event of death befalling him before the completion of his tomb, it sometimes happened that the original plan was modified in detail and the building brought to an abrupt finish, either in order that he might occupy it with the minimum delay or possibly so that his relatives might save themselves the expense necessary for further work on it. Equally, if he lived to see his tomb well advanced towards completion, he might enlarge it and provide himself with a bigger and more imposing resting-place than that which he had originally contemplated.

The motive which prompted the ancient Egyptian to devote such labour to the construction of his tomb was his belief that the attainment of the after-life which he desired was dependent on the fulfilment of two primary conditions: his body must be preserved from disturbance or destruction, and the material needs of both himself and his *ka* must be supplied. This motive remained constant throughout the whole course of Egyptian history. Changes in the form of the tomb occurred not infrequently as a result of experience gained or of new religious developments, but the fundamental purpose of the tomb continued unaffected.

In early predynastic times the dead were buried in shallow pits dug in the desert sand. The body, laid on its side in a contracted posture with the knees drawn up to the chest and the arms bent at the elbows, was wrapped in a reed-mat or in a goat-skin. Around it were placed some personal belongings, such as necklaces, bracelets, hunting implements and pots containing food and drink. The first important innovation in tomb construction was the roofing of the pit with timber. The shape of the tomb, which had been oval, was changed to rectangular, probably because shorter timbers would be required for spanning the pit from side to side. In some instances the walls were coated with mud-plaster or covered with wooden boards lashed together with leather thongs at the corners, thereby forming a kind of coffin. Towards the end of the period the walls were often lined with sun-baked bricks faced with mud-plaster, and the body, still contracted, might be put in a small wooden coffin. No examples of early superstructures have been discovered, but it is unlikely that they consisted of anything more substantial than a heap of sand supported at the sides by a wooden frame. Experience must have shown that a heap of sand was always liable to be blown away, with the result that the body and its appurtenances would be exposed and soon suffer robbery and destruction, while a timber roof merely made it easier for a thief to enter the tomb by boring a tunnel through the wall.

From the beginning of the dynastic era, the kings and nobles overcame the risk of their graves being destroyed by the elements by building over the burial-pit a superstructure composed of sun-baked mud-brick. This form of tomb has become known in modern times as a mastaba – an Arabic word meaning a bench. It was so named because, when engulfed in drift-sand to nearly its full height, it resembled the low bench built outside the Egyptian house of the present day where the owner sits and drinks coffee with his friends.

Some of the most interesting mastabas of the Ist Dynasty, and certainly the most informative for tracing the early stages in the architectural development of the pyramid, were excavated at the northern end of the necropolis at Saqqara by W.B. Emery between the years 1935 and 1956. The oldest mastaba in this group, which is also the simplest in design, is dated to the reign of Aha, the second king of Upper and Lower Egypt. Below ground-level, it consisted of a shallow rectangular pit, which was roofed with timber and divided by cross-walls into five separate compartments. The middle compartment (fig. 2: 1) probably contained the body, enclosed in a wooden coffin, while some of the most intimate possessions were placed in the adjoining chambers. So far, it was only an enlarged version of the predynastic tomb. Above these chambers and covering a considerably greater area was a brick superstructure, the interior of which was divided into twenty-seven cells, intended for the storage of wine-jars, food-vessels, hunting implements, and other necessities of life. The outer faces of the walls of the superstructure, which inclined inwards from the base to the top, were built in the form of alternate panelled projections and recesses (fig. 2: 2). Some of the later mastabas in the group were surrounded by a low terrace, to the upper surface of which were attached by means of wooden pegs life-size heads of cattle modelled in clay and provided with real horns (Plate 2). Approximately three hundred and fifty heads were placed on the terrace of a mastaba dated to the reign of Djet, the fourth king of the Ist Dynasty. Their purpose is open to conjecture, but it has been suggested that they represented cattle from the owner's herd which were slaughtered at the time of his death so that they could accompany him to the next world. The shape of the roof can only be conjectured, for no large mastaba of this period has yet been found with its roof intact, but the evidence afforded by contemporary subsidiary tombs suggests that it was convex. Two walls (fig. 2: 3 and 4),

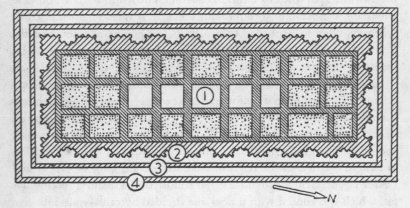

Figure 2. Mastaba dated to the reign of King Aha

also built of brick and separated by a mud-packed pavement, enclosed the building. A coating of white lime-stucco, decorated with coloured geometric patterns, was laid over both the superstructure and the enclosure walls.

Dug in the ground about forty yards outside the north wall was a boat-shaped cavity lined with mud-brick, which had contained a wooden boat intended for the use of the deceased owner in his afterlife. Between the boat and the mastaba stood two groups of dummy buildings, made of rubble cased with mud and overlaid with limestucco, but when found they were so badly damaged that it was impossible to decide whether they had been models of religious or of secular buildings.

Mastabas of this kind were almost certainly close copies of noblemen's houses and royal palaces, thus demonstrating that the tomb was regarded as the place where the dead were believed to dwell. Without doubt, the arrangement of the cells in the superstructure was adapted to fit the particular requirements of the tomb, but they must have represented the various rooms in the residence. Corridors, which would have weakened the building, were unnecessary, because it was thought that the spirit of the deceased could pass unhindered through material barriers. By an extension of this concept it was also supposed that the spirit could enter the dummy buildings outside the tomb even though they were completely solid. Attendants who had been members of the owner's household were sometimes buried in small mastabas arranged in rows outside the enclosure wall of the main tomb (Plate 3), evidently in the belief that they could continue in his service in the after-life. They were certainly buried at the same time as their masters, but not alive as might be supposed. In all probability their death was the result of a lethal dose of poison accepted voluntarily as a duty required by their terms of employment.

Whether or not some of the elaborate mastabas at Saqqara were built for the kings of the Ist Dynasty is a problem which has not yet been solved. That many of these kings, and at least two of their successors in the IInd Dynasty, possessed 'tombs', albeit of a different pattern, at Abydos is however not open to doubt. If, as is not unlikely, a king built residences for himself in different parts of the country, he could well have constructed more than one 'tomb' for the use of his spirit in the after-life. The choice of Abydos for a cenotaph may have been prompted either by its sacred associations (pp. 13-14) or by the fact that it was the ancestral home of the early kings, while Saqqara, it may be argued, was the natural burial-place because of its proximity to Memphis, the capital and consequently the site of the chief royal residence. A further possibility is that the 'tomb' at Abydos was intended for the king in his capacity of ruler of Upper Egypt and the mastaba at Saqqara was the counterpart symbolizing his rulership over Lower Egypt. This explanation would account for the difference in design of the two buildings, which would otherwise be difficult to understand, and would be compatible with the general conception of providing the dead king with an alternative residence.

Many years ago the late Professor G.A. Reisner advanced the theory that the almost totally destroyed superstructures of the royal 'tombs' at Abydos from the reign of Djer, the third king of the Ist Dynasty, onwards were brick-built monuments which rose in two or three deep steps to the summit, but his hypothetical reconstructions have never gained general recognition among Egyptologists. Indeed, H. Ricke, in a more recent study, came to the conclusion that the superstructures were low flat-topped mounds of sand supported at the sides by walls of mud-brick. J.-P. Lauer is in general agreement with Ricke, but considers that Ricke's estimate of the height (about 4 feet) should be approximately doubled and suggests that the top was curved.

One of the many difficult problems which confront an archaeologist excavating badly damaged buildings composed of brick and partly filled with sand and rubble is to trace the design of the interior. Architectural elements of considerable size may not be distinguishable from filling material unless there is some reason for suspecting their existence at an early stage in the process of dismantling the ruined structure. Thus, in the excavation of the Saqqara group of mastabas, it was not possible to recognize at first a feature of considerable importance embodied in the core of the superstructures of at least some of the earliest tombs. This feature was a rectangular mound of sand and rubble, overlaid with a casing of bricks, which had been erected on ground-level directly above the central pit and beneath the innermost storage cells of the superstructure (fig. 3). It is not hard to imagine that this mound represented the pile of sand which, in predynastic times, had been placed over the simple pit-graves. Some magical significance had no doubt been ascribed to it, even though in origin its purpose was purely utilitarian, and consequently it was retained when a new pattern of tomb was introduced. A mound of sand and rubble covered with a layer of bricks must, however, have provided an insecure basis for that part of the superstructure which stood above it, and it is not surprising that, before the end of the Ist Dynasty, a firmer platform was devised by surrounding the mound on all four sides with

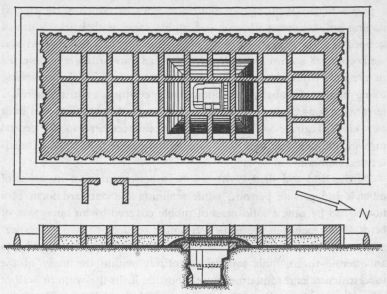

Figure 3. Ist Dynasty mastaba with central mound

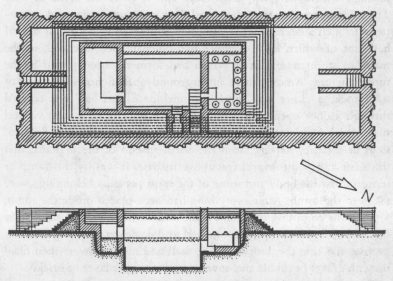

Figure 4. Ist Dynasty mastaba with stepped central mound

a perpendicular wall, against the outer sides of which were erected sloping embankments of sand and rubble cased with bricks laid in a stepped fashion (fig. 4; Plate 4). With this support, the mound was well protected against any tendency to spread outwards when subjected to pressure from above by the weight of the roof and intervening filling of the mastaba. As an additional precaution against this risk a terrace composed of brick and sand with stepped outer faces was built as a kind of girdle which gave further reinforcement to the central mound without depriving it of its essential nature as a separate architectural element.

By the IInd and IIIrd Dynasties the superstructures of mastabas of officials and private persons, while retaining the outward form of a house, had become a solid mass of rubble covered by an outer skin of brick. The recesses in the walls were often reduced to two – one near each end of the eastern wall, the southern recess being developed into an offering-room, built sometimes entirely within the body of the superstructure and sometimes purely outside it. In the western wall of this offering-room there was a niche which served as a false door, through which the spirit could leave and re-enter the tomb at will. The substructure, on the other hand, had increased in size and importance to such a degree that it was often composed of a kind of central hall, out of which led a number of side-chambers, intended, in the main, to store those objects which had formerly been placed in the superstructure. Among these underground apartments, hewn out of solid rock, a closet was sometimes included. The hall was entered through a door opening southwards at the bottom of a deep vertical shaft which had been driven down from the ground-level. A flight of steps or a ramp, starting from the northern end of the mastaba, met this shaft at a point several feet above its base. It was by this ramp or staircase that the body and some of the most personal belongings were taken to the tomb. After everything had been placed inside the tomb, a portcullis consisting of a heavy slab of stone, which had previously been supported by props, was allowed to slide down two perpendicular grooves flanking the doorway. The shaft and stairway were then filled up with gravel or rubble and covered with an outer layer of brick.

To account for the transference of the store-rooms from the superstructure to the substructure, it is fair to deduce that measures to provide greater protection for the body and its belongings had become imperative. The introduction of the mastaba had coincided with a marked elaboration in the equipment of the tomb, and, as a consequence, the risk of robbery must have been substantially increased. While this equipment was mainly stored in a brick structure above the ground or in shallow pits beneath the centre of the structure, tomb-breakers would have experienced little difficulty in forcing a way to their quarry. Deeper burial, however, would certainly present the robber with a serious hindrance, but it would also complicate the task of the tomb-builder.

In 1901 Alessandro Barsanti discovered at Saqqara beneath the mortuary temple of King Unas, at a depth of about 21 feet below ground-level, a vast subterranean tomb approximately 130 yards in length and embodying more than seventy chambers hewn in the rock on each side of a central corridor. Within this tomb were clay jar-stoppers with seal impressions of Hetepsekhemui and Rēneb, the first two kings of the IInd Dynasty, whose order of sequence is uncertain. In every probability this tomb may be ascribed to whichever of these two kings was the later. A second tomb of comparable design lying about 140 yards to the east of the first was excavated in 1937-8 by Selim Bey Hassan and this tomb has been attributed, also on the basis of seal impressions, to the third king of the Dynasty, Ninetjer. The owner of a IVth Dynasty tomb at Saqqara, named Shery, recorded in his inscriptions that he was the overseer of the priests in charge of the tombs of Sened and Peribsen, the fifth and sixth kings of the IInd Dynasty and, since Shery is unlikely to have been buried far from his place of work, it may be deduced that the tombs of these two kings are also at Saqqara and await discovery. The fact that Peribsen possessed a 'tomb' at Abydos, which was found by Émile Amélineau in 1897-8 and re-excavated three years later by Sir Flinders Petrie, cannot be regarded as a hindrance to the acceptance of this theory if, as many authorities suppose, the practice of building tombs in more than one place had already been established by the kings of the Ist Dynasty. Khasekhemui, the last of the line of nine or possibly ten kings who comprised the IInd Dynasty, also built a 'tomb' at Abydos, but hitherto no evidence is available to show that he had a second tomb at Saqqara. The design of this 'tomb' is reminiscent of the two earlier tombs found at Saqqara, but it is smaller in size, its length being only 75 yards. Situated roughly half-way along its main axis is a chamber measuring 17 feet by 10 feet and built entirely of dressed limestone. Peribsen's 'tomb' consisted of a rectangular chamber 24 feet in length by 9½ feet in breadth, surrounded by a corridor on the outer sides of which lay a series of small cells. Apart from Khasekhemui's chamber both these 'tombs' were built of mud-brick. Nothing remains of the superstructures either at Saqqara or at Abydos, but doubtless they also were made of mud-brick.

Many mastabas of the IVth Dynasty were still built of brick, but it was the introduction into general use of stone, previously reserved for royal monuments, which marked the most significant development of this period. Even in the brick mastabas, the offering-room and subterranean chambers were often faced with stone. The stone employed for the purpose was a fine-quality limestone quarried at Tura and Masara, on the east bank of the Nile, roughly opposite Zawiyet el-Aryan. This limestone was also used to face the superstructures of the stone mastabas, while a stone of inferior quality taken from neighbouring quarries was used to build their inner cores.

In their substructures, the IVth Dynasty mastabas, whether made of brick or of stone, present many new features. Both types often had a single room with a deep recess in one of its walls for a coffin made of wood or stone. In the south-east corner of this room the stone mastabas sometimes had a pit, the purpose of which is not certainly known, but it was probably intended to hold the viscera, which had been removed from the body of the deceased in order to help in its preservation. After the burial, the entrance to this room was blocked by a heavy limestone portcullis. The vertical shaft leading to the top of the superstructure was then filled with rubble and its mouth covered with a slab of dressed stone. The ramp adjoining the shaft, which was regularly found in the IInd and IIIrd Dynasties, was generally omitted from the stone mastabas, though it was frequently retained in those made of brick.

The superstructures of IVth Dynasty mastabas sometimes embodied two notable innovations which did not, however, become general until the Vth Dynasty. The first was a statue of the owner of the tomb, occasionally accompanied by statues of other members of his family, and the second was the decoration of the stone walls of the offering-rooms with scenes carved in relief and painted. The statues were placed in a chamber built within the body of the mastaba and known in modern times as the serdab – an Arabic word meaning a cellar. It was so called because, having no doors, windows or apertures of any kind, apart from a hole or narrow slit in one wall approximately on a level with the face of the statue, scarcely any light was admitted into the interior.

Decorated offering-rooms were only the beginning of a process of development whereby, in the Vth and VIth Dynasties, the inside of the superstructure was gradually filled with chambers and columned halls, all of which had their walls covered with reliefs. One famous mastaba of the VIth Dynasty contained more than thirty chambers so decorated (Plates 5, 6). Among the scenes most commonly carved on the walls were those which showed servants bearing offerings of food and drink to their deceased master, harvest scenes, manufacturing processes, the owner of the tomb inspecting his estates or hunting, and a wide variety of other episodes closely associated with his occupations during life.

The important developments in the mastaba from the IVth Dynasty onwards were a direct result of the realization that the measures which had been taken to defeat the elements and the robber had also defeated their own ultimate object, namely the preservation of the body. An inevitable consequence of burying the body in a deep chamber far from the drying influence of the hot sand was that it decomposed unless some method of embalmment was employed. Even in the Early Dynastic Period attempts were sometimes made to imitate the external form of the living body by wrapping each limb separately and inserting under the wrappings linen pads soaked in resin and moulded to the shape of the individual members. A further development, for which evidence is available from the IVth Dynasty, was the painting in green of the facial features on the outside of the wrappings covering the head. The earliest intact mummies now known date from the Vth Dynasty. The first (which was destroyed when the museum of the

Royal College of Surgeons was bombed in the Second World War) was found at Meidum by Sir Flinders Petrie in the season 1891-2. The second was excavated at Saqqara by the Antiquities Service of the Egyptian Government in 1966. This mummy lay in a finely decorated tomb on the south side of the causeway leading to the pyramid of Unas which belonged to a Leader of Singers named Nefer and his father, Kaha. The body had been placed in a coffin lying on its back, with the face turned sideways towards the east. Wrapped in linen bandages, it was covered with a layer of green-coloured plaster, which had been carefully modelled to the shape of the body. The plaster on the face resembled a mask on which the features were delineated and a moustache was represented above the upper lip. Attached to the chin was a ceremonial beard made of stiff linen.

There can be no doubt that the Egyptians were fully aware of the inadequacy of their precautions to preserve the body from molestation and decay. As an additional safeguard for the continuation of life after death they therefore resorted to magic.

In the cult of the dead, the Egyptians believed that, without depriving the deceased person of the virtues of the prototype, a model could be substituted for any article which it was not practicable to supply in actuality. For instance, in some IInd Dynasty mastabas dummy vases were used instead of vessels filled with provisions and were thought to be equally beneficial to the owner of the tomb. Similarly, a statue or even a figure carved in relief was considered to be an effective substitute for the human body in the event of its destruction. One of the best known mastabas of the IIIrd Dynasty was provided with figures of the deceased owner, a high official named Hesy-Rē, carved in relief on wooden panels which fitted into the recesses on the east side of the superstructure. The figures were certainly intended to enable Hesy-Rē to leave and re-enter his tomb. Outside panels of this kind were, however, very vulnerable and the serdab was devised so as to give the figure better protection without any corresponding loss of efficacy. Even greater security was obtained by the introduction of stone figures to take the place of those made of wood. As a variant to the complete figure in the serdab, but not necessarily instead of it, a stone representation of the head of the dead person was sometimes, in the IVth and

Vth Dynasties, placed in the bottom of the tomb-shaft or at the entrance to the burial-chamber rather than inside it. These so-called reserve heads were undoubtedly portraits of their owners (Plate 7), perhaps given by the king to privileged members of the court, male and female, as a mark of special favour. The ears, in the surviving examples, are generally broken off and in some instances an incision has been scored in a line running from the top to the back of the skull. Nicholas Millet has suggested that these mutilations were the result of the treatment to which the heads were subjected in the sculptors' workshops. The purpose of the heads, he believes, was to serve as prototypes which were used for making moulds for casts. A mould would be made of linen dipped in water with size or very thin plaster, which set hard when dry. In order to remove it, the sculptor would cut it from 'the top of the cranium down to the base of the neck, with an adze, knife or chisel, leaving in some cases the cranial groove peculiar to this class of sculpture. The ears would often break off while the shell was being wrenched off the head.' While this explanation would account for the injuries to the heads, it would not provide a reason for placing them outside the burial-chamber. Hermann Junker, who directed the Austrian excavations in the Giza necropolis, put forward the suggestion, which has never been seriously challenged, that the heads were intended to help wandering souls to identify their tombs and to return to their bodies. The location in the tomb would thus be comparable with that occupied by a statue in a serdab.

When once the principle of substitution by means of a representation had been recognized, it was but a step to extend its scope to cover not only individual objects, such as food-vessels or statues, but also composite scenes illustrating episodes in the life of the deceased which he wanted to enjoy again in the after-life. Scenes depicting him hunting, fowling, or inspecting his estates were therefore believed to provide him with the means to continue these pursuits after his death. Likewise, scenes of harvesting, slaughtering of animals, brewing, and baking were thought to guarantee a constant supply of the commodities thus produced.

In order to eliminate any risk of the spirit of the deceased failing to recognize his statue, it was usually inscribed with his name and titles in hieroglyphs. Similarly, in the scenes carved in relief, short explanatory inscriptions were inserted as a kind of commentary, often giving the names of the persons represented and sometimes describing the actions which they performed. These persons were generally relatives of the deceased or his servants, who were thus assured of an after-life in the service of their master.

In spite of all the different devices for securing subsistence which were included in the equipment of the tomb, a regular supply of fresh provisions was always thought essential for the well-being of the deceased. They were laid on a low flat altar, which stood in front of the false door built into the west wall of the offering-room constructed on the east side of the superstructure. This position probably resulted from the practice of building mastabas on the high desert west of the Nile, so that the deceased, when looking out of the false door, would be facing the valley whence the offerings were usually brought.

Possibly the first offerings were presented by a son who, in providing for his deceased father's needs, symbolized Horus, the son of Osiris. Subsequent offerings would generally be brought by mortuary priests (like Shery mentioned above in connection with the royal tombs of the IInd Dynasty) who were engaged by written contract and paid for their services. Payment took the form of land bequeathed by the deceased to the priests. As an instance, one of the sons of Chephren, the builder of the second pyramid at Giza, bequeathed at least twelve towns as a mortuary endowment of this kind. Such land, having become the property of the priests, would be passed on by them to their heirs, who would also inherit the accompanying obligations with respect to the tomb. Experience must, however, have shown that even the most binding contracts would not be observed for longer than a limited period, and, at an early date, the so-called funerary stela was introduced into the tomb to serve as a substitute for the actual offerings. This stela contained a magic formula declaring that the deceased had received the daily offerings in abundance; above the formula there was generally a scene, carved in relief, showing him seated at a table heaped with offerings presented to him by members of his family. While not intended to dispense with the regular supply of fresh provisions, the stela, by means of the magic power of its written word, provided the deceased with a valuable method of reinsurance against starvation and neglect.

However primitive and materialistic the Egyptian conception of the after-life may seem, it must be conceded that it was responsible for the production of some of the greatest artistic masterpieces in antiquity. Without the impetus provided by a practical motive, it is doubtful whether a fraction of the statues, reliefs, or inscriptions which are now so universally admired would ever have been produced.

CHAPTER TWO

STEP PYRAMIDS

Until the end of the Early Dynastic Period both kings and nobles, to judge from the evidence now available, were buried in tombs built of brick. In the IIIrd Dynasty, however, the kings began to use stone – a material which had previously been used only for isolated parts of buildings. The construction of the first tomb of this kind has always been ascribed to Imhotep, the architect of Zoser, who is credited by Manetho with having been the inventor of the art of building in hewn stone. Some indirect confirmation of his connection with Zoser's tomb is provided by the occurrence of his name on the pedestal of a statue which was found outside the tomb when it was excavated. His achievements became legendary among later generations of Egyptians, who regarded him not only as an architect but as a magician, an astronomer, and the father of medicine. In Saite times he was deified, being considered the son of Ptah, while the Greeks identified him with their own god of medicine, Asklepios.

The site which Imhotep selected was a stretch of high ground at Saqqara overlooking the city of Memphis. It covered an area measuring approximately 597 yards from north to south and 304 yards from east to west. A short distance to the north lay the large cemetery of Ist and IInd Dynasty mastabas which included those mentioned in the preceding chapter. Zoser was buried not in a mastaba, but beneath a monumental step pyramid (Plate 8). It was the central and dominating feature of a large complex of stone buildings and courtyards intended for various ceremonies connected with the after-life of the king (fig. 5). Around the perimeter of the complex was a massive stone enclosure wall. Tura limestone was used throughout for the outer facings of the buildings and local stone for their inner cores.

Although most of the subterranean parts of the Step Pyramid had been thoroughly explored during the nineteenth century it was not until the inter-war years that anything was known about the surrounding buildings. Time and deliberate destruction had reduced everything except the pyramid itself to ruined heaps of masonry over which lay a thick layer of sand. Scientific excavations, followed by painstaking restoration by C.M. Firth, J.E. Quibell, and J.-P. Lauer, working for the Antiquities Service of the Egyptian Government, have now enabled a fairly complete picture to be formed of the whole complex as it appeared at the time of Zoser's burial.

In its final form the Step Pyramid was a massive structure rising in six unequal stages to a height of 204 feet. Its base measurements were approximately 411 feet from east to west and 358 feet from north to south. Before attaining these dimensions, however, it had undergone a number of changes of plan, some of which can be clearly detected, while the remainder are admittedly hypothetical and cannot be demonstrated without dismantling a considerable part of the building. Those alterations which can be proved lie in the places where the monument has been most severely damaged and where, in consequence, surfaces which were once covered by later layers of stone have now become exposed. It is an instance, by no means unique, of archaeological knowledge being gained at the expense of artistic loss.

It is clear that the nucleus of the monument is a solid box-like structure consisting of a core of local stone faced with an outer layer of dressed Tura limestone (figs. 6 and 7: 1). This nucleus, 26 feet in height, has usually been regarded as a mastaba of unique shape with a square ground-plan, each side being oriented approximately to face one of the four cardinal points and measuring about 207 feet. When completed, it was extended by about 14 feet on all four sides and a

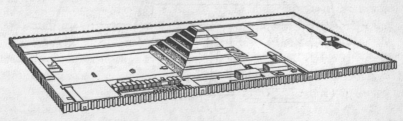

Figure 5. The Step Pyramid enclosure

second facing of dressed limestone was added (figs. 6 and 7: 2). The height of this extension, however, was about 2 feet less than that of the original mastaba, and so a step mastaba was formed (fig. 6: 2). A further enlargement added about 28 feet to the east side only, making the tomb oblong with the longer axis running from east to west (figs. 6 and 7: 3).

Before the facing of this accretion had been dressed, an entirely different design was adopted. The mastaba, which was extended by $9\frac{1}{2}$ feet on each side, became the lowest stage of a four-stepped pyramid (figs. 6 and 7: 4). On its northern side a beginning was made with the construction of a mortuary temple, but before either building had been finished it was decided to extend the pyramid further towards the north and west (figs. 6 and 7: 5). If this enlargement had been completed the height of the pyramid would have been increased and the number of steps would have been augmented to six, but this plan also was abandoned at the level of the fourth step. The sixth and last extension of the pyramid added a little to each side; the six steps were completed and the whole building was cased with a final layer of dressed Tura limestone (figs. 6 and 7: 5′).

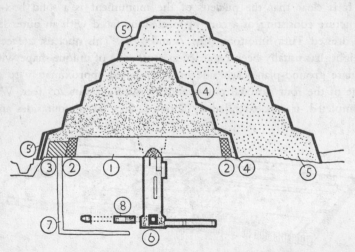

Figure 6. The Step Pyramid, section looking south

The substructure of the Step Pyramid consists of a deep shaft giving access to a maze of corridors and rooms forming a hypogeum without parallel among the other pyramids of the Old Kingdom. Owing to the fact that the construction of some of these subterranean apartments was never finished, it is not always easy to detect which were part of Zoser's design and which were additions by later explorers or robbers. The main plan of Zoser's hypogeum and the successive stages of its construction can, however, be determined with certainty (fig. 7). First, a shaft, approximately 23 feet square, was sunk to a depth of about 28 feet into the limestone substratum. A tunnel, with its ceiling 23 feet below the surface of the ground, was then driven northwards from the shaft for a distance of about 66 feet. At that point, having passed the

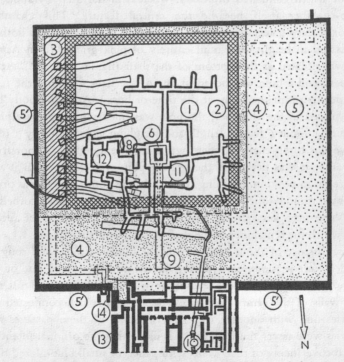

Figure 7. The Step Pyramid, substructure and ground-plan

37

northern limits of both the mastaba and the four-stepped pyramid, the tunnel was continued for a further 70 feet in the form of an open trench, its floor sloping gradually upwards until it reached ground-level (fig. 7: 9). Work on the shaft was then resumed until it had reached a total depth of 92 feet (fig. 7: 6). Concurrently with the deepening of the shaft, the floor of the tunnel was lowered so that it became a ramp with a progressively steeper gradient. The floor was not, however, lowered to the full depth of the shaft, but only to a point about 40 feet above its base.

In design, the vertical shaft and ramp of the substructure of the Step Pyramid resembled the corresponding elements of the contemporary private mastabas. In the latter, however, a door at the bottom of the shaft gave access to a central hall surrounded by a number of rooms, one of which contained the body, whereas in the Step Pyramid the tomb-chamber itself became the central feature. This chamber, approximately 9 feet 9 inches in length and 5 feet 6 inches both in width and in height, was built entirely of pink granite from Aswan and was situated at the bottom of the shaft (figs. 6 and 7: 6). At its northern end a hole was bored in one of the slabs spanning the roof, in order to admit the body at the time of burial. After the body had been placed in the chamber, the hole was filled with a granite plug, measuring about 6 feet in length and weighing approximately 3 tons. Above this tomb-chamber there was a room entered by a door from the ramp; it was here that the granite plug was stored until it was lowered into position. Nothing remains of this room, but it was probably built of limestone blocks. Its roof, which may have been corbelled, must have been very strong, because it bore the weight of the rubble with which the remainder of the shaft was subsequently filled.

At a distance of about 70 feet from the tomb-chamber and roughly parallel with its sides, four long galleries were hollowed out of the native rock. Flights of steps leading down from doors in the east and west walls of the ramp gave access to passages which connected the galleries one with another (fig. 7: 11). Some of these passages and galleries were never finished, but it is likely that the original intention was to cover many of their walls with panels of small blue-glazed tiles, so arranged as to resemble the reed-mats which hung on the walls of

Zoser's palace. Tiled panels of this kind were found in the east gallery (fig. 7: 12), which was discovered only in 1928, and in two rooms near the south-east corner of the tomb-chamber (figs. 6 and 7: 8). The panelling on the west wall of the east gallery was interrupted in three places by limestone reliefs of the king performing religious ceremonies (Plate 9). Around the outer edge of the recesses containing these reliefs there were inscriptions giving the king's name and his titles. Similar inscriptions also flanked a doorway separating the two rooms decorated with blue tiles. Both this doorway and some of the tiles were taken to the Berlin Museum in 1843 by the German Egyptologist Richard Lepsius.

It is probable that, when Zoser's monument was first planned, the substructure was intended to consist only of the two chambers at the bottom of the shaft, the four surrounding galleries, and the connecting passages, but, after the superstructure had been enlarged for the first time, eleven vertical shafts were sunk into the ground on its east side to a depth of about 108 feet. At the bottom of each shaft a corridor was directed westwards under the superstructure (figs. 6 and 7: 7). Two fine alabaster coffins, one of which contained the remains of a child, were found at the far end of the fifth corridor from the north, while limestone pedestals for similar coffins remained in some of the other corridors. It is clear therefore that these shafts and corridors were tombs, almost certainly those of members of the royal family. Possibly each tomb was originally intended to have its independent superstructure, but ultimately they were all buried under the third extension of the monument, and the only means of access to them was by a long stairway leading to the northernmost tomb.

Until the fifth extension of the superstructure, the subterranean chambers and corridors were reached by descending the open trench and ramp from the north side (fig. 7: 9). The open trench, however, was blocked with rubble when the superstructure was extended north-wards, and it became necessary to dig a new tunnel in its place. Beginning with a flight of steps situated some distance to the north of the final superstructure (fig. 7: 10), the tunnel followed a line to the west of the former trench and curved eastwards to join the original ramp near its upper end. Its course seems unnecessarily circuitous, and it is difficult to understand the motives which prompted such an expenditure of labour.

With the exception of the mortuary temple and the serdab, the buildings surrounding the Step Pyramid are without any known precedent or parallel. The mortuary temple (fig. 7: 13) in its ground-plan is reminiscent of a brick temple found at Saqqara by W.B. Emery in 1954 within the enclosure wall of a mastaba dated to the reign of Qaa, the last king of the Ist Dynasty. Both temples moreover were built to the north of their respective tombs. This orientation is notable, almost every similar edifice in the true pyramids being situated, like the offering-room of the normal mastaba, east of the tomb. Zoser's mortuary temple, a large rectangular building attached to the lowest step of the pyramid, was entered through a doorway in its eastern wall. No doors were fitted into this entrance, but an imitation of an open door was carved in the stone wall adjoining the northern jamb. Many other buildings in the complex were fitted with similar imitation doors, often carved to fit the exact measurements of the doorway. Beyond the entrance a long corridor with numerous turns led to two open courts, from one of which the staircase descended towards the substructure of the pyramid. At the southern end of each court there were three gangways opening into a wide gallery. Short walls, flanked on the north side by fluted engaged columns, formed the divisions between the gangways. Engaged columns with various decorations constituted, like the imitation doors, one of the most characteristic features in the architecture of this complex. Their design, which will be discussed at a later stage in the description of this complex, was invariably suggested either by the single stem of some plant or by a number of stems bound together. Two rooms on the west side of the open courts, each with a stone basin in its floor, and a sanctuary with two recesses sunk into the face of the pyramid, complete the few elements of this temple which are sufficiently preserved to be recognizable.

It is impossible to divine with any certainty the archetype by which Imhotep was guided when designing this mortuary temple, but it is tempting to regard it as a stone representation of the royal palace at Memphis. This explanation would be in keeping with the generally accepted opinion that most of the other buildings in the complex were copies of constructions in the palace compound. Whatever may be the true explanation, it is noticeable that most of the principal architectural features (e.g. courts, ablution rooms, and the recesses in the sanctuary) occur in pairs, suggesting that the temple was designed for the celebration of some ritual which had to be repeated. Such a ritual would have been performed for the king, once as ruler of Upper Egypt and a second time as ruler of Lower Egypt.

The serdab, which has suffered relatively little damage, is situated a short distance to the east of the entrance to the mortuary temple (fig. 7: 14). It is built entirely of dressed Tura limestone, its front wall inclining inwards at an angle of 16° from the perpendicular to correspond with the angle of the lowest step of the pyramid, which provides its back wall. Placed inside is a cast of a limestone statue of the king seated on a chair, the original having been transferred to the Cairo Museum at the time of its discovery (Plate 10). He is dressed in a long robe, which leaves only his hands, his feet, and the top of his shoulders exposed. On his head is a long wig covered by a linen head-dress. The eyes, probably made of rock-crystal set in copper sockets, and part of the artificial beard attached to his chin – a symbol of royalty – have now disappeared. Two holes were cut in the front wall of the serdab opposite the face, either to allow the smoke of incense to reach the statue or to enable the statue to look out.

Outside the serdab lies a small enclosure with two entrances, a narrow one at the south-east corner and the main one on the north. Sculptured representations of wooden doors were carved on the walls at each side of the main entrance, giving the impression of doors swung open so that the serdab could be seen from the open court outside the enclosure.

Two large rectangular buildings with curved roofs dominated the whole area lying east both of the serdab court and of the pyramid (fig. 5). Each was composed of a solid core of masonry overlaid with dressed Tura limestone. The southern face of each building was decorated with four engaged columns, which, together with a broad pilaster at each side, supported a cornice following the curve of the roof. In the more northern of the two buildings vertical flutings were carved on both the engaged columns and the pilasters. In the southern, the engaged columns were similarly fluted, but the pilasters were ribbed. The capitals of the engaged columns resembled two large pendent leaves, a design found only in this complex. Near the top of the engaged columns were two square holes and, in the southern building, a pair of bosses into which brackets supporting insignia may have been fitted. An alternative explanation that the holes were intended for wooden imitations of the horns or the tusks of an animal seems less probable.

Situated asymmetrically near the middle of the southern face of each building was an entrance giving access to a narrow passage which led, by way of two right-angled turns, to a small cruciform sanctuary. Three niches, intended either for offerings or for statuettes, were sunk into the walls of the sanctuary. In the northern building there were also two niches in the wall at the end of the passage. The stone ceilings of the passages were carved to resemble the log rafters with which similar corridors were roofed in buildings composed of wood and

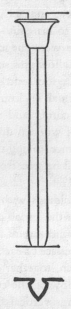

Figure 8. Engaged papyrus column

mud-brick. West of the entrance, concealed from view behind the stone facing, there was a second passage leading to a small chamber which may once have contained a statue.

In front of the two buildings were open courts, the southern being considerably the larger. Surrounding the courts was an enclosure wall, in the east side of which, near the corner of each building, there was a broad recess. In the northern court this recess was decorated with three engaged columns, each representing a single papyrus stem and flower (Plate 11 and fig. 8). The recess in the southern court contained only one engaged column, which appears to have represented a lily.

The precise purpose which these buildings were intended to serve in Zoser's after-life has never been satisfactorily explained. At one time they were believed to be the tombs of two of his daughters, Intkaes and Hetephernebti, whose names were carved on some stelae found nearby, but recent excavation has failed to reveal anything of a funerary character in their composition and a different explanation must be sought. The decoration of the recesses in the courts seems to provide a clue, for it is known that the lily and the papyrus were the emblems of Upper and Lower Egypt respectively. Possibly, therefore, the southern building represented the predynastic national sanctuary of Upper Egypt, which was situated at Hierakonpolis, while the northern building represented the corresponding sanctuary of Lower Egypt at Buto. The presence of an altar, shaped like a horse's hoof, in the court of the southern building would certainly imply that the buildings fulfilled a religious rather than a secular function.

South of the enclosure wall of the southern building lay another oblong court, the east and west sides of which were occupied by a series of dummy chapels composed of solid masonry (fig. 5). In front of each chapel was a small court provided with an imitation open door. A projection from the middle of its south wall screened a niche sunk into the base of the chapel façade. Architecturally, the façades of ten out of the thirteen chapels on the west side bore a striking resemblance to the façades of the northern and southern buildings. They consisted of three engaged columns, decorated with vertical flutings and supporting a curved cornice, the ends of which joined two broad pilasters. The capitals of these engaged columns, like those of the northern and southern buildings, were composed of two pendent leaves (fig. 9). A single round hole, cut between the leaves, probably supported a bracket holding an emblem. The façades of the remaining chapels of the west side and all those on the east seem to have been plain, except for a torus moulding at the top and sides.

This court and its surrounding buildings were designed to provide Zoser with the setting necessary for repeating in his after-life his jubilee ceremony, known in Egyptian as the *heb-sed*. Every king of Egypt was entitled to celebrate the *heb-sed* after occupying the throne for a certain number of years, the period varying from time to time. The origin of the festival is very obscure, but it seems to have been a relic from the remote past when kings reigned for only a limited period before being ceremonially put to death. Underlying this primitive custom was doubtless the belief that it was essential for the welfare of the kingdom that the physical vigour of its king should be unimpaired. The *heb-sed*,

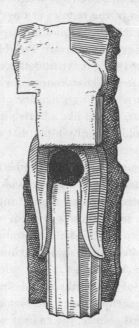

Figure 9. Capital composed of pendent leaves

by enabling the king to regain his vigour through the exercise of magic, obviated the necessity of replacing him by a younger man.

One of the most important elements in the *heb-sed* was a re-enactment of the coronation. In this ceremony a procession led by a priest would enter those of the chapels surrounding the *heb-sed* court in which were gathered the gods of the *nomes* of Upper Egypt. Having obtained from each god consent to the renewal of his kingship, the king would be conducted to the more southern of two thrones, placed on a dais beneath a canopy, in order to be crowned with the white crown of Upper Egypt. A similar ceremony would be repeated in the chapels of the gods of the Lower Egyptian *nomes* before the king ascended the northern throne to receive the red crown of Lower Egypt. The unification of the two kingdoms would be symbolized at a later stage by lacing lotus (or lily) and papyrus flowers around a stake driven into the ground.

The significance of another ceremony in the *heb-sed* is not so apparent. The king, carrying a flail, would run a fixed course, accompanied by 'the priest of the souls of Nekhen'.[1] One of the reliefs discovered in the Step Pyramid seems to show Zoser performing this rite (Plate 9). It may have been derived from a primitive belief that the fertility of the fields depended in some way on the physical agility of the king.

In addition to the chapels already described, the *heb-sed* court of the Step Pyramid still preserves at its southern end the coronation dais. The façades of the second and third chapels on the west side near the dais contained recesses approached by flights of steps. Possibly they were intended for statues of the king, the more southern statue as king of Upper Egypt and the more northern as king of Lower Egypt. The proximity of these recesses to the dais suggests that the buildings to which they belonged represented the pavilions where the king remained while the priests performed the ceremonies preceding the double coronation.

A passage leading from the south-west corner of the *heb-sed* court connected it with a smaller court in which stood a building of medium size. Its outer walls, built with a slight batter, were undecorated, apart

1. The 'souls of Nekhen' were the prehistoric kings of Upper Egypt.

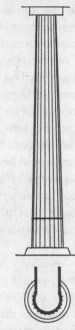

Figure 10. Engaged fluted column

from having a torus moulding on the southern face. Internally, it consisted of an imposing entrance hall, three inner courts and a group of side-chambers. Projecting from the middle of the west side of the entrance hall were three tongue-walls, two of which terminated in engaged columns decorated with vertical flutings (fig. 10). The two alcoves formed by these tongue-walls may have contained statues, but whether they were images of the king or of gods cannot be deduced while the function of the building remains obscure. Its relation to the *heb-sed* court would seem to imply that its use was in some way associated with the *heb-sed*. Possibly it was the pavilion in which the king resided for the duration of the ceremonies and to which he retired between the various episodes in order to change his vestments. In support of this explanation both A. Hermann and H. Ricke have pointed out that the ground-plan shows many affinities with that of a small house of the time of Zoser which has been excavated at Saqqara.

More difficult to understand is the purpose of a maze of corridors and chambers which led out of the *heb-sed* court at the south-east corner. In the absence of any distinctive architectural features, it has been conjectured that they too had some connection with the *heb-sed*.

A corridor linked the *heb-sed* court with the eastern end of a colonnade, close to a gateway in the enclosure wall (Plate 8) – the only entrance into the complex. This colonnade consisted of a long, narrow passage running westwards between a series of alcoves formed by tongue-walls which projected from each side (Plate 12). These tongue-walls, of which there were forty, terminated in engaged columns with a ribbed decoration, the ribs varying in number from seventeen to nineteen (fig. 11). Within the alcoves there may have

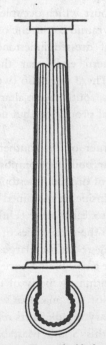

Figure 11. Engaged ribbed column

been statues of the king, those on the south side representing him as king of Upper Egypt and those on the north side as king of Lower Egypt. Since, however, the alcoves so nearly correspond in number with the forty-two *nomes*, it has been suggested that each contained a double statue of the king and a *nome*-god, but, although groups of this kind are known in the IVth Dynasty, excavation has revealed no trace of such sculpture in this colonnade. The whole building was covered with a flat stone roof, carved on the underside to imitate rounded logs of wood. Slits cut at an oblique angle in the side-walls near the roof admitted beams of light which may have been directed on the sculpture in the alcoves.

Attached to the western end of the colonnade was a small transverse vestibule. Its roof, which resembled in pattern that of the colonnade, was supported by eight ribbed columns joined in pairs by cross-walls. In its west wall was a reproduction in stone of an open door giving access to a large open court which occupied the whole area from the south face of the Step Pyramid to the enclosure wall. The side-walls of the court were made of dressed limestone, decorated with recessed panelling. At its northern end, near the pyramid, was an altar approached by a ramp. There were also two constructions, each in the form of a pair of hooves, south of the altar. Possibly they marked the limits of some ceremonial procession, but no evidence of its nature has hitherto come to light.

In the south-west corner of the southern court adjoining the enclosure was a rectangular building composed almost entirely of solid masonry. Its outer walls of dressed limestone were decorated at the top with a frieze of cobras. Inside, it contained only two elongated chambers set at right angles to each other. Unless this building was connected in some way with the ceremonies of the southern court, it must have served as the offering-room for a large mastaba, the superstructure of which, with its longer axis running exceptionally from east to west, was mainly concealed within the body of the enclosure wall. Its position on the north side of the mastaba would correspond with the orientation of the mortuary temple in its relation to the Step Pyramid.

The substructure of this South Mastaba shares many features in common with the Step Pyramid. A tomb-chamber, made of blocks of pink granite, was built at the bottom of the vertical shaft. Its only entrance was a hole (which was subsequently stopped with a granite plug) in the flat roof. Immediately above the tomb-chamber was a second room, intended for storing the plug before the burial, its roof supporting the rubble-filling of the shaft. The side-ramp, however, instead of entering this room like its counterpart in the Step Pyramid, skirted it on the south side and gave access directly to the galleries, all of which were situated east of the tomb-chamber. In one gallery there were three separate reliefs of the king engaged in the performance of religious ceremonies. In a parallel gallery, a short distance to the west, the backs of three doors were carved in the limestone facing of the wall. Their position, approximately behind the reliefs, suggests that the panels containing the reliefs were regarded as false doors through which the king was in the act of emerging. The walls of several of these galleries were covered with the blue-glazed tiles imitating mural hangings made of reeds (Plate 13).

Since Zoser was almost certainly buried under the Step Pyramid, it is difficult to account for the construction within the same complex of a second tomb having every appearance of being intended for him. We know that the kings of Egypt did sometimes build more than one tomb – Seneferu, the first king of the IVth Dynasty, had at least two pyramids – and the reliefs on the false doors of the South Mastaba are strong evidence that Zoser intended the tomb for his own use. The granite tomb-chamber, however, measured only 5 feet 3 inches square, which could not have contained the body of a person of normal stature unless in a contracted position – a manner of burial which is unlikely to have been used for a royal person in the IIIrd Dynasty. It has therefore been suggested that the tomb was either a dummy, intended for use in the symbolic sacrifice of the king during the *heb-sed*, or the actual burial-place of his entrails, which were removed from the body to aid its preservation.

Two parallel structures of solid masonry covered nearly the whole of the west side of the complex. The outer wall of the first structure, where it faced the south court, was decorated with recessed panelling, which gave it a uniform appearance with the walls on the south and east sides of the court. The second structure, which was higher than the first, had a curved roof resembling the roof of the South Mastaba. It may therefore have been the superstructure of a row of tombs belonging to Zoser's attendants, but, owing to the friable nature of the underlying rock, complete excavation has hitherto been impossible. Beyond these two structures was the thick enclosure wall.

The area between the mortuary temple and the northern enclosure wall may never have been finished, its only recognizable features being a large terrace with courts and a platform, measuring approximately 50 feet square, cut out of the native rock. This platform, which was faced with dressed limestone, was nearly in line with the north–south axis of the pyramid, and it is very possible that it served as an altar. The body of the enclosure wall on this side was built in the form of cells with dividing walls of stone. Since no trace of any object which might have been placed in these cells was discovered during excavation, it is unlikely that they were ever used for the purpose of storing funerary equipment. Beneath them, however, were subterranean chambers containing bread, fruit and other means of subsistence for life in the next world.

The enclosure wall of the Step Pyramid complex measured approximately 33 feet in height and had a peripheral length of more than a mile (fig. 5). It was composed of a thick inner core of masonry faced, partly inside and entirely outside, with dressed Tura limestone. On the outside, at intervals of $13\frac{1}{2}$ feet, there were rectangular bastions, all of uniform size apart from fourteen which were larger. On each of these larger bastions, which were spaced irregularly around the wall, an imitation was carved of closed double doors, giving the bastions the appearance of towered gateways. The only actual doorway, which has now been rebuilt (Plate 8), was situated near the southern corner of the east side, where two towers flanked a narrow passage leading to the entrance colonnade. Imitations of double doors, but in an open position, were also carved on the walls inside the towers. The whole outer face of the wall was panelled, and its upper half was decorated with small rectangular insets arranged vertically in rows of eight. These insets undoubtedly represented apertures of a similar pattern found in walls of mud-brick into which were fitted pieces of wood, perhaps for bonding purposes or for keeping the wall dry, but it is difficult to understand why the insets in this enclosure wall should have been confined to the upper half.

Walls composed of alternating projections and recesses are found in Egyptian tombs dating from the earliest dynastic times. The brick mastabas of the Ist Dynasty which lie a short distance to the north of the Step Pyramid are only one group of the many examples known. In those mastabas, however, the enclosure walls were not panelled but plain (fig. 2). The bastions and the fourteen gateways in Zoser's wall may have had their counterpart in the enclosure wall of his palace. It is, however, not impossible that the whole wall was a stone copy of the famous 'White Walls' built around Memphis by Menes. The 'White Walls', it must be supposed, were made of mud-brick overlaid with white gesso.

To review the Step Pyramid as a whole: it is certainly not an exaggeration to describe it as one of the most remarkable architectural works produced by the ancient Egyptians. That later generations regarded it with exceptional esteem is clear, not only from the veneration which they accorded to Imhotep, but also from hieratic graffiti on the passage walls of the northern and southern buildings, which record the admiration felt by some Egyptians who visited the monument more than a thousand years after it was built. No other known pyramid was surrounded with such an array of imposing buildings to supply the needs of the king in his after-life. In their place the kings who ruled two dynasties later were content with pictorial representations carved in relief. As an example, the pyramid complex of Sahurē, the second king of the Vth Dynasty, contains only reliefs of the *heb-sed*; it has no court with buildings specially designed for use in the ceremony.

Doubts have sometimes been entertained whether so high a degree of architectural perfection could have been achieved without having been preceded by a long process of development. There is, however, no evidence that stone had been employed in any earlier building, except for the construction of isolated parts. Moreover, the Step Pyramid displays many features which suggest that its builders lacked experience in the use of stone. Small blocks which could be easily handled were used instead of the massive slabs found in later buildings, showing that the technique of quarrying and manipulating heavy pieces of stone had not then been mastered. Again, engaged columns were probably not the outcome of artistic preference, but of doubt regarding the strength of the free-standing pillar. In decoration too the patterns chosen were copied from the wood, reed, or brick elements of earlier buildings; independent forms suited to stone had not yet been evolved.

Although the prototypes of the papyrus and the lily columns, which decorated the recesses in the eastern façades of the courts of the northern and the southern buildings, are evident at a glance, it is not easy to recognize what the sculptor was endeavouring to reproduce in the case of the ribbed and the fluted columns. H. Ricke has expressed the opinion that the ribbed columns, which are found only in the entrance colonnade, are not in reality columns but merely representations of buffers or fenders made of palm-ribs and laid as a cover over the exposed ends of brick walls in order to protect them from damage. J.-P. Lauer, however, maintains that these columns are imitations of wooden pillars representing bundles of reeds or palm-ribs which had been used as supports in more primitive constructions. This explanation, he believes, would account for the traces of red paint which remain on the columns, because red was the colour used to represent wood, whereas green would have been employed to represent the stems of plants.

Before attempting to summarize the principal theories of their origins, it is necessary to note that the fluted columns, in their occurrence in this complex, show certain differences. Those attached to the façades of the northern and southern buildings and the chapels in the *heb-sed* court were slender (tapering from about 1 foot 9 inches at the foot to 11½ inches at the top), lacked bases, and had the so-called pendent leaf capitals (fig. 9). The columns in the mortuary temple and the pavilion behind the *heb-sed* court, on the other hand, were thicker (about 2 feet 6 inches at the foot and 1 foot 8 inches at the top), were provided with circular disc-bases, and had rectangular block-capitals (fig. 10). All these columns were painted red from the top to a narrow band (lacking in the columns of the *heb-sed* court) 2 feet above the base, which was white, and black from the band downwards. Both Lauer and Ricke are in agreement in regarding the black colour as representing a protective covering of leather placed on the lower portions of similar columns made of softer materials. They are also essentially in agreement in interpreting the white band as a representation of a strip of metal, probably copper, which was intended to reinforce the lower part of the column. They regard the columns as reproductions in stone of the trunks of trees, perhaps conifers, the flutes being merely stylized representations of the incisions made in the wood by the curved cutting-edge of the tool used for dressing the surface. Ricke, who argues that the term 'column' is architecturally incorrect, has explained the so-called pendent leaf capitals (fig. 9) as being composed of a block representing the exposed end of a purlin supporting the framework of the roof and two cleats which were intended to strengthen the joint of the purlin with the framework and with the column. The corrugated surface of the cleats, he believes, may be explained, like the flutes of the columns, as a reproduction of the grooves made in the wooden prototype by the metal tool. The outward curve of the tips of the 'leaves', he suggests, was a device for deflecting rain-water away from the joint.

Although Lauer and Ricke differ widely in their interpretation of several details, including the nature of the objects placed in the holes beneath the pendent leaf capitals, they concur in their views on two fundamental matters: both agree that the ribs on the columns of the entrance colonnade represent stems, probably palm-ribs, and that the fluted columns imitate trunks of trees. P.E. Newberry, who was a botanist as well as being an Egyptologist, however, maintained that these two columns shared a common prototype in an umbelliferous plant, the *Heracleum giganteum*, the hollow stems of which, when green, are ribbed but, when dry, are fluted. In support of this identification he claimed that the pendent leaf capitals were imitations of the petioles of the leaves which hang down over the stem (fig. 12). This explanation is attractive for many reasons: it places the ribbed and the fluted columns in the same category as the papyrus and the lily columns, each being a representation of a single stem of a plant; the *Heracleum giganteum*, when fully grown, possesses sufficient strength to have been used in primitive structures for the framework over which reed-matting was placed; neither the papyrus nor the lily, by reason of the weakness of their stems, could have been used, at least singly, as

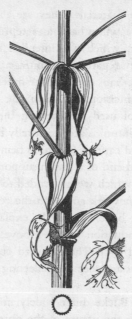

Figure 12. Stem of the Heracleum giganteum

supports, but if the Egyptians were already employing the *Heracleum giganteum* for structural skeletons it would have been simple, when reproductions in wood or stone took the place of the actual plant, to introduce variations, and the papyrus and the lily, because of their symbolical significance, would have been the most obvious plants to choose; lastly, the resemblance of the petioles to the pendent leaves of the capital seems too close to have been accidental.

Newberry's interpretation of the columns would probably have received more general acceptance than has yet been accorded to it if he could have shown that the *Heracleum giganteum* grew in Egypt, but, although this plant is widely distributed in its occurrence, there is no evidence that it has ever flourished in the Nile valley. (Newberry was aware of this difficulty and had previously suggested another umbelliferous plant, the *Silphium*, which was almost certainly a North African species of *Ferula*, either *Ferula communis* or *Ferula tingitana*, both of which have tall, rigid stems fluted externally.) Several other plants, however, which were once common in Egypt have long become extinct there, and it is conceivable that the *Heracleum giganteum* belongs to this class. On architectural grounds it may be argued that the pendent leaf capital is found only in the engaged columns of the northern and southern buildings and the *heb-sed* court, but the petioles, unlike the flowers of the papyrus and the lily, were without symbolical meaning and their omission from the engaged columns of the pavilion and the mortuary temple could be understood as an artistic variation. A stronger case can be presented against the theory that the ribbed columns also owed their origin to the *Heracleum giganteum* because their capitals (fig. 11) appear to have no clear parallel in the plant itself, unless it be that the stem was slit vertically at the top and the strips, still attached at the base, were folded downwards over the outside in order to double the thickness and thus provide greater strength. It must however be conceded that the absence of any indication of a tie at the base of the capital is difficult to reconcile with this explanation.

Size, architectural design, and decorative elements were not the only respects in which Zoser's pyramid excelled the tombs of his predecessors. It was also equipped on a scale never attempted before. In spite of being subjected to plundering over a period of at least four thousand years, it has yielded in the course of excavation thousands of beautifully shaped vases and dishes made of alabaster, schist, porphyry, breccia, quartz crystal, serpentine, and many other stones. Considerable quantities still await removal from the tombs of the royal family, where they may be seen lying in heaps reaching from the floor to the ceiling. No food or other commodity was placed in most of these vessels; their very presence, possibly in conjunction with the recitation of a magic formula by the priest, was enough to ensure a constant supply of their appropriate contents for the king.

Before its destruction, the enclosure must have contained a considerable number of statues. Only the seated figure of Zoser in the serdab has been preserved substantially intact, but fragments of other statues have also been found. At the northern end of the *heb-sed* court there is a limestone pedestal on the top of which are carved eight human feet; it must therefore have supported a group of four statues, possibly those of the king, queen, and two princesses. In the same court there were found three large monolithic figures, only one of which had been finished. At first sight these figures resemble caryatides, but it is highly unlikely that they were designed to stand as independent columns; they were probably intended to be built into niches. Fragments of other statues, including at least one of the king, were discovered outside the enclosure wall and in a recess in the south wall of the entrance colonnade. All these statues, and possibly several more which have now disappeared without trace, were made not to commemorate the persons whom they represented, but to provide their spirits with a substitute for their bodies during the various ceremonies performed within the pyramid enclosure. Since only two royal statues dating from an earlier period – both representing a predecessor of Zoser, Khasekhem – have hitherto been discovered, it is highly probable that Zoser's reign marked a big advance in the production of sculpture in the round. The figure in the serdab, if it may be regarded as typical, suggests that the collection of statues once contained in the enclosure was of a quality comparable with the finest masterpieces of the succeeding dynasties.

Before the recent excavations nothing remained visible of Zoser's monumental works except the pyramid itself, stripped almost entirely of its outer casing; inside also the pyramid had suffered grievously. All the rubble-filling of the central shaft and part of the blocking built into the side-ramp after the burial were systematically removed by ancient plunderers, so that today it is possible to stand on the granite roof of the tomb-chamber and, with the aid of a powerful electric torch, to see the underside of the lowest layer of stones which covered the mouth of the shaft when the first mastaba was built. Beneath these stones the plunderers, when removing the rubble-filling, had constructed a stout wooden platform, only a few fragments of which now remain. That the stones, lacking the support of either the filling or the platform, have not collapsed into the shaft is little short of miraculous.

Apart from the stone vessels, nothing has been preserved of Zoser's tomb furniture. In the tomb-chamber, however, some human remains were found; although there is no proof that they belonged to Zoser, the method of their burial would have been consistent with the practice of his time. The eleven tombs of the royal family were similarly plundered, leaving only the two alabaster coffins already described. One of these coffins – that containing the skeleton of a child – was lined with six layers of wood, each less than a quarter of an inch in thickness. They were laid with their grains running alternately in vertical and horizontal directions, and were held together by small wooden pegs. Some gold rivets, found in the innermost layer, suggest that this wooden lining was originally overlaid with gold.

It is impossible to estimate with any accuracy when the plundering of the Step Pyramid was begun. The graffiti in the northern and southern buildings suggest that the surrounding structures were substantially intact during the New Kingdom, but it does not follow that the tomb itself had not been robbed of its most valuable furniture by that time. The three reliefs of Zoser in the eastern gallery may provide evidence that access could be gained to the subterranean chambers and corridors during the Saite Period. Each relief has been divided by ink lines into squares, indicating that a scale reproduction of it was planned. Since the Saites are known to have modelled some of their sculpture on the works of the Old Kingdom, it is not unlikely that they were the artists who drew these grids over the reliefs. Other intruders were guided by baser motives, and a steady process of denudation probably continued without hindrance until the present century.

The Service des Antiquités, under the direction of J.-P. Lauer, has done a considerable amount of restoration work within the enclosure. The entrance colonnade, the south-east corner of the enclosure wall including the portal (Plate 8) and isolated parts of several other buildings have been reassembled.

Although none of Zoser's successors in the IIIrd Dynasty has left a monument comparable in magnificence with his pyramid enclosure, there is clear evidence that they followed the example which he had set in building tombs of a step pyramid form. One of these kings chose a site close to the south-west corner of Zoser's complex and laid out an enclosure roughly equal in length to the enclosure of the Step Pyramid, but only about two-thirds of its width. The excavation of this site was undertaken by Zakaria Goneim on behalf of the Service des Antiquités of the Egyptian Government in 1951–5 and through his labours a very considerable amount of information was obtained, although he was unable to complete the task before his premature death in 1959. Between 1963 and 1976 work on a limited scale was continued intermittently by J.-P. Lauer.

Inscribed clay stoppers of jars discovered in this pyramid showed that it was built by Sekhemkhet, a king who is otherwise known only from three representations carved in relief on a rock at Wady Maghara in Sinai and mistakenly attributed by Egyptologists in the past to Semerkhet, the penultimate king of the Ist Dynasty. How soon after his accession Sekhemkhet began to build his pyramid is unknown, but, if he has been correctly identified with a king whose personal name is

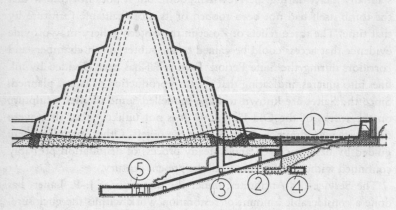

Figure 13. The pyramid of Sekhemkhet, section looking west

given as Zoser-Ti or Zoser-Teti in the king-lists, his reign lasted for no longer than six years and it is not surprising that a very considerable amount of the projected work was never carried out. Planned on a base measuring about 395 feet square, the superstructure (fig. 13) would probably have risen by seven steps to a height of about 230 feet. Since the monument was used as a quarry in later times it is impossible to estimate the height to which it had been built when work was abandoned; all that has survived to the present day is a few layers of the inner core nowhere higher than about 23 feet above ground-level. In order to reach the required depth for the substructure an open trench with sloping floor was cut in the rock, its shallow end being situated far beyond the northern face of the pyramid (figs. 13 and 14: 1). When the trench had been hewn to a depth of about 40 feet below the surface of the rock it was continued as a tunnel for a further 29 feet before this plan was abandoned, probably because the rock at that level was found to be unsound. The trench was then filled with rubble to about half its depth and a second tunnel was cut immediately above the first.

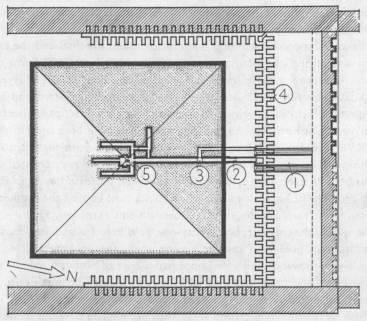

Figure 14. The pyramid of Sekhemkhet, substructure and ground-plan

Although the floor of the new tunnel continues the gradient of the trench, its flat ceiling is horizontal as far as a point 38 feet, measured on the incline, from the entrance where an arch, rounded on the underside, 3 feet in thickness and 13 feet in height, is carved in the rock which forms the south wall of this section of the corridor (figs. 13 and 14: 2). Beyond the arch, the ceiling, roughly curved, slopes at about the same angle as the floor, but its continuity is interrupted by ertical shaft, about 9 feet square in section and 41 feet in height, which rises through the rock and the core of the pyramid (figs.13 and 14: 3). Shafts comparable in design and position were constructed in mastabas of this period at Beit Khallaf, their purpose being to enable heavy stone portcullises to be lowered to the corridor and block it after the body had been placed in the tomb. In this pyramid the shaft had been blocked, though not to its full height, by large stones, which had been dropped down from above, those dropped first lying on a thick bed of *tafl* – an Arabic word meaning marl, shale or clayey rock – which had been piled on the floor of the corridor.

Four unexpected discoveries were made when the shaft and the *tafl* bed were being cleared. At the top of the shaft, bones and horns of animals, including cattle, rams and gazelles, had been placed in layers separated by fine sand. Beneath these layers were sixty-two papyri, most of which were written in demotic – a cursive script indirectly derived from hieroglyphics and first known to have been used in the XXVth Dynasty. Some of these documents dated from the reign of Ahmose II in the XXVIth Dynasty. The third discovery consisted of hundreds of stone vessels, which had also been buried in layers in the *tafl* bed. The bed itself stretched more than a yard beyond the northern limit of the shaft and on the floor beneath this extension, against the east wall of the corridor, lay twenty-one gold bracelets and armlets, an imitation in gold of a bivalve scallop shell, the gold overlay of a sickle-shaped wand which had once had a core of wood, hundreds of gold beads and other items of jewellery, including 420 small faience beads, all plated with gold, a needle and a pair of tweezers, both of which were made of electrum. It is difficult to explain how this treasure came to be buried in the corridor. Was it put there for some ritual purpose or by a thief who failed to return and recover his loot? Whatever the true explanation may be, if the treasure does date from the time when the pyramid was built, it is the oldest sizeable collection of gold jewellery at present known.

A doorway in the west wall of the corridor immediately beneath the shaft (figs. 13 and 14: 3) gives access, by way of an L-shaped passage, to a series of 132 subterranean magazines (fig. 14: 4) arranged in staggered fashion on each side of a level corridor running first from east to west and continued at both ends with arms extending southwards. From the doorway leading to these magazines the sloping corridor tinues downwards until it becomes flat at a point only a few yards short of the burial-chamber (figs.13 and 14: 5), a roughly hewn compartment measuring about 30 feet from north to south, 17 feet in width and 16½ feet in height. Recesses extending from floor to ceiling, each 6½ feet in depth, were cut approximately in the middle of the east and west walls, but their purpose is not evident. A doorway in the south wall of the burial-chamber leads to a blind gallery, one of four similar galleries, the northernmost of which would probably have been accessible by a connecting passage from the sloping corridor if work had not been terminated when the passage had been tunnelled to within 8½ inches of the corridor. It may be conjectured, on the analogy of Zoser's pyramid, that the walls of some at least of these galleries would ultimately have been decorated with blue-glazed tiles and possibly also with carved representations of the king performing religious ceremonies.

In spite of the unfinished condition of this pyramid, hopes were raised in the course of its excavation that it would prove to contain the body of the king. Not only was the corridor sealed in three places, at its entrance, below the shaft and at the doorway of the burial-chamber, by thick blocking walls of stone, which were still intact, but also there was no trace of any tunnel by which robbers could have circumvented these obstacles. Most significant of all, however, seemed to be the fact that a closed sarcophagus, on which a wreath had been placed, was discovered in the burial-chamber. This sarcophagus, carved from a single rectangular block of alabaster, was exceptional in one respect: instead of having the whole top as a lid, it had, at one end, a sliding panel which could be raised and lowered by a rope passed through a U-shaped boring at the top of the panel. Rib-shaped tenons on the sides and the base of the panel fitted into grooves cut in the sides and base of the aperture in the sarcophagus. Some plaster which could be seen in the grooves suggested that the panel had not been moved since it was ceremonially closed at the time of the funeral. All these indications, however, proved deceptive: the sarcophagus when opened was found to be empty. Unless it is to be assumed that the body and its costly appurtenances were stolen with the connivance of those in charge of the burial, it seems necessary to suppose that the tomb, or at least the sarcophagus, was intended as a dummy.

Too little work has been done on the clearance of the enclosure to show how far the construction of the various buildings had progressed when operations were brought to an end, presumably because of the king's death. Exploratory pits sunk at intervals along the perimeter and elsewhere in the enclosure revealed that it was honeycombed with retaining walls of stone, which boxed in rubble and *tafl*. Extensive terracing had been employed not merely to fill depressions but to raise the general level of the ground by about 30 feet, so that the buildings would stand high enough to be seen from Memphis. Some idea of the magnitude of the work involved can be gained from the results of an examination of the foundation of the western enclosure wall. This subterranean structure, which was 66 feet in thickness and 27 feet in height, served both as a platform for the wall above it and as the retaining wall of a terrace. The pyramid itself was founded on bed rock and, although the surviving part of its superstructure rises to a height of about 23 feet, it would all have lain below the level of the raised ground. It was for this reason that it was called the 'buried pyramid' before the name of its builder was known.

As first planned, the enclosure measured about 287 yards from north to south and 207 yards from east to west. If those dimensions had been retained, the pyramid would have stood in the middle of the area. Subsequently, however, the enclosure was enlarged by extending the east and west walls by about 206 yards to the north and 103 yards to the south, where the ground fell away. From north to south the enclosure was thus 598 yards in length and almost identical with that of Zoser, but it was only two-thirds of its width.

A considerable part of the original north wall still remains standing; it is composed of a thick core of local stone faced with fine limestone. Like the enclosure wall of Zoser's pyramid, it is panelled and rectangular bastions project outwards from its northern side. It is in fact almost an exact copy of Zoser's wall, both the panels and the bastions being of the same measurements as the corresponding features in the Step Pyramid enclosure, and doubtless imitations of closed double doors would have been carved on the irregularly spaced larger bastions if they had been completed. Greater economy in the use of Tura limestone as well as in its composition is however to be detected in the construction of Sekhemkhet's wall: the outer skin is only one course in thickness (about 1 foot) and each block is about twice as high (approximately 20 inches) as the facing-blocks in Zoser's wall. When it was decided to enlarge the enclosure, this wall, which had been built to the level of the sixth course, was left to serve as the southern retaining wall of a terrace, which appears to reach as far as the new northern boundary of the complex. The excavator stated that the eastern and western walls, in their northern extensions, were not in direct alignment with the earlier walls, each being stepped in by about 6 feet. Further excavation is required to verify this strange feature and it may also bring to light at least the foundations of other constructions within the enclosure, only one of which has yet been explored, though some walls on the north side of the pyramid, probably belonging to the mortuary temple, have been located.

Like Zoser, Sekhemkhet built a mastaba on the south side of his pyramid, but its superstructure was not concealed in the core of the enclosure wall. It was constructed of stone blocks and it stood on the terrace about half-way between the pyramid and the original enclosure wall, its main axis running from east to west. Before its almost complete demolition the superstructure measured about 34 yards in length and 17 yards in breadth. The substructure, which has been excavated by J.-P. Lauer, consists of a vertical shaft under the western end of the superstructure, a sloping corridor and a level passage leading to a small tomb-chamber measuring $11\frac{1}{2}$ feet in length and $8\frac{1}{2}$ feet in breadth. The shaft, sunk through rock to a depth of about 95 feet, penetrates the roof of the level passage near its junction with the sloping corridor. It was filled with sand and rubble when the tomb was closed. Nevertheless, the ancient robbers were able to bore a tunnel through the blocking of the sloping corridor, skirt the base of the shaft and reach the tomb-chamber. No doubt they removed most of its contents, but they left a few fragments of gold foil embossed with a reed-mat pattern, some stone vases, pottery, animal bones and a badly decayed wooden coffin of a IIIrd Dynasty design. The gold foil may have been the overlay of an inner coffin of wood or of a box containing jewellery which had been reduced to dust. Inside the coffin, which measured only 3 feet 11 inches in length and 2 feet 4 inches in breadth, lay the skeleton of a child of eighteen months to two years, perhaps a son of Semerkhet, but it is improbable that the mastaba was built to be his tomb. Unfortunately the discovery leaves the questions raised by Zoser's South Mastaba still unanswered.

Not the least valuable result of the excavation of the pyramid of Sekhemkhet was the light which it shed on the date of another step pyramid, the so-called Layer Pyramid at Zawiyet el-Aryan (Plate 14). G.A. Reisner, who examined this pyramid some years after it had been excavated by Alessandro Barsanti, at first ascribed it to the IIIrd Dynasty; subsequently he revised his opinion in favour of the IInd Dynasty. Its superstructure, of which only the lowest courses of the inner core have been preserved (Plate 15), covers an area 276 feet square. In every probability the architect planned a monument with six or seven steps, but it seems that the building was never completed. A flight of steps to the north of the superstructure, about 13 yards from the north-east corner, descends to a rock-cut tunnel which runs to a point outside, and approximately in line with, the middle of the north face where it joins the base of a vertical shaft (fig. 15: 1), 62 feet 6 inches in depth. At the same level in the shaft two other tunnels have their entrances, one in the south wall leading by way of a horizontal corridor and a second flight of steps to the tomb-chamber (fig. 15: 2) measuring approximately 12 feet (north-south) by 8 feet 9 inches and 9 feet 10 inches in height, and the other in the north wall giving access by a connecting passage to a long transverse corridor (fig. 15: 3) running from east to west with short arms at each end directed southwards. Thirty-two compartments, all oriented towards the pyramid and about 15 feet in length, were cut in the inner wall of this corridor. At a higher level in the shaft another corridor, a *cul-de-sac*, was tunnelled southwards (fig. 15: 4).

Although the design of the substructure of this pyramid differs in detail from the pyramid of Sekhemkhet, it is essentially similar and the surviving remnants of the two superstructures are almost identical. Perhaps the resemblance would have been even closer if the work on

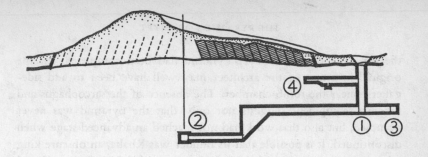

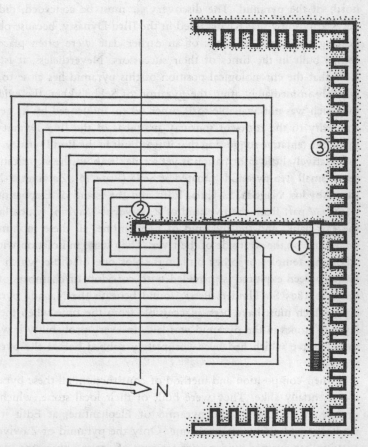

Figure 15. The Layer Pyramid of Zawiyet el-Aryan, section looking west and plan

the substructure of the Layer Pyramid had been completed, for the original intention of the architect may well have been to add side-galleries near the tomb-chamber. The absence of the sarcophagus and funerary equipment suggests not only that the pyramid was never occupied, but also that work had not reached an advanced stage when discontinued. It is possible that its builder was Khaba, an obscure king whose name was inscribed on some stone vessels which Reisner found in a group of IIIrd Dynasty brick mastabas situated on a plateau to the north of the pyramid. The discovery, it must be conceded, did not necessarily show that Khaba ruled in the IIIrd Dynasty, because objects bearing the names of kings of an earlier date were often placed in tombs built in the times of their successors. Nevertheless, it is now clear that the chronological position of this pyramid lies close to, and possibly immediately after, the pyramid of Sekhemkhet, the evidence of which was not available to Reisner when, influenced by its general similarity to the rock-cut stairway mastabas of the IInd Dynasty, he made the tentative suggestion that it was built in the IInd Dynasty.

Relatively little information is yet available about the significance of seven small step pyramids situated at Seila (Plate 16), Zawiyet el-Mayitin, Abydos, Nagada, El-Kula, Edfu and the island of Elephantine at Aswan. Apart from the pyramid of Zawiyet el-Mayitin, which lies on the east bank, and the pyramid of Elephantine, all these monuments were built on the west side of the river. They stand in isolation without adjoining temples or other buildings. Not one of those which have hitherto been explored is provided with corridors or chambers of any kind. In 1895 Sir Flinders Petrie found beneath the Nagada pyramid a pit which must have been inaccessible from the time when the first layer of stones in the pyramid was laid. In every probability it was an earlier grave which had been completely robbed before the pyramid was built.

In their composition and method of construction, all these pyramids are essentially alike. They were built of their local stone, which was granite in the case of the pyramid of Elephantine; at Edfu it was sandstone and elsewhere limestone. Only the pyramid of Zawiyet el-Mayitin has retained evidence of a casing of dressed limestone, part of which is still visible at the base; it may originally have covered the whole pyramid. Some fragments of dressed limestone were found at both Seila and El-Kula, but not enough to prove that either pyramid had once had an outer casing. Each pyramid in the group consists of a trapezoidal nucleus, which tapers upwards on all four sides and to which were added thick coating layers of masonry. The layers incline inwards towards the nucleus, their tops forming the steps. The stones in the coating layers are generally, but not invariably, laid in inward-inclining courses. Most of the pyramids have three steps, but, when complete, the pyramid of Seila had four and possibly the pyramid of Zawiyet el-Mayitin had the same number. Base measurements, apart from those of the pyramids of Seila (99 feet square) and Zawiyet el-Mayitin (74 feet square) are approximately 60 feet in each direction.

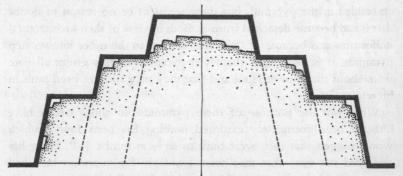

Figure 16. The pyramid of El-Kula, section looking south-east

They vary in height, in their present state of preservation, from about 13 feet, at Abydos, to about 27 feet at El-Kula (fig. 16). With the possible exception of the pyramid of Seila, the sides of which face north, south, east and west, all the pyramids in the group are oriented so that their sides are parallel to the river. This orientation has resulted in the corners (not the sides) of the pyramids at El-Kula and Abydos facing the four cardinal points.

Similarity in design and construction would alone suggest proximity in date for all seven pyramids. They clearly belong to the same stage in technical achievement as the step pyramids of Zoser and Sekhemkhet and the fact that they are square at the base points to a date not earlier than that of Sekhemkhet. A discovery which seems to give a closer indication of the date was made in 1909 by a French expedition working at Elephantine. The aim of the expedition was to find evidence of a Jewish community which had settled on the island in the fifth century B.C. Documents written by members of the community in Aramaic, which had been found earlier in the excavations, mentioned a Jewish temple, and the director, C. Clermont-Ganneau, had mistakenly supposed that a tumulus on the west side of the island, which eventually proved to be the pyramid, was the substructure of the temple. In the course of subsequent excavations, his successor, J.-E. Gautier, found a large granite cone near the tumulus which bore an inscription on its base naming Huni, the last king of the IIIrd Dynasty. It was not embedded in the pyramid, but there seems to be no reason to doubt that it had become detached from it. Both in view of their architectural uniformity and because of their resemblance to the other known step pyramids, it is likely that the seven pyramids in this group all date from about the time of Huni and that they may all have been built in his reign.

What was the purpose of these pyramids? In those which have hitherto been completely explored nothing has been found which would suggest that they were built to serve as tombs. J.-P. Lauer has expressed the view that they were cenotaphs for queens, which had been erected in their places of birth while their real tombs were built near those of the kings in the Memphite necropolis. Another archaeologist with long experience of working on pyramids, Dieter Arnold, regards the pyramids as representations of the primordial hill, the hieroglyphic sign for which depicts a step pyramid. It is, moreover, known that several places in Egypt claimed to be founded where the hill had emerged from the waters of chaos. Werner Kaiser, Director of the German Institute of Archaeology in Cairo, and his assistant Gunter Dreyer, who carried out a survey of all seven pyramids in 1979, concluded that they were either cenotaphs for the king or, more probably, emblems of his power set up in the vicinity of his provincial residences. They were all, according to their opinion, the work of Huni. Personal appearances by a king in Middle and Upper Egypt were probably rare in very early times and monumental reminders of his authority might have helped to retain the allegiance of the people. Although the employment of a pyramid for such a purpose would have no parallel in later times, the explanation is not unattractive, but it is only a hypothesis, which is all its authors claim for it. Perhaps its most obvious weakness is that it does not take into account the fact that the pyramid of Seila was not only not far from the capital at Memphis but was actually within sight of the much larger and more imposing pyramid of Meidum, the first builder of which is generally believed, though without proof, to have been Huni. It would have been a more conspicuous reminder of the king's power. A small pyramid at Seila would seem superfluous. Besides the known pyramids which have not yet been properly explored, there may be others in a ruined condition concealed under the sand, but still capable of shedding light on the true purpose of these problematical monuments. Without more information than is now available, uncertainty and speculation are likely to continue.

CHAPTER THREE

THE TRANSITION TO THE
TRUE PYRAMID

At the beginning of the IVth Dynasty an important development occurred in the design of the royal tomb: the step pyramid was superseded by the true pyramid, a monument with a square base and sides sloping inwards to a point at the summit. By a lucky chance it is possible to trace this development in the badly damaged pyramid at Meidum which lies about thirty miles south of Memphis. In its present condition the monument resembles a high rectangular tower rather than a pyramid (Plate 17). This shape is not entirely fortuitous, but is partly due to the method of its construction, the main features of which became known through Sir Flinders Petrie's excavations in 1891. Subsequent investigations, conducted at different times by G.A. Wainwright, Ludwig Borchardt, and Alan Rowe, have added many important details to Petrie's discoveries.

Like Zoser's pyramid, the pyramid of Meidum attained its final form after undergoing a number of transformations. The initial building may have resembled a mastaba with a square base or it may have been a small step pyramid, the superstructure of which would now be concealed within the surviving core. Some blocks recovered in the course of excavation bore drawings scratched by the quarrymen which showed buildings with two, three and four steps, possibly representing successive alterations in the original design. It is difficult to judge how much reliance can be attached to such sketches, but what may be regarded as supporting evidence for changes in form will be cited after the structure of the pyramid has been described.

The first ascertainable form of the superstructure is that of a seven-stepped pyramid (fig. 17: 1). It was achieved in the same way as in the seven small step pyramids mentioned in the last chapter, by constructing a central tower-like building with inward-sloping sides, which

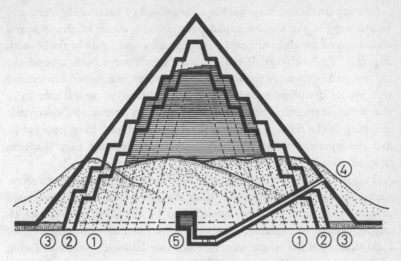

Figure 17. The pyramid of Meidum, section looking west

served as both the nucleus and the top step of the pyramid. Six thick coatings of masonry, diminishing in height from the centre outwards, were then built against the four sides of this nucleus, their upper portions supplying the six remaining steps. Each of the coatings, which inclined inwards at an angle of about 75°, consisted of a core of local stone cased from top to bottom with Tura limestone. Only those parts of the casing which covered the steps were dressed, the remainder being left in the rough.

When the seven-stepped pyramid had been completed, a considerable enlargement was undertaken, thereby converting it into a pyramid with eight steps. Each step in the overlay was built to a level somewhat higher than the corresponding step in the previous design. When the new step had reached the level of the old, a number of courses of blocks were laid across both steps to bond the two structures together (fig. 17: 2). What had been the platform at the top of the seven-stepped pyramid became the seventh step and the height of the pyramid was raised by about 45 feet. Again the material used was local stone cased with Tura limestone, which was dressed where it was exposed.

The superstructure now visible is composed of parts of the third and fourth steps of the seven-stepped pyramid, the whole of the fifth and sixth steps of the eight-stepped pyramid and a small part of the seventh step (fig. 17: hatching). If the coatings which were built around the nucleus had been more firmly bonded together, the ruined superstructure would doubtless have assumed a very different appearance from that which it presents today. In the course of its destruction, systematic stripping of the sides, coating by coating, would have been impossible, and the pyramid would probably have been reduced to a shapeless heap of stones.

This pyramid was not, however, destined to remain as a step pyramid, although it is evident that both the seven- and the eight-stepped designs were, in their turn, intended to be final. For reasons which cannot readily be explained, the steps were filled in with a packing of local stone, and the whole structure was overlaid with a smooth facing of Tura limestone. By this means, the monument was transformed into a geometrically true pyramid (fig. 17: 3). Substantial portions of the lower half of the ultimate form still remain intact.

A remarkable feature of this monument is that the casing and the backing-stones of the true pyramid, unlike those of the seven- and eight-stepped pyramids, do not rest directly on the underlying rock. They rest on a kind of platform of stone blocks under which, in places, a layer of sand has been laid in order to fill up unevennesses in the rock and thus bring the top surface of the platform to a uniform level. Sand, if dry and properly compacted, is known to provide an effective foundation material, and there is no reason to suppose that its use in this pyramid was a contributory factor to its partial collapse, as one writer mistakenly tried to show. In an investigation carried out in 1983-4 the whole of the northern face was cleared of sand and débris down to the bottom without revealing any sign that movement had occurred.

Although Sir Flinders Petrie was able to determine correctly how the pyramid was constructed, he could only do so insofar as it was possible from the outside. For that reason he was unable to offer any proof that a mastaba or a small stepped pyramid lay in the middle of the monument. It was largely in the hope of verifying this theory that Petrie's assistant, G.A. Wainwright, bored a tunnel through the masonry at the base of the pyramid from the east face almost to the tomb-chamber. It was a laborious task, spread over two seasons between 1910 and 1912, but it enabled him to study the foundations of the eight successive coatings already identified and to discover two more coatings, the faces of which were 16 and 33 feet respectively inwards from the eighth face. He continued his tunnel for a further 21 feet without finding another face or anything except compact masonry, which must cover an area about 103 feet square at the centre of the pyramid. Is it the base of a stepped mastaba such as exists in the Step Pyramid of Zoser? No one can be sure. The additional coatings may be simply structural elements which are continued upwards to different heights within the visible nucleus. On the other hand, it is possible that they are the outer faces of a square stepped structure such as can be seen in the Step Pyramid of Zoser or else the middle and the outermost coating of a small initial pyramid with three steps.

The entrance to the pyramid at each stage of its development was in the northern face (fig. 17: 4). From a point in the outermost casing, situated a little above the lowest step of the penultimate design, a corridor leads downwards at an angle of about 28°, first through the core of the superstructure and then into the substratum of rock. At a distance of about 190 feet from the entrance, the gradient ceases and the corridor continues on an even plane for a further 31 feet. Near the bottom of the gradient there is a pit in the floor, but its purpose is not apparent. Beyond the pit there may have been a wooden door, the frame of which would have fitted into grooves cut in the walls, roof, and floor of the corridor. Two recesses, each about $8\frac{1}{2}$ feet in width and 4 feet in depth, open out of the sides of the level section of the corridor, the first on the east and the second on the west. The purpose of these recesses too is obscure, but it is tempting to think that they were intended for storing, during the construction of the pyramid, stone plug-blocks which would have been too large to be lowered down the corridor after the burial. The area of both recesses would have been sufficient for manoeuvring blocks of considerable size, and the space left vacant when they had been moved into position could have been filled with masonry. Some limestone blocks found in the recesses may actually have been used for this purpose. Such a method of sealing the passages to the tomb-chamber may well have led to the invention of the side portcullises found in the next pyramid to be described.

At the end of the corridor a vertical shaft leads upwards, emerging in the floor of the tomb-chamber at its north-east corner (fig. 17: 5). Built partly in the rock, but mainly in the core of the superstructure, it measures 19½ feet from north to south and 8½ feet from east to west. It is constructed entirely of limestone and its floor was paved with slabs of limestone, most of which have now disappeared. On the east and west sides, its roof consists of seven overlapping layers in the form of a corbel vault. In the south wall there is a hole made by robbers in search of hidden treasure. Both in the shaft and in the chamber there are wooden baulks which may have been used for some purpose by the builders or, alternatively, may have been required for moving heavy funerary equipment, such as a stone sarcophagus. No trace of such a sarcophagus was, however, found in 1882 by Sir Gaston Maspero, the first archaeologist to enter the pyramid in modern times.

The buildings belonging to this pyramid were arranged according to what subsequently became the standard design for an Old Kingdom pyramid complex, the essential elements of which were always the pyramid itself and at least one subsidiary pyramid standing on high ground within an enclosure, a mortuary temple, a sloping causeway, and a building on the western fringe of the cultivation. The valley building was connected with the river by a canal dug in order to enable the funeral procession of boats to reach the complex without a long journey overland.

A wide mud-plaster pavement, bounded by a stone wall, surrounded this pyramid. Between the south face and the wall lay the earliest known subsidiary pyramid. Its stepped superstructure, about 88 feet square at the base, is now reduced to a few stones which cover a severely destroyed substructure. The final extension of the main pyramid having obstructed the northern entrance to the subsidiary pyramid, a shaft, 4 feet square and 11½ feet in depth, was sunk on its southern side and from the base of the shaft a horizontal passage, 22 feet in length, with a curved ceiling was cut through the rock to the pyramid-chamber. Within the enclosure on the north side was a large mastaba – an unusual feature in such a position – which has completely disappeared. Built against the middle of the east face of the pyramid, and still almost intact, is the mortuary temple composed entirely of Tura limestone. It is a very simple building, covering an area little more than 34 feet square and rising to a maximum height of 9 feet. A door in the southern corner of its front wall opens into a passage set

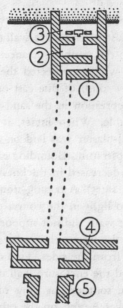

Figure 18. Mortuary temple of the pyramid of Meidum

at right angles to the door (fig. 18: 1); beyond lies a single chamber running parallel with the passage (fig. 18: 2) and an open court which backs directly on to the pyramid. No carvings of any kind decorate the walls of the passage or the chamber, neither of which has any opening for light except the door. In the middle of the court, opposite the door leading from the chamber, there is a low limestone altar intended for the daily offerings of food and drink for the dead king (fig. 18: 3). Two tall monolithic slabs of limestone with rounded tops, mounted on low rectangular bases of similar material, stand one on each side of the altar. Although no inscriptions have been carved on these slabs, it is clear from their shape that they were designed as funerary stelae which might have been expected to bear the various names and titles of the king. The absence of such an inscription, together with the fact that the stones forming the lowest courses of the temple walls have been left undressed, would strongly suggest that the building was never finished.

An open space measuring about 80 feet in width separated the mortuary temple from the eastern enclosure wall (fig. 18: 4). At a point in the wall nearly opposite the temple entrance, a narrow opening gave access to the causeway which connected the pyramid area with the building situated slightly south of due east on the edge of the valley (Plate 17). A shallow depression in the sand is the only indication of this causeway now visible. When intact, it measured 235 yards in length. Its floor of mud-plaster was laid on a bed, 10 feet in width, hewn out of the rock substratum. Bounding each side was a stone wall, 7 feet in height, which decreased in thickness from 5 feet at the base to 4 feet at the top (fig. 18: 5). A coping-stone with the upper surface rounded, which came to light in the course of Flinders Petrie's excavations, showed that the walls did not support a roof. The only break in these walls was near the upper end, where two doors allowed the causeway to be entered from the sides. Two deep recesses at the junction of the causeway and the enclosure wall may once have contained statues of the king, the southern as king of Upper Egypt and the northern as king of Lower Egypt; on the other hand, they may have been used for the performance of some ritual during the funeral ceremony. At the lower end of the causeway, close to where it joined the valley building, there was a double door, the pivots of which fitted into two sockets cut in the rock beneath the mud-plaster floor. It is difficult to account for the presence of a door in such a position, but it may be surmised that it was intended to debar those not entitled by their office to proceed further than the valley building.

Complete excavation of the valley building has so far proved impracticable owing to the sodden condition of the ground, caused by a rise in the level of the Nile bed since the days when this pyramid complex was built. Its walls are reduced nearly to ground-level and the simplicity and modest dimensions of the mortuary temple would certainly suggest that the valley building also was unpretentious.

No contemporary inscriptions giving the name of the builder of this pyramid have been found at Meidum. In the passage and chamber of the mortuary temple, however, there are a number of graffiti, scribbled on the walls by visitors during the XVIIIth Dynasty, which show that the pyramid was at that time considered to be the work of Seneferu, the first king of the IVth Dynasty. As an example, one of these graffiti may be translated as follows: 'On the twelfth day of the fourth month of summer in the forty-first year of the reign of Tuthmosis III, the Scribe Aakheperkāre-senb, son of Amenmesu [the Scribe and Ritualist of the deceased King Tuthmosis I], came to see the beautiful temple of King Seneferu. He found it as though heaven were within it and the sun rising in it. Then he said: "May heaven rain with fresh myrrh, may it drip with incense upon the roof of the temple of King Seneferu."' Other graffiti in the temple dating as early even as the VIth Dynasty mention the name of Seneferu, but do not state explicitly that the temple belonged to him.

The information given in the graffiti alone would be considered sufficient to enable the pyramid of Meidum to be attributed to Seneferu if no other pyramid with a comparable claim were known. Twenty-eight miles north of Meidum, at Dahshur, there are, however, two pyramids (Plate 18), both of which were certainly built by Seneferu. Before the question of ownership can be discussed more fully, it is necessary to describe the chief architectural features of these two pyramids. Although the southern pyramid was no doubt planned as a geometrically true pyramid, it was not completed as such; at a point somewhat above half its height the angle of its incline decreases abruptly from 54° 31' 13" to 43° 21' (figs. 19 and 20). It has, therefore, been variously named the 'Bent', 'False', 'Rhomboidal' and 'Blunted' Pyramid.

A survey of the pyramid published in 1964 by V. Maragioglio and C.A. Rinaldi showed that the original intention was to build a pyramid covering a smaller area and having a slope of about 60°. Cracks, however, developed in the outer casing and in the chambers and

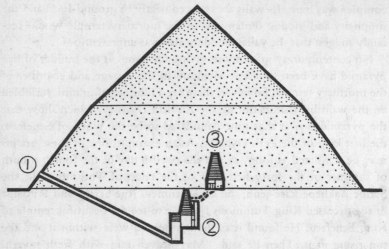

Figure 19. The Bent Pyramid, section looking east

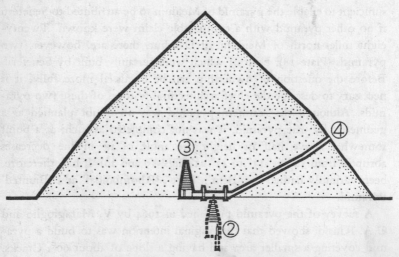

Figure 20. The Bent Pyramid, section looking south

78

passages, so that it became necessary to change the design, but not before the building had reached a height of at least 112 feet. In order to prevent further movement, substantial additions were built to all four sides of the pyramid, increasing its length at the base to 620 feet, and the slope of the whole structure was reduced to 54° 31′ 13″. In spite of these measures, fresh cracks must have appeared and, in consequence, another change was made in the design: at a perpendicular height of about 162 feet the angle of its slope was reduced to 43° 21′ and the same angle was retained to the top of the pyramid. Some loss has occurred at the summit; its present height is about 333 feet.

Approximately 800 years after the time of Seneferu, Ammenemes III of the XIIth Dynasty built a pyramid to the east of the Bent Pyramid, apparently with comparable results. Dieter Arnold, who conducted the first exhaustive exploration of the pyramid, reported that its architect had overestimated the carrying properties of the clayey strata in which its chambers and corridors were excavated. Cracks developed in the course of the work and eventually the king decided to build another pyramid in the Faiyum. The Bent Pyramid was built, according to Maragioglio and Rinaldi, on ground consisting of 'compacted clay, with flint pebbles'. In their opinion 'the pyramid nucleus rests directly on the clay while the backing-stones rest on a foundation platform which was built around the nucleus and presents an upper surface sloping towards the inside'. It has been calculated that, when work was discontinued on the first design at a height of 112 feet, foundation pressure on one square foot would have been no more than $6\frac{1}{4}$ tons and yet the cracks had already appeared. The second and the third stages in the construction increased the pressure, each by about 2 tons, so that the final pressure amounted to about 10 tons per square foot – considerably above the limit of 6 to 8 tons per square foot foundation pressure on shale (*tafl*) recommended in modern textbooks. If these calculations are correct, it seems necessary to conclude that the measures taken to rectify the cracks were bound to make them worse.

No other major pyramid has preserved so much of its outer casing as this pyramid. That it is in that exceptional state is largely due to the way in which it was built. The stones in the lower part are laid in courses which incline inwards and downwards and, in that respect, this pyramid resembles the step pyramids. Rectangular blocks of stone laid in that fashion gave a building greater cohesion and also reduced the amount of trimming necessary to bring their outer surfaces into alignment with the slope of a pyramid. The stones above the change of angle are not only smaller than those below, but they are laid in approximately level courses.

Internally, the Bent Pyramid is unique among the pyramids of the Old Kingdom in having two separate entrances (figs. 19–21: 1 and 4).

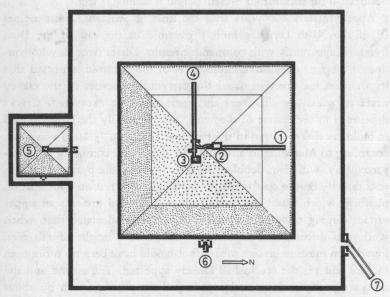

Figure 21. The Bent Pyramid, plan

An aperture approximately in the middle of the northern face and at a height of about 39 feet above ground-level gives access to a narrow low-roofed corridor, which descends initially at a gradient of 28° 22′ and subsequently at 26° 20′, first through the core of the pyramid and then into the subterranean rock (figs. 19 and 21: 1). At a distance of about 241 feet 6 inches from the entrance, the corridor becomes level for a further 2 feet 8 inches, where a corbelled roof suddenly rises to a height of 41 feet 6 inches and a kind of lofty, narrow vestibule, 16 feet 2 inches in length, is formed. Immediately beyond lies the lower of two chambers, measuring 20 feet 6 inches from north to south and 16 feet 6 inches from east to west, with a height of about 57 feet (figs. 19 and 21: 2). The most remarkable feature of this chamber is its corbelled roof, which is made by stepping a few inches inwards each of the fifteen upper courses of all four limestone walls, leaving at the top a span only 5 feet 3 inches long and 1 foot wide. In the south wall of the chamber, opposite the entrance, there is a passage 10 feet in length leading to a deep pit, which, until it was excavated in 1946–7 by Abdessalam Hussein, was filled with cut blocks of stone and paved. Above the pit a blind shaft rises perpendicularly to a height of 42 feet 6 inches; a second passage, vertically above the first, runs from the roof of the chamber to a point higher up in the shaft. Two blocks of stone were placed in recesses in the shaft, one on the north side immediately below the opening from the upper passage and the other on the south side near the top of the shaft, apparently for the purpose of closing the shaft, but neither of these trap-doors had been lowered into position. Like the pit, the floor of the chamber was built up with blocks of stone to a height of 20 feet 6 inches above the floor of the vestibule.

A second corridor with its entrance at a height of about 110 feet from the ground and about 15 yards south of the middle of the west face of the pyramid leads to the upper chamber (Plate 19; figs. 20 and 21: 4). It is the only known instance during the Old Kingdom of such a corridor running from any direction except the north. Sloping first at a gradient of 30° 09′ and then at a gradient of 24° 17′ it descends through the core of the superstructure for a distance of 212 feet until it reaches ground-level, where it continues horizontally for a further 66 feet to join the chamber (figs. 20 and 21: 3). This chamber is not built immediately above the one connected with the northern entrance, but lies to the south-east. It has a corbelled roof, and its floor, like that of the lower chamber, was built up to a height of about 14 feet by layers of small blocks of stone. When this blocking was removed in 1946–7 it was found that a kind of framework of thick cedarwood poles had been constructed against the walls and across the part of the chamber which had previously lain beneath the floor (Plate 21). What motive could have prompted the builders to place the framework in this position is uncertain, but the stoutness of the poles and their arrangement suggest that it was intended to counter lateral pressure on the walls and thus provide support until the floor had been built up. Structural weaknesses must have become apparent while the pyramid was being built, because, as Perring observed, plaster had been used by the builders to fill up cracks which had developed in the walls of the lower chamber, and similar repair work had also been carried out in the upper chamber.

Until 1951 access to the upper chamber could not be gained by way of the corridor, which had remained partly blocked with stones, and its entrance was sealed with the outer casing of the pyramid. The only means of approach was through a roughly hewn passage running from a hole in the south side of the roof of the lower chamber to a point in the horizontal section of the upper corridor. To Perring belongs the credit of being the first to describe a pair of portcullises which he saw in the upper corridor, one on each side of the mouth of the passage leading from the lower chamber.[1] They were considerably wider than the corridor (fig. 22: 1) and were not constructed in the normal way to drop perpendicularly, but to slide sideways across the corridor (fig. 22: 2) from recesses in the side-walls. A wooden prop (fig. 22: 3) was probably used to keep the portcullis from sliding into position prematurely. Only the outermost of the two portcullises, however, had been closed (Plate 19); the one nearer to the chamber still remained in its recess. Since the closed portcullis was plastered not only on the outer side but also on the inner side, Perring concluded that it must have been closed at a time when the passage leading to the lower chamber and also the two sloping corridors were open; otherwise the workmen who laid the plaster would have been trapped within the pyramid. Perring's observations have since been confirmed and it is evident that the passage was not the work of later robbers, as the roughness of its fashioning would at first suggest. It would not be the only example of such a passage being hurriedly hewn through the masonry of a pyramid; the Great Pyramid offers a striking parallel, which will be considered in the next chapter.

1. H. Vyse, *The Pyramids of Gizeh*, Vol. III, p. 69.

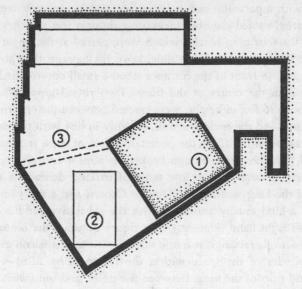

Figure 22. The Bent Pyramid – portcullis in open position

Apart from some 'cordage and ancient baskets' of uncertain date which Perring discovered in one of the corridors, the only objects which have been recovered from the Bent Pyramid are the dismembered remains of a bird, identified as an owl, and parts of the skeletons of five bats, all wrapped together and placed inside a wooden box laid in a cavity in the floor of the upper corridor. No trace of a sarcophagus was found either in the upper or in the lower chamber. The name of Seneferu, written in red ochre, was however identified on a block lying beneath the floor of the upper chamber and also on a stone at the north-east corner of the outer casing.

At a distance of about 60 yards to the south of the pyramid and within its stone enclosure wall a second and much smaller pyramid was built (fig. 21: 5). Each of its sides measures about 174 feet at the base. When complete it rose to a height of 106 feet 9 inches, but the top 38 feet and most of the outer casing are now missing. Internally it consists of a corridor which descends steeply from an entrance above ground-level in the centre of the northern face, a short horizontal passage with a portcullis and an ascending passage opening westwards into a corbel-roofed chamber measuring about 7 feet 8 inches square. Two of the four plug-blocks, which were placed at the upper end of the ascending passage, failed to slide down the passage; they are still in the pyramid. In front of the entrance stood a small one-roomed chapel with a pit in the centre of the floor. Two round-topped limestone stelae, about 16 feet in height, were erected between the eastern side of the pyramid and the enclosure wall, roughly in line with the east-west axis of the pyramid. Only the pedestal of one of these monoliths has survived, but the other, though broken, is almost entirely preserved. Carved on its outer face in low relief of striking delicacy is a seated figure of the king wearing the Double Crown and a short linen garment of a kind usually associated with the *sed* festival, and holding a flail in his right hand (Plate 20). The figure occupies the bottom left-hand corner of a rectangular frame surmounted by the falcon of Horus, the remainder of the space within the frame being filled with the names and titles of the king. Between the stelae, and somewhat further to the east, traces of what may have been a brick altar were found, but its date could not be ascertained.

Subsidiary pyramids of this kind, varying in number, are regularly found within the main pyramid enclosures. It has generally been supposed that they were built for the queens. Some may have been used for that purpose, but others could not possibly have been tombs. In this instance it seems likely that it was intended to fulfil the same function as the South Mastaba in the Step Pyramid enclosure, and consequently it has been conjectured that it was built as a tomb for the king's entrails, which were removed from the body during mummification, and perhaps also for his *ka*.

The original plan of the Bent Pyramid does not seem to have included a mortuary temple worthy of the name, but only an open offering-place with an altar and two limestone stelae (figs. 21: 6, and 23: 2 and 3). Fragments of the stelae recovered during excavation show that they were nearly twice as high as those outside the subsidiary pyramid, similar in shape and decorated with the king's names and titles. The altar, formed like the hieroglyphic sign for an offering, consisted of three limestone blocks with an alabaster offering-table

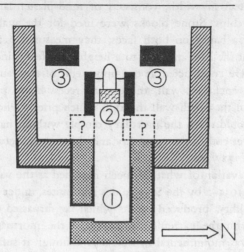

Figure 23. Mortuary temple of the Bent Pyramid

inserted in a cavity cut to receive it in the top surface of the blocks. At
an early date the offering-place was enclosed within protecting walls
of brick and, perhaps even earlier, an antechamber was built further
towards the east with its entrance in the south-east corner (fig. 23: 1).
The altar was also roofed over with flat slabs of stone resting on two
stone walls. Some reconstruction work was undertaken at a later date,
possibly during the Middle Kingdom, and the general plan was modified in detail, but these changes had little effect on the fundamentally
simple character of the initial offering-place. An even simpler structure
to house a limestone offering-table, which was also protected by walls
of brick, was located outside the northern entrance to the pyramid.
Small chapels in such a position were a common feature in subsequent
pyramids; perhaps they were the architectural descendants of the northern mortuary temples of step pyramids.

In almost every respect the causeway with its unroofed corridor
resembled the causeway of the Meidum pyramid, except in so far as it
was considerably longer and it joined not the eastern enclosure wall

but the northern wall near the eastern end (fig. 21: 7). The pavement, about 10 feet in width, consisted of mud-plaster laid on a bed of limestone chips. Stone blocks were used for the walls, which were built with a batter on both faces; they measured 6 feet 6 inches in thickness at the base and rose to a height of 6 feet 2 inches. Two deep recesses were constructed at the upper end of the causeway where it joined the enclosure wall, the eastern recess being provided with a doorway in the north wall through which priests who lived near the pyramid could reach the mortuary temple without having to go first to the lower end of the causeway and then return between its walls, a distance of 772 yards.

The excavation of what has been regarded as the valley building in the season 1951-2 by the Service des Antiquités, under the direction of Ahmed Fakhry, produced results which far surpassed expectations. In contrast with the extreme simplicity of the mortuary temple, this building was monumental in size and, although it suffered systematic destruction at a time which cannot yet be determined, enough has been preserved of the decoration to show that it would have borne comparison with anything now known of its kind dating from the Old Kingdom. Rectangular in its plan (fig. 24) and surrounded by an enclosure wall, the entire building was composed of local stone and faced with Tura limestone; the floor was paved with mud-plaster. In front of the entrance, which was in the middle of the southern façade, lay a narrow court, the long outer wall of which was a continuation of one of the walls of the causeway. At each end of this wall, on the outer side, stood a limestone stela decorated with the names and titles of the king; in shape and size they resembled the stelae outside the subsidiary pyramid. The building itself was divided into three main parts: an entrance hall flanked on each side by two chambers, an open court, and six shrines at the back of a pillared portico. Its floor dimensions were approximately 51 yards from north to south by 28 yards 1 foot from east to west. Scenes were carved in bold relief on the walls of the entrance hall, on the rectangular monolithic pillars and on the side-walls of the portico and at least the two westernmost shrines. Statues of the king, larger than life-size, were attached to niches in the back walls of some, and possibly all, of the shrines; they were thus in the nature of figures carved in very high relief and not free-standing sculptures like the seated statue of Zoser in the serdab of the Step Pyramid. Some idea of the destruction wrought in later times to these sculptures may be gained from the bare fact that more than 1,400 decorated fragments were recovered in the course of excavation but very few pieces of sufficient size to enable their scenes to be interpreted in detail. The best preserved were the reliefs forming a kind of dado in the entrance hall and on the side-walls of the portico which showed female offering-bearers personifying the royal estates and bringing produce from the estates to the pyramid (Plate 22). Among the many other scenes in the building, of which only fragments have been preserved, were episodes in the *heb-sed* and representations of the king performing various ritual ceremonies in the presence of the gods.

Until further investigations have been conducted towards the east some doubt must be felt concerning the precise identification of this building. In later pyramids, as at Meidum, the valley buildings are located on the eastern fringe of the desert where it joins the cultivation. This building, however, lies in a depression at some distance from the

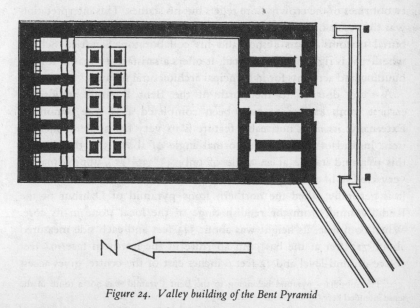

Figure 24. Valley building of the Bent Pyramid

cultivation and consequently was not directly accessible by canal from the river. H. Ricke expressed the opinion that another building might have stood at the edge of the valley on a site now occupied by the tomb of a sheikh. The present building, he believed, represented the temple in which the funerary rites of Seneferu as king of Lower Egypt were performed, while the corresponding ceremonies on his behalf as king of Upper Egypt were celebrated in the mortuary temple. An important difference between the two ceremonies was that the rites of Lower Egypt alone required four chapels for the viscera and two chapels for royal crowns, relics of very ancient royal mortuary customs practised respectively at Buto and Saïs. Ricke considered that the four easternmost shrines in this building were intended for the rites of Buto (one for each of the deities known as the Four Sons of Horus, under whose protection the viscera were regularly placed) and the two westernmost shrines for the rites of Saïs. In support of his theory he claimed that the two groups of shrines differed in their decoration and also in the size of the niches in their back walls; only the shrines of the viscera, the walls of which he believed were plain, contained statues, while the two shrines of the crowns bore reliefs but no statues. This interpretation was the result of an extensive study into the history of early Egyptian burial customs by its author and his collaborator, Siegfried Schott; whether it is right or not in detail, it offers a satisfactory reason for the building and accounts for its principal architectural features.

A short distance to the north of the Bent Pyramid stands the earliest tomb known to have been completed as a true pyramid.[2] Externally, its most noticeable feature is its very flat angle of inclination. Instead of rising at the normal angle of about 52°, the sides of this pyramid incline at an angle of only 43° 36′ 11″, approximating very closely in this respect to the upper portion of the Bent Pyramid. It is generally called the northern stone pyramid of Dahshur or the Red Pyramid, from the reddish tinge of the local stone in its core. When complete, its height was about 343 feet and each side measured about 722 feet at the base. An aperture in the northern face, 94 feet above ground-level and 12 feet 6 inches east of the centre, gives access

2. The subsidiary pyramid belonging to the Bent Pyramid was not a tomb in the sense intended here.

to a corridor which descends at an angle of about 27° 56' through the masonry core of the pyramid (fig. 25: 1). Approximately 206 feet from the entrance, the slope ends and the corridor continues horizontally for 24 feet 5 inches to the threshold of the first of three chambers, one beyond another.

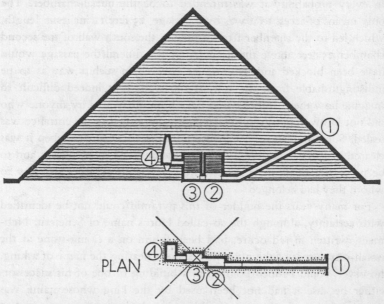

Figure 25. The northern stone pyramid of Dahshur, section looking west and plan

The first two chambers (fig. 25: 2 and 3) are almost identical in size and in design, each measuring about 27 feet 6 inches from north to south and nearly 12 feet from east to west. Both have corbelled roofs rising to a height of about 40 feet. The eleven overlapping courses of the roofs, which begin at a height of 11 feet 8 inches above the floor and converge at the top to within 1 foot 2 inches, are confined to the east and west walls; the north and south walls are vertical. In its position the second chamber (fig. 25: 3) is exceptional; no other major pyramid has a chamber in the superstructure placed directly under the apex. This instance apart, chambers in the inner cores of pyramids were located out of axis so that they would not be subjected to the direct pressure of the superincumbent masonry. The third chamber (fig. 25: 4), the floor of which has been removed to a depth of 14 feet, measures 13 feet 9 inches from north to south and 27 feet 5 inches from east to west; its corbelled roof rises to a height of nearly 50 feet. In every probability it was intended to be the burial-chamber. The only means of access to it was by a passage, 23 feet 11 inches in length, which led to the chamber from a hole in the south wall of the second chamber 25 feet above the floor. After the funeral the passage would have been blocked and its entrance covered in such a way as to be indistinguishable from the rest of the wall. It is indeed difficult to imagine how the chamber could have been discovered by anyone who did not know about its existence and location before the entrance was sealed. Some human remains were found in the chamber when it was cleared in 1950, but, although they were believed to be ancient and to be parts of a single male skeleton, there was no evidence to show to whom they had belonged.

For many years the builder of this pyramid could not be identified with certainty, although the so-called Horus name of Seneferu, Nebmaet, written in red ochre, had been found on a casing-stone at the north-east corner of the pyramid. A stone bearing the name of a king, however, could be incorporated in a building of one of his successors either because it had not been used by the king whose name was written on it or because the building in which it was first embodied had been dismantled and its stones re-used by a later king. As an example, the pyramid of Unas, the last king of the Vth Dynasty, contained blocks inscribed with the name of his predecessor, Isesi. All doubts about the ownership of the northern stone pyramid of Dahshur were, however, dispelled in 1982, when a joint expedition of the Egyptian Antiquities Organization and the German Institute of Archaeology in Cairo, under the directorship of Rainer Stadelmann, found larger than life-size representations of Seneferu carved in relief when they were excavating the mortuary temple on the east side of the pyramid. These sculptures show the king wearing the same kind of *sed*-festival dress as he wears in the reliefs on the stelae of the Bent Pyramid. Even before the excavation was completed, it was evident that this temple was more elaborate architecturally than the temple of the Bent Pyramid and consequently it could be assumed that it was later in date.

Additional confirmation of the ownership by Seneferu of the two Old Kingdom pyramids at Dahshur is provided by inscriptions found in their vicinity. As long ago as 1905 Ludwig Borchardt published a decree which, he was informed, had been discovered on the edge of the cultivation near the northern stone pyramid. It was dated in the twenty-first year of the reign of the VIth Dynasty king, Pepi I, and its purpose was to exempt from certain duties and taxes the priests of the 'Two Pyramids (called) Kha Seneferu'. A priest named Duarē, who lived in the Vth Dynasty and whose mastaba was built to the east of the Bent Pyramid, bore the title 'Overseer of the Two Pyramids of Seneferu', while his son, Ankhmarē, was described as 'Overseer of the Southern Pyramid of Seneferu'. The same designation of what can only be the Bent Pyramid is inscribed on the figure of a priest of the Middle Kingdom which was actually found in the valley temple of the pyramid. In all probability 'Southern Pyramid' had only a local application with reference to Dahshur. It does not preclude the possibility that the pyramid of Meidum, which was farther south, could also have been built by Seneferu, although it is hard to imagine why one king should build three pyramids.

A theory which has been accepted by many Egyptologists is that the outer covering of the pyramid of Meidum alone was the work of Seneferu, while the inner step pyramids belonged to his predecessor, the little known king Huni, who was once thought to have been the owner of the Bent Pyramid. In favour of this theory it may be argued that the engineering feat of building three pyramids, embodying approximately nine million tons of stone without taking into account the stone used in the temples, causeways and enclosure walls, would have required greater technical and physical resources than are likely to have been available to one king in the Old Kingdom. It may also be argued that two pyramids could be understood to symbolize Seneferu's sovereignty over Upper and Lower Egypt, but a third pyramid would seem to have no justification. Huni, to whom the Turin King-list ascribes a reign of twenty-four years, must surely have built a pyramid somewhere, but it does not follow that it was the step pyramid at Meidum; other possible locations, particularly a large enclosure to the west of the pyramids of Zoser and Sekhemkhet, must be explored first and be found lacking before the absence of an alternative tomb can be considered as a valid reason for associating him with the pyramid of Meidum. It is, moreover, necessary to remember that no single mention of his name has yet been found at Meidum, and no members of his family nor any of his functionaries seem to have been buried there. One of his most powerful officials named Metjen, who did not die until the reign of Seneferu, was buried at Saqqara. Admittedly, Seneferu was reputed to have been a beneficent king, but it must be questioned whether his sense of piety towards his predecessor would have led him to transform the design of his tomb; later kings, whose predecessors' monuments were incomplete at the time of their death, were generally content to make only summary additions in brick and plaster, and in one instance, in the Vth Dynasty, a valley building and a causeway built by one king were actually usurped by a successor.

On the whole, it seems less improbable that Seneferu built three pyramids than that the Egyptians of the XVIIIth Dynasty were mistaken when they attributed the pyramid and mortuary temple of Meidum to him. If, as Stadelmann has persuasively argued, the length of Seneferu's reign, as recorded in the Turin King-list, should be emended from twenty-four years to thirty-four, the average amount of constructional work done in each year would have been somewhat less than in the case of the Great Pyramid, which was built during a reign lasting twenty-three years. Regnal years throughout most of the Old Kingdom were reckoned in terms of censuses (of cattle), which were normally held in alternate years. According, however, to the entries which have survived for the reign of Seneferu on the fragment of the official annals of the early Egyptian kings, known as the Palermo Stone, the seventh and the eighth censuses were held in successive years. No further entries for his reign have survived, but it has been conjectured that the censuses continued annually, and not biennially, for the rest of Seneferu's reign. Since his highest known census is the seventeenth, it has generally been accepted that his reign consisted of seven biennial and ten annual censuses extending over twenty-four years (or twenty-three if the first census was held in his first year on the throne), thus confirming the record in the Turin King-list. The case for assuming that a census was held annually from the eighth year onwards is, however, not very strong and since it cannot be reconciled with the archaeological evidence it is hard to believe that the departure from the biennial custom in the eighth year was not exceptional and consequently that the king-list is not, in this instance, as in some other records of reigns, accurate.

Distinctive structural features in the three pyramids provide firm ground for establishing the order in which they were built, but there still remain some questions of a more general kind to which no certain answers can yet be given. It has already been noted that the technique of laying stones in courses inclining inwards, found in all the step pyramids, was also used in the construction of the lower part (but not the upper) of the Bent Pyramid. If technique were the only criterion, it might be difficult to determine the relative positions of the inner pyramid at Meidum and the lower part of the Bent Pyramid, but the step-design of the former leaves no room for doubt that it is the earlier. The stones in the northern stone pyramid at Dahshur are laid in level courses; since that method was regularly used in subsequent pyramids, the order of sequence of the two Dahshur pyramids is clear. The Meidum pyramid at its different stages of construction has technical affinities with both the Dahshur pyramids: the stones of the inner step pyramid are laid in inclined courses, while those of the outer pyramid are flat (fig. 26). The outer pyramid must therefore be later than the Bent Pyramid, but its precise chronological relationship with the northern stone pyramid is harder to determine.

If all the available information – technical, archaeological and epigraphical – be marshalled, the picture which emerges has a fairly clear outline. Seneferu, early in his reign, began to build his step pyramid at Meidum. Why he chose a place so far from Memphis is not clear, but perhaps it was for the same unknown reason as that which prompted one of his predecessors to build a chamberless pyramid at the neighbouring Seila. Seneferu's eldest son, Nefermaet, and his wife, Itet, and another son named Rehotep, who was High Priest of Heliopolis, and his wife, Nofret, together with some other members

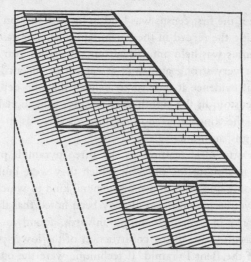

*Figure 26. The pyramid of Meidum, sketch of section showing
details of construction*

of the royal family, were all buried in brick mastabas near the pyramid,
which suggests that, when they died, the king intended to be buried
in the Meidum pyramid. He seems, however, to have changed his
mind and, as a result, instead of having a step pyramid he began to
build a true pyramid, the Bent Pyramid, at Dahshur, much nearer
Memphis. Stadelmann has suggested that the reason for holding the
eighth census in the year after the seventh may have been the need to
increase revenue in order to pay for a second pyramid, but there is
nothing to confirm that surmise, though it cannot be ignored. The
mastabas in the vicinity of this pyramid, unlike those at Meidum, were
almost exclusively tombs of priests and functionaries, all later than
Seneferu. Nothing daunted, he built yet another pyramid at Dahshur
with the flattest slope of any pyramid in Egypt. Dates on some of its
casing-blocks show that it was being built at the time of the sixteenth
census and therefore very near the end of his life. Its architect seems to
have been his eldest surviving son, Kanofer, who was eventually buried
with some other sons and daughters of the king in brick mastabas
which lie to the south-east of the pyramid. While the northern stone

pyramid was being built, the step pyramid of Meidum was being converted into a true pyramid and a small mortuary temple was built on the east side, the original northern temple presumably having been dismantled. Dated blocks from the casing of the pyramid show that the conversion was in progress during the years of the fifteenth, sixteenth and seventeenth censuses. Some of the casing at the base of the pyramid was not dressed, as also were the outer walls of the mortuary temple, and the stelae in the temple were not inscribed, so it is likely that the king died shortly before the work was finished.

If the human remains which were found in the third chamber of the northern stone pyramid are left out of account, on the ground that there is nothing by which they can be positively identified, it is not possible to deduce in which of the three pyramids Seneferu was buried. Only two facts seem to be beyond dispute: his original intention was to be buried in the step pyramid at Meidum, and he would not have embarked on building a third pyramid at a late stage in his life if he had not intended that pyramid, and not its two predecessors, to be his tomb. In the last chapter an explanation will be offered for the transformation of the step pyramid into a true pyramid, but it will not explain why Seneferu should have built a second true pyramid at Dahshur when the Meidum pyramid in its converted form would have served the same purpose. It is not inconceivable that Seneferu was buried at Meidum if the northern stone pyramid complex was not finished in time, but it is hard to believe that the Bent Pyramid became his sepulchre when it had been superseded by the northern stone pyramid and by the Meidum pyramid in its final form. Nevertheless even as late as the Middle Kingdom the mortuary cult of Seneferu was maintained at two pyramids, each of which had its resident priesthood. The king must have made endowments of land for their support and consequently there is no doubt that he did not discard at least one of the two pyramids in which he was not buried. Nor was there any reason for his doing so. A statue, once the necessary magical rites had been performed on it, could serve as an effective substitute for the body, and the spirit of a dead person could occupy it at will. Similarly, a cenotaph could serve as a substitute for the actual tomb. The fact that only two mortuary priesthoods of Seneferu are attested, both at

Dahshur, does not rule out the possibility of a third in distant Meidum. Even without priests the pyramid could still function as a residence when the king wished to visit those who were buried in its vicinity and it could also fulfil the other purposes which will be discussed in the last chapter.

CHAPTER FOUR

THE
GIZA GROUP

Seneferu's son and successor to the throne was Khufu, better known as Cheops, the Greek form of his name (Plate 23). Inspired possibly by the magnitude of his father's constructions, he chose a plateau, situated on the edge of the desert about five miles west of Giza, and erected at its north-west corner a pyramid of even vaster dimensions. Two later kings of the IVth Dynasty, Chephren and Mycerinus, followed his example by building their pyramids on the same plateau, a short distance to the south. Together, these three pyramids constitute possibly the most celebrated group of monuments in the world (Plates 24, 25).

The pyramid of Cheops, or the Great Pyramid, marks the apogee of pyramid-building in respect of both size and quality. No exact computation of the amount of hewn stone contained in it is possible, because the centre of its core consists of a nucleus of rock, the size of which cannot be precisely determined. It has, however, been estimated that, when complete, the core of local stone and the outer facing of Tura limestone were composed of about 2,300,000 separate blocks, each averaging some two and a half tons in weight and reaching a maximum of fifteen tons.

Many attempts have been made by writers on the Great Pyramid to illustrate its size by comparison with other famous buildings. It has, for instance, been calculated that the Houses of Parliament and St Paul's Cathedral could be grouped inside the area of its base and still leave considerable space unoccupied.[1] According to another estimate there would be room for the cathedrals of Florence, Milan, and St Peter at Rome, as well as for Westminster Abbey and St Paul's Cathedral.[2] It has also been reckoned that, if it were sawn into cubes measuring a

1. Somers Clarke and R. Engelbach, *Ancient Egyptian Masonry*, frontispiece.
2. E. Baldwin Smith, *Egyptian Architecture as a Cultural Expression*, p. 96.

foot in each dimension and these cubes were placed in a row, they would extend over a distance equal to two-thirds of the earth's periphery at the equator. One computation of this kind has been attributed to Napoleon during his campaign in Egypt. When some of his generals returned from climbing to the top of the pyramid, Napoleon, who had declined to make the ascent himself, greeted them with the announcement that, according to his calculations, the three pyramids on the Giza plateau contained enough stone to build a wall, measuring 10 feet in height and 1 foot in width, around the whole of France. The mathematician Monge, who was among the savants accompanying Napoleon on this campaign, is alleged to have confirmed this calculation.[3]

No monument in Egypt has been surveyed and measured so often and with so much care as the Great Pyramid. Even before the theories regarding the supposed esoteric significance of its angles and dimensions had been invented, Edmé-François Jomard, another of Napoleon's staff of savants, Colonel Howard Vyse and J.S. Perring (1837-8) and other pioneers of Egyptian archaeology had measured the monument with as high a degree of accuracy as is required by most modern excavators. The first exhaustive survey of the monument was, however, conducted by Sir Flinders Petrie, who spent the greater part of two seasons (1880-82) at the task. His published results remained the standard work on the subject until 1925, when they were partly superseded by a fresh survey undertaken with the help of more modern instruments by J.H. Cole of the Survey Department of the Egyptian Government.[4] From this survey it was ascertained that the following were the original measurements of the four sides at the base: north, 755.43 feet; south, 756.08 feet; east, 755.88 feet; west, 755.77 feet. While, therefore, no two sides were absolutely identical in length, the difference between the longest and the shortest was only 7.9 inches. Each side was oriented almost exactly in line with true north and south

---

3. J. Capart and Marcelle Werbrouck, *Memphis à l'ombre des pyramides*, p. 47.
4. *Survey of Egypt*, Paper No. 39: 'The Determination of the Exact Size and Orientation of the Great Pyramid of Giza', Cairo, 1925. The measurements in this report are given in metres and decimal fractions of a metre; they have here been translated into feet and decimal fractions of a foot for the sake of uniformity.

or east and west, the following being the estimated errors: north side, 2′ 28″ south of west; south side, 1′ 57″ south of west; east side, 5′ 30″ west of north; west side, 2′ 30″ west of north. As the accuracy of this orientation implies, the four corners were almost perfect right angles, their exact measurements being: north-east, 90° 3′ 2″; north-west, 89° 59′ 58″; south-east, 89° 56′ 27″; south-west, 90° 0′ 33″. When complete, it rose to a height of 481.4 feet, the top 31 feet of which are now missing. Its four sides incline at an angle of about 51° 52′ to the ground. The area covered by its base is 13.1 acres.

Although the Great Pyramid, when viewed from a distance, gives the impression of being preserved substantially intact, closer observation reveals that it has suffered severely at the hands of despoilers. About a dozen courses and the capstone, possibly made of granite, have been removed from the apex. The whole of the outer facing of Tura limestone, with the exception of a few pieces at the base, has been stripped off the sides. In the north face, a little below the original entrance, there is a large aperture roughly cut in the core. According to Moslem tradition, this aperture was made during the latter part of the ninth century at the command of the Caliph Ma'mun, son of Harun al-Rashid of Arabian Nights fame, in the mistaken belief that the pyramid contained hidden treasure. Until that time the pyramid, though doubtless robbed of its former contents, had probably remained structurally intact. Subsequently it became a copious and convenient quarry, providing the stone required for bridges over irrigation canals, houses, walls, and other buildings in the neighbourhood of Giza and Cairo.

The chambers and corridors of the Great Pyramid, if their arrangement is to be understood, must be considered in conjunction with its structural development. In contrast with the pyramid of Meidum, the transformations which the Great Pyramid underwent in the course of construction were mainly, if not entirely, internal; its ultimate external shape and dimensions were probably those intended from the beginning. The entrance is in the north face at a height of about 55 feet, measured vertically, above ground-level (fig. 27: 1; Plate 26). It is not situated exactly midway across the face, but at a point about 24 feet east of the centre. From the entrance a corridor, measuring about

3 feet 5 inches in width and 3 feet 11 inches in height, descends at a gradient of 26° 31′ 23″ first through the core of the pyramid and then through the rock. At a distance of about 345 feet from the original entrance, the corridor becomes level and continues horizontally for a further 29 feet before terminating in a chamber (fig. 27: 2). On the west side of the level section of the corridor, near the entrance to the chamber, there is a recess, the cutting of which was never completed. The chamber also is unfinished, its trenched floor and rough walls

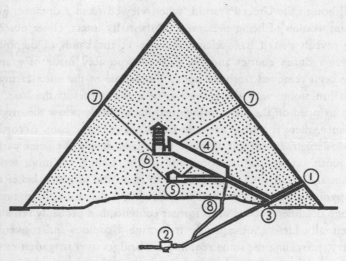

Figure 27. The Great Pyramid, section looking west

resembling a quarry (Plate 27). A square pit sunk in the floor may represent the first stage in an unfulfilled project for deepening the chamber. According to Vyse and Perring, who measured the chamber in 1838, its dimensions are: height 11 feet 6 inches; east-west, 46 feet; north-south, 27 feet 1 inch.

In the south wall of the chamber, opposite the entrance, there is an opening to a blind passage, roughly hewn in the rock and obviously unfinished. The presence of this passage suggests that, if the original plan had been executed, there would have been a second chamber beyond the first and connected with it by a corridor. Such an arrangement would have as a parallel the northern stone pyramid at Dahshur, the main difference being that in the latter the second chamber lies directly beneath the apex and the first to the north of it, whereas in the Great Pyramid both chambers would have been situated south of a point perpendicularly under the apex.

It is of some interest to compare the half-finished rock-chamber with the brief but graphic description of the subterranean part of the Great Pyramid given to Herodotus when he visited Egypt in the middle of the fifth century B.C. Beneath the pyramid, he was told, were vaults constructed on a kind of island, which was surrounded by water brought from the Nile by a canal. On this island the body of Cheops was said to lie. No trace, however, of either the canal or the island has yet been found, and it is most unlikely that they ever existed. Although the pyramid had almost certainly been opened and its contents plundered long before the time of Herodotus, it may easily have been closed again during the Saite Period, when a number of ancient monuments were restored. The story which Herodotus relates – the veracity of which he does not claim to have confirmed from his own observations – may well have been embroidered by generations of pyramid guides extending over the greater part of two centuries.

At the time when the decision was made to alter the original project and to substitute a burial-chamber in the body of the pyramid for the one under construction in the rock, the superstructure had already been built to a height of several feet. A hole was therefore cut in the masonry-roof of the earlier Descending Corridor at a point about 60 feet from the entrance and a new Ascending Corridor was hewn upwards through the core (fig. 27: 3). The mouth of this corridor was filled, after the burial, with a slab of limestone, so that it became indistinguishable from the remainder of the roof at the upper end of the Descending Corridor. The block could not, however, have been securely fastened, because it collapsed when Ma'mun's men were boring their tunnel nearby. According to Moslem historians it was the noise made by the fall of this block to the floor of the Descending Corridor which enabled the tunnellers to locate the pyramid corridors, their previous operations having been directed too far to the west.

The Ascending Corridor, which is approximately 129 feet in length corresponds in width and height with the Descending Corridor; its gradient of 26° 2′ 30″ also tallies to within a fraction of a degree. At its lower end, immediately above the gap left by the missing limestone slab, are three large plug-blocks made of granite and placed one behind another (Plate 28). These plugs, which completely fill the original corridor, were bypassed by Ma'mun's men, who simply cut a passage through the softer limestone of the west wall as far as a point beyond the uppermost plug. Borchardt, while making a detailed study of the walls of this corridor, observed that the stones at the lower end were laid approximately parallel with the ground, whereas nearly all those at the upper end were parallel with the gradient of the corridor. From this fact he deduced that the point at which the angle changed marked the height to which the pyramid had already been built when it was decided to transfer the tomb-chamber to the superstructure. Borchardt also noticed that the joints of the stones at the lower end were irregular, whereas the stones at the upper end fitted closely – a feature which certainly supports his contention that the lower part of the corridor was cut through rough core-masonry already laid, while the upper part was built *pari passu* with the construction of the pyramid. The only stones in the upper part which are not laid parallel with the gradient are the so-called 'girdle-stones', a name used to describe either single stones or two stones, one above the other, through which the corridor has been hewn. These 'girdle-stones', placed at regular inter-vals of 17 feet 2 inches, may offer a clue to the structural composition of the Great Pyramid which will be discussed in a later chapter.

When the Ascending Corridor was being constructed, the builders probably intended the burial-chamber to occupy a position in the centre of the superstructure and at no great height above ground-level. Such a chamber was actually built at the end of a passage leading from the top of the Ascending Corridor (fig. 27: 5). Called by the Arabs the 'Queen's Chamber' – a misnomer which it has retained – this chamber lies exactly midway between the north and south sides of the pyramid. Its measurements are 18 feet 10 inches from east to west and 17 feet 2 inches from north to south. It has a pointed roof, which rises to a height of 20 feet 5 inches. In the east wall there is a niche with corbelled sides: its original depth was only 3 feet 5 inches, but the back has now been cut away by treasure-seekers. Its height is 15 feet 4 inches and the width at the base 5 feet 2 inches. Presumably it was designed to contain a statue of the king, which may, however, never have been placed in position.

There are many indications that work on the Queen's Chamber was abandoned before it had been completed. The floor, for instance, is exceedingly rough; if the chamber had been finished it would probably have been paved with finer stone. Again, in the north and south walls there are small rectangular apertures from which shafts run horizontally, the northern for a distance of 6 feet 4 inches and the southern for 6 feet 8 inches, and then turn upwards, the northern at an angle of approximately 37° 28′ and the southern at about 38° 28′ (fig. 27: 6). These apertures were not cut at the time when the chamber was built – an omission which can only be explained on the hypothesis that the chamber was never finished – but in 1872 by an engineer named Waynman Dixon, who had been led to suspect the existence of the shafts by their presence in the King's Chamber above. Unlike those in the King's Chamber, however, the shafts leading from the Queen's Chamber seem to have had no outlet in the outer surface of the pyramid; the absence of such an outlet provides further evidence of an alteration in the original plan. Possibly the same explanation also accounts for the different levels in the floor of the passage which connected the Ascending Corridor with the chamber. At first the passage is only 3 feet 9 inches in height, but nearer the chamber a sudden drop in the floor increases its height to 5 feet 8 inches.

The abandonment of the plan to place the burial in the Queen's Chamber is generally believed to have led to the addition of two of the most celebrated architectural works which have survived from the Old Kingdom, namely the Grand Gallery and the King's Chamber. J.-P. Lauer has, however, shown that the Grand Gallery must belong to the same constructional phase as the Queen's Chamber.

The Grand Gallery (fig. 27: 4 and fig. 28) was built as a continuation of the Ascending Corridor. It is 153 feet in length and 28 feet in height. Its walls of polished limestone rise vertically to a height of 7 feet 6 inches; above that level each of the seven courses projects inwards about 3 inches beyond the course on which it rests, thus forming a corbel vault of unparalleled dimensions. The space between the uppermost course on each side, measuring 3 feet 5 inches in width, is spanned by roofing slabs, every one of which is laid at a slightly steeper angle than the gradient of the gallery. Sir Flinders Petrie, commenting on this method of laying the slabs, says it was done 'in order that the lower edge of each stone should hitch like a pawl into a ratchet cut in the top of the walls; hence no stone can press on the one below it, so as to cause a cumulative pressure all down the roof; and each stone is separately upheld by the side-walls across which it lies'.[5] At the foot of each wall a flat-topped ramp, 2 feet in height and 1 foot 8 inches in width, extends along the whole length of the gallery. A passage measuring, like the roof, 3 feet 5 inches in width runs between the two ramps. At the lower end of this passage there is now a gap, caused by the removal of a bridge, probably made of planks resting on baulks of timber for which sockets can be seen in the side-walls. The bridge linked the floor of the passage with that of the Ascending Corridor and also covered the mouth of the passage leading to the Queen's Chamber. In the gap, the lowest stone in the western ramp has been removed, revealing a shaft which descends partly perpendicularly and partly obliquely, first through the core of the pyramid and then through the rock, until it emerges in the west wall of the Descending Corridor (fig. 27: 8). Its apparent purpose and the significance of some other peculiar features in the Grand Gallery will be considered after the King's Chamber has been described.

A high step at the upper end of the Grand Gallery gives access to a low and narrow passage leading to the King's Chamber. About a third of the distance along its length the passage is heightened and enlarged into a kind of antechamber, the south, east, and west walls of which are composed of red granite. Four wide slots have been cut in both the east and west walls of the antechamber, three extending to the floor and one – the northernmost – stopping at the same level as the roof of the passage. The long slots were intended to hold three granite portcullises, no traces of which have survived. According to Borchardt, these portcullises, each weighing about $2\frac{1}{4}$ tons, were de-

5. W. M. Flinders Petrie, *The Pyramids and Temples of Gizeh*, p. 72.

signed to be lowered by ropes which ran over cylindrical beams mounted above the slots. Three semicircular depressions, into which the lower halves of the ends of the beams fitted, are still to be seen at the top of the west wall, and also four long grooves on the face of the south wall of the chamber along which the ropes passed. Spanning the antechamber and fitting into the short slot, there still remain two blocks of granite, one resting on the other; a third block may originally have filled the space between the upper block and the ceiling. Without such a barrier, robbers could, by climbing through the gap, have passed unhindered over the first two portcullises.

The King's Chamber, built entirely of granite, measures 34 feet 4 inches from east to west, 17 feet 2 inches from north to south, and 19 feet 1 inch in height. In the north and south walls, at a height of about 3 feet above the floor, are the rectangular apertures of shafts which differ from those of the Queen's Chamber only in penetrating the core of the pyramid to the outer surface, the northern at an angle of $31°$ and the southern at an angle of $45°$ (fig. 27: 7). The reason for having these shafts will be explained when the purpose of the pyramid is discussed in the last chapter. Near the west wall stands a lidless rectangular granite sarcophagus which once contained the king's body, probably enclosed within an inner coffin of wood. In appearance it is rough, many of the scratches made by the saw when cutting it being still clearly visible. Sir Flinders Petrie discovered that the width of the sarcophagus was about an inch greater than the width of the Ascending Corridor at its mouth; he therefore concluded that it must have been placed in position while the chamber was being built.

The roof of the King's Chamber has no clear architectural parallel. Above its flat ceiling, which is composed of nine slabs weighing in aggregate about 400 tons, there are five separate compartments, the ceilings of the first four being flat and the fifth having a pointed roof. The purpose of this construction, it appears, was to eliminate any risk of the ceiling of the chamber collapsing under the weight of the super-incumbent masonry. Whether such extreme precautions were required by the character of the building may be debatable; they have, however, been justified by subsequent events. Every one of the massive slabs of granite in the ceiling of the chamber and many of those in the relieving compartments have been cracked – presumably by an earth-quake – but none has yet collapsed.

Access to the lowest of the relieving compartments is gained by a passage leading from a hole at the top of the east wall of the Grand Gallery. When or by whom this passage was cut is unknown; the first European to mention it was a traveller named Davison who visited the pyramid in 1765. The four upper compartments were not discovered until 1837–8, when Colonel Howard Vyse and J.S. Perring forced a way to them by hollowing out a shaft from below. Some of the walls in these upper compartments are composed of limestone; since they were not intended to be seen their surfaces were not dressed and, in consequence, many of the blocks still retain the red ochre markings painted on them at the quarry. Among these quarry-marks are the only instances of the name of Cheops found in the pyramid.

Owing to its upward slope, the blocking of the Ascending Corridor of the Great Pyramid after the funeral presented unusual difficulties. In other pyramids the corridors either slope downwards or are approxi-mately level, so that they could easily be packed with large plug-blocks which would have been stored outside the pyramid until required. The Descending Corridor of the Great Pyramid could have been blocked in this way, but not the Ascending Corridor. Not only would the task of raising heavy granite plugs through the hole in the roof of the Descending Corridor have caused many mechanical difficulties, but plugs so inserted would have served no useful purpose because they could not have been firmly secured. No alternative remained, there-fore, but to store the plugs somewhere in the pyramid while it was under construction and to move them down the Ascending Corridor after the body had been put in the burial-chamber. That such a method was adopted is clear from the fact that the three plugs which still remain in position at the lower end of the Ascending Corridor are about an inch wider than its mouth and, consequently, could not have been introduced from the Descending Corridor. Two problems, how-ever, arise from this deduction: where were the plugs stored before being lowered down the Ascending Corridor, and how did the men who must have pushed the plugs from behind escape from the pyramid after completing their work?

Until Petrie discovered that the horizontal passage leading to the Queen's Chamber was an inch too small in both width and height to hold the plugs, it was generally supposed that they had been stored in that chamber. The necessary width and height could have been found in the gap between the top of the Ascending Corridor and the lower end of the Grand Gallery passage, but the length of the gap would have been insufficient to accommodate the plugs if placed end to end. Lack of height would also exclude the passage leading to the King's Chamber, and, in consequence, the chamber itself. Petrie therefore concluded that the plugs were stored in the Grand Gallery passage, where all the requirements of space would have been satisfied. Such an explanation, as Petrie recognized, was open to the objection that the plugs, by blocking the passage, would have obstructed the funeral procession – which must have either climbed over the plugs or proceeded up the side-ramps – but considerations of size seemed to preclude any other solution. A further corollary to Petrie's conclusion was that the Grand Gallery itself must have formed part of the second, and not the third, constructional phase, when it was intended to locate the burial in the Queen's Chamber.

Borchardt, while accepting Petrie's main thesis that the plugs were stored in the Grand Gallery, observed that it did not account for the existence of fifty-six horizontal sockets, fifty-four of which were cut in two rows of twenty-seven, one row on the upper surface of each ramp. The two remaining sockets were cut on each side of the high step at the upper end of the gallery. They alternated in size, the longer being about 1 foot $11\frac{1}{4}$ inches and the shorter about 1 foot $8\frac{1}{2}$ inches. Two other features which Petrie had not explained were, first, twenty-five vertical sockets in each of the side-walls directly above the horizontal sockets, apart from two neighbouring pairs at the lower end of the gallery and the pair on the high step, and, secondly, a continuous groove running the whole length of the gallery on both sides in the lower part of the third projecting lap from the bottom of the corbel roof (fig. 28). The vertical sockets had been filled with insets of stone, which suggested that they had been superseded by those cut horizontally. Across each inset and extending beyond it on both sides are some shallow incisions.

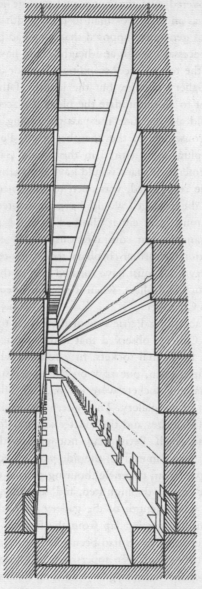

Figure 28. The Great Pyramid, Grand Gallery

In order to explain the significance of these features, Borchardt suggested that they were connected with timber scaffolding surmounted by a sloping platform which was as wide as the gallery at the level of the grooves in the side-walls. When it was first designed, the platform was supported by single uprights, which were attached at the base to the vertical sockets. If that interpretation is accepted, it was probably because the structure proved to be unstable that the uprights were increased in number and were set in the horizontal sockets on the ramps, three lashed together side by side in the longer sockets and two in the shorter. The plugs, Borchardt maintained, were stored on this platform until after the funeral, when they would be used to block the Ascending Corridor.

Notwithstanding its ingenuity, Borchardt's explanation is open to some clear objections, one being the formidable mechanical difficulty involved in lowering the plugs some 14 feet from the platform to the floor of the corridor. His explanation of the use of the vertical sockets also is not convincing. It seems far more likely that they were constructed to receive the ends of beams placed across the gallery to prevent the plugs on the floor of the sloping corridor from sliding down prematurely into the Ascending Corridor.

Lauer, although in general agreement with Borchardt on the construction of the scaffolding, has interpreted its employment differently. It was not, he believes, an elaborate structure for storing about twenty-five plugs, but a device for enabling the plugs, which were stored on the floor of the Grand Gallery passage, to be hauled to the top of the gallery so that they could be used as building material for constructing the antechamber and the King's Chamber. In order to facilitate the operation, wooden poles were attached by tenons to pairs of wooden uprights located opposite each other and each plug in turn was hauled up the slope by a rope which passed over one pole after another until it reached the top. Three or four plugs, however, were left at the bottom of the gallery until they were needed for blocking the Ascending Corridor. The original intention to fill the corridor with plugs must have been abandoned as impracticable. To have succeeded in moving even three plugs into position was a remarkable achievement, because they are rather less than half an inch narrower than the corridor and the gap between the tops of the plugs and the ceiling of the corridor is only about 1¼ inches.

From the moment when the first plug was introduced into the upper end of the Ascending Corridor, the workmen who were charged with the task of transferring the plugs to their final position would have been unable to leave the pyramid by the normal way. They had, however, provided themselves with a means of escape down the shaft which leads from the bottom of the Grand Gallery to the Descending Corridor (fig. 27: 8). It is idle to speculate whether this shaft was constructed with or without the knowledge of Cheops, but the burial of living persons was certainly not practised by the Egyptians of the Pyramid Age. The shaft would have been completely concealed at the time of the funeral by the lowest stone in the western ramp, which is now missing. The removal of the stone would have presented no difficulty to the workmen when the time came for making their descent. After the last of the workmen had reached the bottom of the shaft, the opening in the west wall of the Descending Corridor would have been covered with a slab of stone so that it would have been indistinguishable from the remainder of the corridor. At the same time also the mouth of the Ascending Corridor beyond the first of the plugs would have been covered with the stone, which fell to the floor of the Descending Corridor when the Caliph Ma'mun was forcing a way into the pyramid.

Some speculation regarding the method of closing the entrance to the pyramid has been caused by a statement made by Strabo. In his *Geographica*, written at about the beginning of the Christian era, he states that the Great Pyramid, 'a little way up one side, has a stone that may be taken out, which being raised up there is a sloping passage to the foundations'. Petrie interpreted this statement as meaning that the Great Pyramid had a flap-door composed of a single slab of stone which swung on pivots near the top of each side. In support of his theory he was able to point out that, both in the northern corridor of the Bent Pyramid and in the pyramid of Meidum, there were sockets cut in the side-walls near the entrance which were apparently intended for holding door-pivots. Owing to the loss of the outer casing, it is impossible to say whether the entrance to the Great Pyramid was provided with similar sockets. It is, however, difficult to believe that the door described by Strabo, if his words have been correctly understood, dated from the time when the pyramid was built. Plugs and portcullises would certainly not have been used to block the corridors of pyramids if subsequent access to the internal chambers was contemplated; a flap-door would have presupposed such access. Possibly the entrance to the Great Pyramid, like the western entrance to the Bent Pyramid, was originally covered with a layer of casing-stones which rendered it indistinguishable from the remainder of the outer surface. When the pyramid was first violated – probably during the period of anarchy which followed the end of the Old Kingdom – the robbers must have forced a way through the blocks covering the entrance. How long it remained open cannot be known, but it may have been sealed and again violated on more than one occasion during the subsequent dynasties, until eventually – possibly under the Saites – a door, corresponding with the one described by Strabo, was fitted. If this highly speculative surmise be correct, it is also necessary to assume either that the existence of the door was forgotten or that the entrance was again blocked with facing-stones at some time during the period between Strabo's visit and the ninth century. No other explanation would account for the inability of the Caliph Ma'mun to find the entrance until he had forced a new passage through the core of the pyramid.

Although the buildings which once completed the Great Pyramid complex have either entirely or partly disappeared, the surviving remnants are enough to show that the general lay-out conformed with the standard pattern. Nothing is now visible of the enclosure wall, but part of the fine limestone pavement which covered the area between the wall and the pyramid has been preserved.

Opposite the middle of the east face of the pyramid stood the mortuary temple, a rectangular building of limestone measuring about 171 feet from north to south and about 132 feet from east to west. It was connected with the upper end of the causeway by a doorway in the east façade (fig. 29: 1). Immediately beyond lay a court paved with black basalt and surrounded by a cloister (fig. 29: 2). The roof of the cloister, to which a stone staircase in the south-west corner gave access,

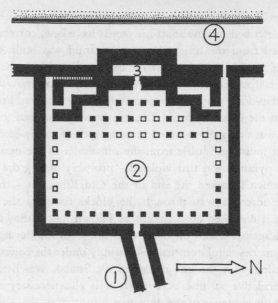

Figure 29. Mortuary temple of the Great Pyramid

was supported by granite columns, all of which were square in section
with the exception of those in the four corners which were oblong. Its
walls were decorated with scenes delicately carved in low relief. On
the west side was a deep cruciform recess. What lay beyond the recess
(fig. 29: 3) is not known; J.-P. Lauer, who succeeded in tracing the
plan of the temple in 1946, conjectured that it was the sanctuary and
that two false doors stood against its west wall. H. Ricke, however,
has suggested that the sanctuary, consisting of an altar flanked by two
round-topped stelae, was erected in the open space between the centre
of the back wall of the temple and the base of the pyramid (fig. 29: 4).
Some statues of the king may have been placed either in the recess or
behind it, but no actual evidence to support this possibility was found.

North and south of the temple, outside the eastern enclosure wall of
the pyramid, are two boat-shaped pits hewn in the rock; a third pit of
the same kind lies on the north side of the causeway near the temple.
All these pits were cleared by Reisner, but with small reward: the first

two yielded nothing and the third only fragments of gilded wood and some rope. A fourth pit, however, provided one of the outstanding Egyptological surprises of this century. Situated on the south side of the pyramid and very close to the enclosure wall, this pit was found by Kamal el-Mallakh in May 1954. It is 103 feet in length and 17½ feet in depth. Unlike the other pits in the complex, it is rectangular. At a depth of about 6 feet from the top, its perpendicular walls are stepped inwards all round the pit. On the surface of the step, which measures about a yard in width, rested the ends of forty-one limestone roofing blocks laid side by side on edge. Manoeuvring these blocks into position over the pit, some of them weighing more than fifteen tons, could not have been a simple task. On the south wall of the pit and on most of the roofing blocks there were masons' graffiti, which included as the name of one of the gangs 'Djedefrē is the ruler'. Djedefrē, whose name occurs several times on the blocks, was Cheops's son and successor, who must have been responsible for seeing that his father's burial was properly carried out.

Inside the pit, undisturbed since it was put there, lay a dismantled, flat-bottomed boat largely built of cedar wood. Time would show that it consisted of as many as 1,224 pieces, the largest measuring about 75 feet in length and the shortest 4 inches. They were in thirteen layers, arranged to some extent methodically. Thus, the bow- and stern-posts with papyriform terminals were placed at opposite ends of the pit, the bow-post being at the western end. The position in the pit of each piece was carefully recorded before it was removed, but, even with the help of all available information, the work of reassembly proved long and difficult, occupying a highly skilled restorer, Hag Ahmed Yusuf, for some fourteen years. The result of his work is a boat in almost perfect condition, 143 feet long (40 feet longer than the top of the pit), which is estimated to have a displacement of about 40 tons (Plate 29). Its main timbers, which are about 5½ inches thick, bear special marks to assist the ancient builder to put them in the right order when assembling the boat. These marks are of two kinds: general, of which there were four, to indicate the main divisions of the boat, and particular, which were usually placed on neighbouring timbers. Joins were usually made either by ropes of halfa grass or by pegs of sycamore wood. The ropes were not in a condition to be re-used when the boat was reassembled after discovery. Copper staples were used instead of pegs in some parts. In its restored state the boat can be seen to have three structures on deck: a small baldachin on the foredeck, an awning amidships and a deckhouse aft. One of its interesting features is a row of palm-tree columns supporting the roof of the deckhouse; all the other columns have lotus-bud capitals. Six pairs of oars were buried with the boat, their length varying from about 25 feet to about 22 feet. Two of the oars are in the stern for steering the boat.

The burial of boats suitable for navigation, although not uncommon in the enclosures of the large brick mastabas of the Ist Dynasty, seems to have been limited in the Old Kingdom to the royal pyramid complexes. Some of these boats may have been used at the time of the funeral, but others were probably intended to provide the dead king with a means of transport in his after-life, the precise region in which they were to be employed being still obscure. In the solar cult, a boat would be required for accompanying the sun-god on his daily journey across the heavens and on his nightly journey beneath the earth; it would also be needed for reaching the region beyond the eastern horizon, where the gods were thought to dwell. Hag Ahmed Yusuf, in his long study of Cheops's boat, formed the opinion that it had been used only once, which would suggest that it was made specially for the king's funeral, perhaps for conveying his body from Memphis to Giza. Its use may become more evident when the second pit is opened if, in accordance with expectations, it contains another boat.

At right angles to the upper end of the causeway, on the south side, lies a row of three subsidiary pyramids, each with a small ruined chapel adjoining its eastern face. Beside the first pyramid there is a small boat-pit. Reisner believed that this pyramid belonged to Cheops's favourite queen who, in accordance with Egyptian custom, may also have been his full-blood sister. Concerning the second pyramid, Herodotus recounts the following legend:

The wickedness of Cheops reached to such a pitch that, when he had spent all his treasures and wanted more, he sent his daughter to the stews, with orders to procure him a certain sum – how much I cannot say, for I was not told; she procured it, however, and at the same time, bent on leaving a monument which should perpetuate her own memory, she required each man to make her a present of a stone towards the works which she contemplated. With these stones she built the pyramid which stands mid-most of the three that are in front of the Great Pyramid, measuring along each side a hundred and fifty feet.[6]

Happily there is no reason for believing that the details of this story bear any relation to historical fact. To judge from the few fragments which have survived, the walls of the chapel of this pyramid, built against the middle of the east face, were decorated with carvings in low relief equal in quality to the reliefs in the king's mortuary temple. This pyramid also, like the first, had a boat-pit, which was not discovered until 1952, but it has since been reburied. The third pyramid was ascribed in later times to Queen Henutsen, who may have been only a half-sister of the king. By the XXIst Dynasty she had been identified with the goddess Isis and had been given the name Isis-Mistress-of-the-Pyramid. At that time also the small chapel adjoining the pyramid was enlarged in order to provide a suitable sanctuary for the goddess.

Placing subsidiary pyramids on the east side of the main pyramid constituted a departure from precedent. Seneferu, both at Meidum and at Dahshur (at least in the complex of the Bent Pyramid – the subsidiary pyramid of the northern stone pyramid has not yet been found), placed the subsidiary pyramid south of the main pyramid. Approximately in that position, south of the Great Pyramid, Junker found, cut in the rock, a short sloping corridor leading to a small chamber, which he believed could represent the substructure of a pyramid for a queen. If that explanation is correct, perhaps the superstructure was never built. Maragioglio and Rinaldi, however, prefer to regard it as the counterpart of a subterranean chamber and its sloping corridor in the pyramid complex of Chephren, which will be described in connection with that monument.

The causeway consisted of a corridor, built either directly on the rock-bed or, in those places where the level of the rock-bed was too low, on an embankment of masonry. According to Herodotus, the

6. *Herodotus*, II, 126 (Rawlinson's translation).

construction of the causeway and the other buildings at the foot of the pyramid occupied ten years. Today nothing of the corridor remains intact, but some of the embankment is still standing in a small quarry, which it bridged, and again at the point where it crossed the edge of the plateau. The lower end of the causeway and whatever may have been preserved of the valley building still lie unexcavated beneath the modern village of Kafr es-Samman. A tunnel was constructed near the middle of the causeway, so that those who wished to cross it could do so without having to make a long detour around either the pyramid or the valley building.

Herodotus, in his description of the causeway, stated that it was built of polished stone on which were carved pictures of animals. The veracity of this statement was doubted by some archaeologists because no traces of carving in relief had been found in any of the IVth Dynasty pyramids or in their adjoining buildings, although they were certainly included in some of the contemporary private mastabas. To account for their absence, it was necessary to suppose that the architects of the period were preoccupied with mastering the technique of using granite and with learning the art of building in megalithic masonry. In the light, however, of the recent discovery that the walls of the mortuary temple were decorated with reliefs, a strong presumption is created in favour of the accuracy of Herodotus's statement regarding the causeway.

South of the causeway, close to the first of the subsidiary pyramids, the Boston-Harvard expedition directed by Reisner found in 1925 the only undisturbed royal tomb of the Old Kingdom hitherto known. It lay at the bottom of a vertical shaft which had been blocked with masonry to its entire depth of 99 feet. Within the chamber were stored the fine alabaster sarcophagus and funerary equipment of Queen Hetepheres, wife of Seneferu and mother of Cheops. Although the sarcophagus proved to be empty, the viscera, which had been removed from the body to help in its preservation, were found in an alabaster chest - the so-called Canopic chest. To explain the absence of the body, since the chamber had never been plundered, Reisner suggested that Hetepheres was buried in a tomb at Dahshur near the northern stone pyramid, which he ascribed to Seneferu, but that soon after her burial robbers had broken into the tomb and removed the body with its jewellery and gold ornaments. Before they were able to steal the remainder of the equipment, however, news of the violation of the tomb had reached the king. Hoping to prevent further despoilment, Cheops, who may not have been told of the disappearance of the body, decided to transfer his mother's tomb - possibly in secret - to Giza, where it would receive the same degree of protection as his own pyramid. As an additional precaution not only was no superstructure built above the new tomb, but a coating of plaster was spread over the stones covering the mouth of the shaft and finally the whole cavity was overlaid with a layer of limestone gravel so that no trace of its presence was visible. The fact that it remained undetected until the twentieth century, when the American excavators literally swept the sand from the rock-bed, is the best testimony to the success of the strategem.

Among the smaller objects found in this chamber were alabaster vessels, a copper ewer, three gold vessels, gold razors and knives, copper tools, and a gold manicure instrument, pointed at one end for cleaning the nails and curved at the other end for pressing down the quick; a toilet-box contained eight small alabaster vases filled with unguents and kohl. Inside a jewel-case were twenty silver anklets, each inlaid with dragonflies of malachite, lapis lazuli, and carnelian. The larger objects included a canopy-frame made of wood cased with gold, and two armchairs and a bed which were partly cased with gold sheeting (Plate 30). On the foot-board of the bed was a panel of gold inlaid with a blue and black floral design. A carrying-chair, also made of wood partly cased with gold sheeting, bore an inscription, written in hieroglyphs of gold set in ebony panels and repeated four times, which read: 'The mother of the King of Upper and Lower Egypt, follower of Horus, she who is in charge of the affairs of the harem[?] whose every word is done for her, daughter of the god [begotten] of his body, Hetepheres.'

No description can do justice to the artistic excellence and technical perfection of the equipment of Hetepheres; in comparison with its exquisite simplicity of design, much of the tomb furniture used in the later periods appears tawdry. Only the woodwork had suffered with the passage of time; inevitably it had either become decayed or shrunk to such a degree that it could not be used when the objects were reconstructed by the experts of the Boston–Harvard expedition before being delivered, in accordance with the terms of the excavators' agreement, to the Cairo Museum. Reisner was of the opinion that at least some of the objects had been used by Hetepheres during her lifetime. There is nothing improbable in the suggestion. Belongings of a personal kind were certainly not placed in the tomb until the time of the funeral, although vases and jars containing stores were often made expressly for the tomb and may well have been deposited there in advance. Whether the objects actually formed part of the furnishings of the queen's apartments in the palace is, however, a matter of only secondary importance. The real interest of the discovery lies in the light which it throws on the practical and artistic achievements of the IVth Dynasty and in the concrete evidence which it provides of the kind of equipment which was once to be found in other contemporary royal tombs.

Not the least significant of the various elements designed to add to the impressive effect of the Great Pyramid was its architectural setting. Other pyramids were surrounded by the tombs of officials and relatives of their owners, but little attention seems to have been given to their lay-out. East and west of the Great Pyramid enclosure wall, however, large cemeteries of mastabas were arranged in parallel rows several feet apart. South of the pyramid only a single row was built, while on the north there were none. The ownership of the tombs was also carefully planned, those in the eastern cemetery being allotted to close relatives of the king and those in the western cemetery – the larger – to officials. Although most of these mastabas have now lost their entire outer casing, it must be supposed that they were all originally faced with Tura limestone; their colour therefore would have been uniform with that of the vast pyramid rising in their midst. H. Junker, who excavated a part of the western cemetery, has aptly remarked that the Egyptian conception of the dead ruler continuing in the after-life to be surrounded by his relatives and loyal followers has never found so vivid an expression as in the arrangement of the tombs in this necropolis. It may be claimed, with equal truth, that the difference between the divine majesty of the ruler and his mortal subjects was never more strongly emphasized than in the contrast between the towering pyramid and the simple flat-topped mastabas.

Cheops's obvious wishes for the architectural setting of his tomb appear to have commanded little respect from subsequent generations. Already in the Vth and VIth Dynasties the symmetry of the original design was being destroyed by the construction of smaller mastabas in the spaces between the rows. The owners of these tombs were either officials of the necropolis or mortuary priests who, during their lifetime, had performed the various duties deemed necessary for securing the well-being of the dead king and his associates. In later times, particularly under the Saites, burial in the vicinity of the three Giza pyramids was believed to confer special benefits on the dead, with the result that the whole area became honeycombed with tombs and the regularity of the earliest design must have been obscured beyond recognition.

South-east of the Great Pyramid complex and near the valley building of the Second Pyramid lies the Giant Sphinx (Plate 31). A knoll of rock, which had been left by the builders of the Great Pyramid when quarrying stone for its inner core, was fashioned in the time of Chephren into a huge recumbent lion with a human head. Perhaps the builders left it because the quality of the stone in that part of the quarry was poor. In order to conceal its defects, it was probably overlaid with a coating of plaster and painted. The length of this colossus is about 240 feet, its height 66 feet, and the maximum width of the face 13 feet 8 inches. On the head is the royal head-dress; other emblems of royalty are the cobra on the forehead, and the beard, now largely missing, on the chin. There was a hole in the top of the head, which may have been a socket for attaching a crown, but it has been filled with cement in modern times and is no longer visible. Although the face has been severely mutilated, it still gives the impression of being a portrait of King Chephren and not merely a formalized representation. A figure, possibly of the king, was carved in front of the chest, but scarcely any trace of it now remains. Between the outstretched paws stands a large slab of red granite bearing an inscription which purports to record a dream of Tuthmosis IV of the XVIIIth Dynasty before he ascended the throne. According to this inscription the prince, when hunting, decided to rest at midday in the shadow of the sphinx. During his sleep the sphinx, which was regarded at that time as an embodiment of the sun-god Harmachis, promised him the Double Crown of Egypt if he would clear away the sand which had nearly engulfed his body. Unfortunately, the latter part of the inscription is too badly weathered to be legible, but it may be surmised that it related how the god's wish was fulfilled and how the prince was finally rewarded with the Crown of the Two Lands. In addition to clearing away the sand, Tuthmosis IV may have repaired damaged portions of the body by the insertion of small blocks of limestone – an operation which was repeated in Roman times, when the sand was once more removed and an altar was erected in front of the figure.

Freeing the sphinx of sand was no doubt a recurrent need and probably there were long periods when it was almost, if not entirely, concealed from view by accumulations of wind-blown sand. Perhaps it was for that reason that it was not mentioned by the classical authors Herodotus, Diodorus and Strabo. A stela in the British Museum records that it was cleared of sand in the time of Nero (A.D. 54-68), while Claudius Balbillus was Prefect of Egypt. Drawings made in the last century show large fissures in the head and head-dress and deep depressions on the neck from sand erosion (Plate 32). That it has survived to the present day in spite of its fragility must be largely due to its having been buried for so much of its existence. The first excavation of the sphinx in modern times was conducted by Captain Caviglia in 1817 at a cost of £450. Subsequently it was cleared of accumulations of sand by Mariette (1853), Maspero (1886), Baraize (1925) and Selim Bey Hassan (1936).

Although the Greeks may have adopted the idea of the sphinx from Egypt, perhaps indirectly by way of Syria, the hybrid which they developed differed widely from its Egyptian counterpart both in form and in attributes. The name also may have been suggested by the Egyptian epithet *shesep-ankh*, 'living image', which the Greeks may have wrongly associated with their own word meaning 'to bind', the sphinx being composed of human and animal elements *bound* together. In Egyptian mythology the lion often figures as the guardian of sacred places. How or when this conception first arose is not known, but it probably dates back to remote antiquity. Like so many other primitive beliefs, it was incorporated by the priests of Heliopolis into their solar creed, the lion being considered as the guardian of the gates of the underworld on the eastern and western horizons. In the form of the sphinx, the lion retained the function of a sentinel, but was given the human features of the sun-god Atum. An inscription carved on the pedestal of a small sphinx in Vienna, which was probably placed in front of a XXVIth Dynasty tomb, puts the following words in the mouth of the sphinx: 'I protect thy chapel of thy tomb, I guard thy gate. I ward off the intruding stranger. I hurl the foes to the ground and their weapons with them. I drive away the wicked one from the chapel of thy tomb. I destroy thine adversaries in their lurking-place, blocking it that they come forth no more.' A possible reason for the identification of the sun-god's features with those of the deceased king may be the Heliopolitan belief that the king, after his death, actually became the sun-god. The Giant Sphinx would therefore represent Chephren as the sun-god and also convey the idea of the lion as the guardian of the necropolis.

Immediately in front of the sphinx lie the ruins of a small temple excavated by Baraize in 1925-32 while clearing accumulations of sand around the Giant Sphinx. It was further explored in 1935-6 by Selim Bey Hassan, who reported that its coarse limestone walls had once been overlaid with granite ashlars. Its chief architectural feature was a colonnaded court paved with alabaster. Both from the method of its construction and from its architecture it is clear that it dates from the same period as the valley building of Chephren. But what was its purpose? Its position in front of the sphinx leaves little room for doubt that the two monuments were related. Ricke and Schott, who made in 1965 a detailed study of the surviving elements of the building on behalf of the Swiss Institute of Archaeology in Cairo, called it the Temple of Harmachis, while conceding that the sphinx was not iden-tified with Harmachis until the New Kingdom. Its architectural form, with sanctuaries at both the east and the west ends and an altar for burnt offerings in the central court, led them to deduce that it was dedicated to the sun-god in his three aspects, as Khepri in the morning, as Rē at mid-day and as Atum in the evening. It is the only known temple dating from the IVth Dynasty which was not erected for the celebration of a funerary cult. It was never finished, probably owing to Chephren's death. The fact that no tombs of its officiating priests have been found suggests that it was never used. By the XVIIIth Dynasty it seems to have been at least partly buried in sand, because a corner of a small temple of Amenophis II was built over its enclosure wall, near the north-west corner.

The valley building of Chephren was itself thought at one time to be a temple connected with the sphinx. Many years ago, however, it was identified as an element in the pyramid complex of King Chephren, the Greek equivalent of the Egyptian name Khaef-Rē by which the builder of the Second Pyramid is usually known. Auguste Mariette, the founder of the Cairo Museum, discovered this building in 1853, but although he cleared the whole of the inside, considerable accumulations of sand were left against the outer walls. A further clearance was made by Mariette in 1869, when the building formed one of the principal show-places to which the distinguished visitors who attended the opening of the Suez Canal were conducted. Finally in 1909–10, the outer walls were freed of sand by the von Sieglin expedition, under the direction of Uvo Hölscher and Georg Steindorff, when excavating the whole of the pyramid complex (Plate 33).

Considering the very early date of the valley building, its condition is truly remarkable. No other building of the IVth Dynasty, with the possible exception of the unfinished mortuary temple of the Meidum pyramid, has survived in a comparable state of preservation. It was built on an almost square ground-plan, measuring 147 feet from east to west and marginally different from north to south owing to a slight outward deviation of its north wall, and it rises to a height of 43 feet. Its immensely thick walls are composed of coarse local limestone faced, both internally and externally, with ashlars of polished red granite from Aswan (fig. 30: 1). The four outer walls are not perpendicular, but have a pronounced batter – a regular feature in buildings of the period. Outside the east wall probably stood a stone kiosk containing a statue of the king. Two doorways in this wall, which may originally have been flanked by sphinxes, give entrance to the building from a terrace cut in the rock. Around each doorway was carved a band of

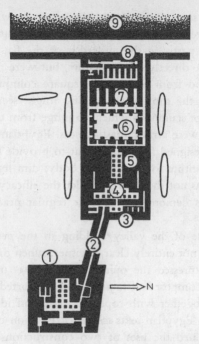

Figure 30. The valley building and mortuary temple of Chephren

hieroglyphic inscription giving the name and titles of the king, but only the last words, 'beloved of [the goddess] Bastet' and 'beloved of [the goddess] Hathor', are preserved; no other inscriptions or reliefs occur anywhere else in the building. Short passages lead from the doorways by way of small but lofty vestibules to a long antechamber, in the floor of which Mariette found a deep pit containing a diorite statue of Chephren – one of the finest examples of Old Kingdom sculpture hitherto recovered (Plate 34). Originally, this statue, which is rather larger than life-size, was probably placed in the T-shaped hall leading westwards out of the antechamber; its transference to the pit, the date of which is uncertain, may have been due to a desire to preserve it from destruction. A total of twenty-three royal statues made of diorite, schist and alabaster once stood against the sides of the hall, seventeen in the stem of the T and six facing eastwards in the cross-piece. Light entered the hall through oblique slits cut partly in the top of the walls and partly in the underside of the flat granite roof; the rays did not shine directly on the statues, but were reflected from the alabaster floor and from the massive square columns of red granite which supported the roof. Such lighting might seem inadequate for the illumination of sculptures which, to judge from the one which has remained intact, were artistic masterpieces. Egyptian sculptures, however, were not designed for display, but to provide the spirit with an imperishable substitute for the human body; dim light or even complete darkness was not thought to hinder the efficacy of the substitute – a fact which is demonstrated by the regular practice of enclosing statues in serdabs.

The precise use of the valley building in the performance of the funerary ritual is not entirely clear. Reisner, when discussing its architectural form, expressed the opinion that it was ultimately derived from a pavilion composed of matting and supported by a framework of poles lashed together with ropes. B. Grdseloff identified it with a building called in Egyptian texts *seh-netjer* (Pavilion-of-the-god). In his opinion it combined the uses of two constructions which normally stood independently when built in association with mastabas of the Old Kingdom, namely the *ibu* (Purification-tent) and the *wabet* (House-of-embalmment). The purification ceremonies in the valley building of Chephren took place, Grdseloff suggested, in a temporary pavilion built on the roof, to which a ramp paved with alabaster gave access from a passage leading out of the north-west corner of the T-shaped hall. Round holes, which he believed had served as sockets for the framework of such a pavilion, are still visible in the paving of the roof. The embalming of the body, he considered, was performed in the antechamber. The Abbé Drioton, while agreeing with Grdseloff's interpretation in general, suggested that his identification should be reversed and that the purification was conducted in the antechamber and the embalmment on the roof. H. Ricke, however, thought that the actual processes of purification and embalmment were carried out elsewhere, probably in brick buildings, and re-enacted as ritual ceremonies in this building. The ritual purification, he believed, took place on the terrace in front of the building and the ritual embalmment in the transverse part of the T-shaped hall.

Purification by washing played an important part in Egyptian ritual at all times. The king, for instance, was ceremonially washed in the sacred lake of the temple of Rē at Heliopolis before he entered the building. Similarly, before his dead body could be taken into the sacred precincts of his tomb, it was necessary that it should be purified by washing. From this purification, moreover, it was believed that the dead king was regenerated, just as the sun-god was thought to be reborn each morning by bathing in the 'Lily Lake' before embarking on his journey across the heavens. According to Ricke it was this episode which was ritually reproduced on the terrace in front of the valley building. Osiris too, according to one tradition, had been revivified by the lustration of his body; the dead king therefore, when identified with Osiris, was thought to derive equal benefit from the same treatment.

During the funeral of the king a ritual re-enactment of the embalmment may well have taken place in the valley building, whether or not the actual operation was performed there. To judge from inscriptional evidence in the tomb of Queen Meresankh III, a grandchild of Cheops, the processes of embalmment occupied several months, two hundred and seventy-two days being given as the interval between her death and her burial. So long a period would not have been necessary unless either her tomb was not ready when she died or some preservative substance with a slow action, perhaps natron or salt, had been employed; wrapping and modelling the various physical members, to which reference has already been made in connection with burials in mastabas, could have been accomplished in a shorter time. The discovery in the tomb of Hetepheres of a so-called Canopic chest containing the viscera proves that the most decomposable organs were removed in the embalmment of a queen at the beginning of the IVth Dynasty; in the case of a king the practice may have existed at a much earlier date.

A third ceremony to be performed in the valley building was the so-called 'Opening of the Mouth'. Priests, at least one of whom would be a son of the dead king, would approach each of the twenty-three statues of the king in the T-shaped hall, sprinkle water over it, fumigate it with incense, offer sacrifices before it, touch its mouth with various implements including an adze and a chisel, rub milk on its mouth, and deck it with the royal regalia. In later times these ceremonies were also performed on the dead body, but possibly this practice was not introduced until after the Old Kingdom. By their execution it was thought that the statue or mummy would be endowed with the faculties of a living person and a statue would become an abode for the *ka* of its owner.

It is unlikely that Chephren would have placed so many statues of himself in this building merely to provide his *ka* with as many reserve 'bodies' as possible. A king required not only a continuation of life after death, but also a continuation of divine life. In order to achieve this divine existence in the next world each of the twenty-six members of which the body was composed must be deified separately and identified with the particular deity who was associated with that member. Ricke and Schott would explain these statues as being intended for the deification of Chephren's physical members individually. Since three deities were each associated with two members, it was not necessary to have twenty-six statues, but only twenty-three, the ceremonies being repeated twice on three of the statues. While the 'Opening of the Mouth' and the deification were being performed, the coffin containing the king's body, they believed, would be placed in the hall and the viscera kept temporarily in four of a group of six long cells, arranged in two storeys and approached by a passage opening out of the south side of the hall. The two other cells, in their opinion, were used for storing the two crowns of Saïs.

After the completion of the three ceremonies, the embalmed body and viscera, and also the two crowns if the explanation of Ricke and Schott be correct, would have been taken out of the valley building by way of the passage which connected the hall with the causeway (fig. 30: 2). On its journey through the passage the cortège would have passed the mouth of a narrow corridor leading to a small chamber built of alabaster. The purpose of this chamber is not evident, but Hölscher conjectured that a porter, whose duty it was to guard the entrance to the causeway, lived in it; Grdseloff, however, suggested that it was used for storing food-offerings required during the three ceremonies.

In order to avoid the necessity of building an embankment across a deep depression which lay directly to the east of the mortuary temple, the causeway was constructed on a ridge of rock which crossed the depression obliquely from south-east to north-west. It was more than a quarter of a mile in length and about 15 feet in breadth. Nothing of its structure is now visible except part of the rock foundation and some blocks of Tura limestone from the walls and floor of its corridor. When standing, its walls rose perpendicularly on the inside, but their outer face had a marked batter. If Herodotus is correct in his statement that the causeway of the Great Pyramid was decorated with reliefs, it must be supposed that the inner walls of the corridor of this causeway also were decorated. It was roofed with slabs of stone laid flat. Perhaps the practice of roofing causeways dates from the time when their corridors were first decorated with reliefs. The causeways of the Bent Pyramid and the pyramid of Meidum, neither of which appears to have been decorated, were certainly not roofed; possibly, therefore, the causeway of the Great Pyramid was the first to be given a roof in order to protect the painted reliefs on its walls. Light was admitted to the corridor through horizontal slits, cut along the middle of the roof. Since rain also would enter through these slits and, unless drained, would run down into the valley building, a channel was sunk in the paving at the lower end of the causeway to conduct the water through an outlet in the side-wall.

When the body of the dead king was transferred to the mortuary temple, no one standing outside the causeway could have witnessed the ceremony. Without doubt, such screening was intentional, although the motive which prompted it cannot be deduced with certainty. The most probable explanation seems to be that it was thought necessary to protect the dead body, after its purification in the valley building, from the gaze of those who were ceremonially impure. Even the fact that the body was already enclosed within a wooden coffin was apparently not considered a sufficient protection against contamination. Persons, other than priests, who were to accompany the bier to the mortuary temple probably underwent ritual purification before joining the cortège. Priests, as their Egyptian name *wab* ('pure') implies, were ceremonially clean at all times.

The mortuary temple, now reduced to ruins, was a low, rectangular building which measured about 370 feet in length and 160 feet in breadth. Its walls were composed of local stone, in part faced on the inside with red granite. Outside, the lowest course was also faced with granite, but the remainder of the building had a facing of Tura limestone (Plate 35). Five pits for boats were hewn in the rock close to the north and south walls. Two of the pits still have well-preserved roofs made of limestone slabs, but no trace of the wooden boats has been found.

Not one of the mortuary temples hitherto excavated has proved to be an exact replica of any other known example. They differ, however, only in arrangement and in architectural detail. From the time of Chephren until the end of the Old Kingdom, every mortuary temple embodied five main features: an entrance hall, an open court, five niches for statues, magazines, and a sanctuary.

In Chephren's temple, the causeway did not lead directly to the entrance hall, but to a corridor, at the southern end of which were two granite chambers. According to Ricke these chambers were constructed for the crowns of Saïs, while a group of four chambers with floors and walls of alabaster situated beyond a vestibule at the northern end of the corridor (fig. 30: 3) were shrines for the viscera. At the funeral the first ceremonies to be performed in this building would thus commemorate two of the ancient burial rites of Saïs and Buto. A narrow passage connected the vestibule with the entrance hall, the latter consisting of two sections, one transverse (fig. 30: 4) and the other longitudinal (fig. 30: 5). Rectangular monolithic columns of red granite, resembling those in the valley building, supported the roofs of both the vestibule and the entrance hall. At each end of the transverse section of the entrance hall, a long and narrow chamber penetrated deeply into the masonry core of the building. Since the end wall in each chamber was composed of a single block of granite Hölscher conjectured that its surface was carved into a figure of the king fashioned almost in the round. If this conjecture is correct, the chambers would have been serdabs of a kind without any known parallel in a royal mortuary temple. Ricke, however, is inclined to regard them as having been built for models of the two barques of the sun-god, the southern for the day barque and the northern for the night barque.

Beyond the entrance hall lay the open court paved with alabaster. Like the court in the mortuary temple of Cheops it was surrounded by a cloister (fig. 30: 6). Traces of a drain, found in the middle of the court, suggest that an altar may have stood there, the drain being required for carrying away the blood of the animals sacrificed and the liquid of the libations offered; on the other hand, the drain may have been used simply for disposing of accumulations of rain-water. Broad piers built of blocks of red granite supported the curved roof of the cloister. Twelve seated statues of the king, each about 12 feet in height, projected outwards from recesses in the outer faces of all the piers, apart from those at the four corners. A single band of hieroglyphic inscription, giving the king's names and titles, was engraved around the openings between the piers, and above each statue was carved a pair of vultures with open wings representing the protecting goddess Nekhbet. The inner walls of the cloister, above a granite dado, were decorated with limestone reliefs, one fragment of which, showing part of a bound Asiatic captive, was excavated by Hölscher, but its connection with this court was only recently recognized by Ricke. Opposite each of the five openings on the west side of the cloister was a deep niche which may have contained a statue of the king (fig. 30: 7). The significance of the five statues – a number which does not vary in any of the subsequent mortuary temples – may be that each bore one of the five official names assumed by the king on his accession. It is, however, equally possible that the number was dictated by the need to represent the king in association with five different cult-symbols.

The open court marked the limit beyond which only the priests were allowed to advance. During the temple ceremonies, secular attendants must have remained in the court while the priests proceeded, by way of the corridor in front of the statue-niches, to the sanctuary (fig. 30: 8). The main feature of the sanctuary was usually a false door in the west wall with a low altar at its foot. Offerings were placed on the altar daily by the priests. Since it was only the spirit of the substance provided and not the actual material which was thought to be of value to the dead, the fact that the offerings remained undisturbed until replaced would not have troubled the minds of the ancient Egyptians. Five magazines lay between the sanctuary and the five statue-niches – a coincidence in number which may not have been accidental. In construction also, the magazines shared with the niches the peculiarity of being the only parts of the temple not paved with alabaster. Within the magazines were stored stone vases and reserve supplies of food, which would be required by the king if the priests neglected their daily duty to provide fresh offerings.

A long ramp led from the north-west corner of the corridor surrounding the open court to the terrace on which the pyramid stood. The position of the entrance to the ramp implies that access to the pyramid enclosure was permitted to persons who were not entitled to enter the innermost parts of the mortuary temple. At the funeral service, therefore, the whole procession may have proceeded to the pyramid (fig. 30: 9) after the 'Opening of the Mouth' ceremony had been performed on the statues in the niches. The masons and workmen who blocked up and sealed the entrance to the pyramid must also have reached the enclosure by way of the ramp; a high wall, which surrounded the pyramid on every side, would have prevented an approach by any more direct route.

Between the pyramid and the surrounding wall there was a pavement about 34 feet in width on the north, east and west sides and somewhat wider on the south side, where a single subsidiary pyramid stood approximately opposite the middle of the king's pyramid. The mortuary temple was separated from the east face of the pyramid by a paved alley-way. In this respect it resembles the Great Pyramid; in later enclosures the two buildings are generally contiguous, so that there is no open space between the false door and the pyramid. Borchardt conjectured that a second false door or a stela stood against the east face of the pyramid, but no trace of its existence was revealed during excavation. In the light of the discoveries at the Bent Pyramid it is perhaps more likely that if anything stood in the alley-way it was a pair of round-topped stelae and an altar.

West of the subsidiary pyramid, the superstructure of which is almost completely destroyed, Abdel Hafiz, working for the Antiquities

Service of the Egyptian Government, in 1960 found a sloping corridor hewn in the rock directly in line with the east–west axis of the subsidiary pyramid and running from east to west. It was blocked with three limestone plugs, and beyond them lay a chamber in which had been placed a wooden box. The contents of the box, which had been arranged in three layers, consisted of a base (appararently of a shrine), four columns and crossbars and a roof, all made of wood, and copper handles which were attached to the roof. Both in its position and in its design, this cavity resembles a subterranean construction in the Great Pyramid complex and it is equally difficult to explain.

The most distinctive external feature of Chephren's pyramid, apart from its size, is the substantial portion of its outer casing which still remains intact near the apex. Some of the casing has also been preserved at the base. The stone employed is, however, different in each place, the upper remnant being composed of Tura limestone and the lower of red granite – a material which was used only as a casing for the bottommost course. Herodotus, in his description of the pyramid, states that 'the lowest layer is of variegated Ethiopian stone',[7] apparently in the mistaken belief that granite was employed not merely as a casing but as a kind of platform on which the pyramid was built. The capstone, which has now disappeared, may also have been made of granite.

Owing to its position on somewhat higher ground, Chephren's pyramid creates the illusion of being taller than the Great Pyramid. In reality, its present height of $447\frac{1}{2}$ feet falls short of that of its neighbour by $2\frac{1}{2}$ feet. Originally, it rose to a height of 471 feet and was therefore about 10 feet lower than the Great Pyramid, when the latter was also undamaged. The area covered by Chephren's pyramid today is approximately $690\frac{1}{2}$ feet square; formerly each side measured $707\frac{3}{4}$ feet, so that the dimensions at the base were about 48 feet less in each direction than those of the Great Pyramid. The faces of the pyramid, which slope at an angle of 52° 20′, rise more steeply than the faces of the Great Pyramid – a fact which explains the small difference in height between the two buildings when compared with the considerable inequality of their base dimensions.

Internally, Chephren's pyramid bears little resemblance to the Great

7. Book II, 127.

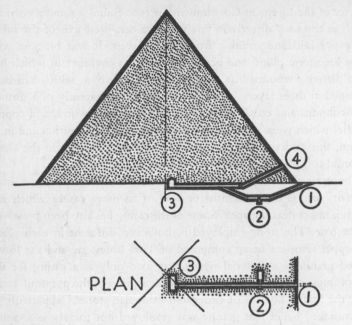

Figure 31. The pyramid of Chephren, section looking west and plan

Pyramid. It has two entrances, one in the north face at a height of nearly 50 feet, and the other directly below, hewn in the rock foundation of the surrounding pavement (fig. 31: 4 and 1). Both entrances are situated at a distance of about 41 feet to the east of the pyramid's main north-south axis. From the upper entrance, a low and narrow corridor descends at an angle of 25° 55' through the core of the pyramid until it enters the rock; here it becomes horizontal and continues on a level plane to the tomb-chamber (fig. 31: 3). The roof, walls and floor of the whole of the sloping section and of a small part of the horizontal section are lined with red granite. Near the end of the granite lining vertical slots have been cut in the walls to receive a portcullis, also made of granite, the damaged remains of which are still in position. The tomb-chamber has been hewn, with the exception of its roof, entirely out of the rock; the pointed gable roof consists of limestone slabs laid at the same angle as the faces of the pyramid. With its longer axis running from east to west, the chamber measures 46½ feet in length, 16½ feet in breadth, and 22½ feet in height. Rectangular cavities were cut near the top of both the north and the south walls, apparently with the intention of constructing shafts from the chamber to the outer surface of the monument, as in the Great Pyramid, but the plan was abandoned when each shaft was only about a foot in depth. Squares marked in red on the walls approximately 5 feet below these cavities suggest that an earlier plan to locate the shafts at about the same height above the floor as those in the Great Pyramid had already been discarded. On the west side of the chamber, a fine rectangular sarcophagus of polished granite has been let into the floor up to the level of its lid. The lid itself, which lies nearby, is broken into two pieces – a condition in which it was found in 1818 by Giovanni Belzoni, the first European explorer to enter this pyramid in modern times. No trace of Chephren's body was discovered in the sarcophagus.

A Canopic chest containing the king's viscera was probably buried in a pit cut in the rock floor of the chamber by the south wall. The pit is shown in Belzoni's drawing of the chamber, but has since been filled up. Originally it was probably covered with one of the limestone slabs with which the chamber was paved.

The lower corridor (fig. 31: 1), at its beginning, follows a course similar to the upper corridor; it is, however, completely hewn out of the rock. After descending at a gradient of 21° 40′, it becomes horizontal for a short distance and then rises steeply to emerge in the floor of the horizontal section of the upper corridor. A granite portcullis stood also in this corridor, but the walls were not lined with granite. In the east wall of the horizontal section, there is a recess opposite which a sloping passage leads down to a chamber, measuring 34 feet 3 inches in length, 10 feet 4 inches in breadth, and 8 feet 5 inches in height (fig. 31: 2). There can be no doubt that this chamber, at the time of its construction, was intended to contain the royal sarcophagus; some explanation for its abandonment must therefore be sought. Two exceptional features which may offer a clue in solving the difficulty immediately strike the eye: first, the chamber is situated very near the entrance to the pyramid, and, secondly, the mouth of the corridor

leading to the chamber lies beyond the northern limit of the superstructure. In other contemporary pyramids, the tomb-chamber is located
approximately beneath the apex and the entrance is situated in the
northern face. If, however, it be supposed that, when the chamber and
corridor were constructed, it was planned to build the pyramid some
200 feet further north, both the chamber and the entrance would have
occupied their customary positions. An alternative explanation would
be that the first intention was to build a pyramid covering a much
larger area and that the northern and eastern limits were moved inwards. In either case a possible reason for the change in plan was the
discovery of a suitable rock foundation for the causeway concealed
beneath the sand on a line south of the one originally chosen.

A problem to which no satisfactory solution has yet been found is
the purpose of the sloping passage which connects the lower apartments with the upper corridor. The only explanation which has been
suggested is that it was used for transferring the sarcophagus from the
old chamber to the new. Petrie, however, showed that the sarcophagus
which is now in the upper chamber was 3 feet 6 inches in width and
therefore about half an inch wider than the upper and the lower
corridors. That being so, it could never have been in the lower chamber and it must have been placed in the upper chamber before it was
roofed. The fact, however, remains that the passage was constructed
and that, after serving its purpose, it was blocked with limestone boulders, many of which have never been removed. Blocking of the same
kind completely fills the lower entrance corridor so that it cannot now
be entered.

West of the pyramid, outside the enclosure wall, lies a series of
galleries which Sir Flinders Petrie identified as the barracks in which
were housed the masons and workmen employed in building the pyramid complex. These galleries are now almost entirely concealed beneath the sand, but Petrie, who surveyed them in 1880–82, has stated[8]
that they numbered ninety-one, each measuring about 88 feet in
length, $9\frac{1}{2}$ feet in width, and 7 feet in height. The walls of the galleries
are composed of rough pieces of limestone faced with a coating of
dried mud; the floor also is overlaid with a coating of the same

8. Petrie, *The Pyramids and Temples of Gizeh*, pp. 101–3.

material. Wide pilasters of hewn limestone serve as terminals to the walls at the entrance end. The east end of each gallery is closed by a single wall running at right angles to the galleries and oriented almost exactly parallel to the west side of the pyramid.

Considered in relation to its predecessors, Chephren's pyramid provides the first recognizable example of a complex in which all the architectural elements of the standard pattern appear in their fully developed form. Earlier complexes, notably that of the Great Pyramid, embody many of its salient features, but they are either not in a comparable state of preservation or, like the mortuary temple of the Meidum pyramid, architecturally still in embryo. In Chephren's pyramid complex, the valley building is largely intact, the foundations of the causeway are plainly visible and enough of the mortuary temple remains to enable its ground-plan to be determined with certainty. Each of these structures, moreover, contains in its design all the basic elements of the subsequent pyramid complexes; modifications in detail and substantial decorative innovations were to be introduced, but the essential skeleton was to remain unchanged.

The third pyramid of the Giza group stands in the south-west corner of the wide plateau. Although it had been ascribed to Mycerinus both by Herodotus and by Diodorus Siculus, who visited Egypt in the middle of the first century B.C., the identification was not confirmed until 1837-8, when Colonel Howard Vyse found the name of Mycerinus written in red ochre on the roof of the burial-chamber in the second of the three subsidiary pyramids within the complex. Further proof was obtained by the expedition of Harvard University and the Boston Museum of Fine Arts, which excavated the site between the years 1905 and 1927 under the directorship of G.A. Reisner.

Contemporary records shed no light on the life and character of Mycerinus. In very late times he seems to have gained a reputation for piety and justice, while Cheops and Chephren were regarded as having been wicked and tyrannical kings. Herodotus, in whose writings this tradition is preserved, speaks of Mycerinus in the following terms:

This prince [i.e. Mycerinus] disapproved the conduct of his father, reopened the temples and allowed the people, who were ground down to the lowest point of misery, to return to their occupations and to resume the practice of sacrifice. His justice in the decision of causes was beyond that of all the former kings. The Egyptians praise him in this respect more highly than any of their other monarchs, declaring that he not only gave his judgements with fairness, but also, when anyone was dissatisfied with his sentence, made compensation to him out of his own purse and thus pacified his anger.[9]

The gods, however, had ordained that Egypt should suffer tyrannical rulers for a hundred and fifty years. The reigns of Cheops and Chephren, according to this legend, had already accounted for a hundred and six years, so that forty-four years of affliction still awaited the Egyptians when Mycerinus ascended the throne. Not to be foiled of their purpose, the gods decided that the reign of the 'just and pious' Mycerinus must be cut short, but not without warning him that this fate was impending. To quote the words of Herodotus:

An oracle reached him from the town of Buto, which said 'six years only shalt thou live upon the earth, and in the seventh thou shalt end thy days'. Mycerinus, indignant, sent an angry message to the oracle, reproaching the god with his injustice – 'My father and uncle,' he said, 'though they shut up the temples, took no thought of the gods and destroyed multitudes of men, nevertheless enjoyed a long life; I, who am pious, am to die soon!' There came in reply a second message from the oracle – 'For this very reason is thy life brought so quickly to a close – thou hast not done as it behoved thee. Egypt was fated to suffer affliction one hundred and fifty years – the two kings who preceded thee upon the throne understood this – thou has not understood it.' Mycerinus, when this answer reached him, perceiving that his doom was fixed, had lamps prepared, which he lighted every day at eventime, and feasted and enjoyed himself unceasingly both day and night, moving about in the marsh-country and the woods, and visiting all the places that he heard were agreeable sojourns. His wish was to prove the oracle false, by turning the nights into days and so living twelve years in the space of six.[10]

There is certainly no reason for believing that the legend quoted by Herodotus is founded on historical fact, although evidence that Mycerinus met an untimely death is to be seen in all the buildings of his pyramid complex. Mycerinus must have intended to follow the example of Chephren by constructing his valley building and part of his

9. *Herodotus*, II, 129 (Rawlinson's translation).
10. *Herodotus*, II, 133 (Rawlinson's translation).

mortuary temple of limestone faced with ashlars of granite and his causeway of limestone. Reisner's excavations, however, have shown that this plan was never realized and that the greater part of the work was either hastily finished in materials of inferior quality or even left incomplete. Only the foundations of the valley building were made of stone; the superstructure was composed almost entirely of crude brick. The causeway consisted of an embankment of stone, upon which was built a brick corridor overlaid, both inside and outside, with white plaster and roofed with wooden logs. In the mortuary temple the foundations and the inner core of some of its walls were composed of limestone. A beginning had also been made with laying floors of granite and with adding granite facings to the walls, but crude brick was again the material used for completing the greater part of the building.

Examples of tombs and monuments left unfinished by the owner, but completed by his son or successor, are not uncommon. It would therefore be only natural to suppose that Shepseskaf, who is believed to have succeeded Mycerinus, was the king who built the crude brick additions to the pyramid complex. Proof that Shepseskaf did, in fact, contribute towards the completion of the complex is provided by an inscription, found in the ruins of the mortuary temple, which states that he 'made it [the temple] as his monument for his father, the King of Upper and Lower Egypt [Mycerinus]'. Both the valley building and the mortuary temple were, however, repaired and slightly modified in design at a later date. These repairs and alterations were attributed by Reisner to the priests who officiated in the temple during the Vth and VIth Dynasties. Their labours, he pointed out, might not have been inspired by consideration of duty alone, but also by motives of self-interest. As mortuary priests, they would have been entitled to enjoy the fruits of the rich endowments bequeathed by the dead king in return for service in his temple; they would also have been qualified to dwell in his pyramid city – a residential enclosure attached to the valley building, the inhabitants of which were exempt from the payment of certain taxes. To secure these privileges, however, it would have been necessary for them to preserve intact the fabric of the buildings and to maintain at least some show of performing the temple services.

Architecturally and in their internal lay-out, both the earlier and the later forms of the buildings differed considerably from those of Chephren, but no fundamental changes in general composition were introduced.

During his excavation of the valley building and the mortuary temple, Reisner discovered a large number of statues and statuettes, most of which represented the king either alone or as a member of a group. Among those found in the valley building were some beautifully carved slate triads composed of the goddess Hathor, the king, and one of the *nome* deities (Plate 36). There can be no doubt that Mycerinus intended to have forty-two of these triads, each showing him in company with a different *nome*-god or goddess, but only four and some fragments were discovered; possibly the remainder were never carved. Another fine piece of sculpture also found in the valley building was a slate group-statue of Mycerinus and Queen Khamerernebty II (Plate 37). As works of art, these statues are worthy of comparison with the best of their kind yet known. They have all been carved in the naturalistic style typical of the Old Kingdom, with the result that a high degree of individuality in points of detail is evident. Of the eight representations of the king's face, no two are exactly alike, but the majority portray the features with slightly bulging eyes, a rounded nose, and a protruding lower lip. In many respects the face resembles that of Chephren, as portrayed in the famous diorite statue (Plate 34), but the cheek-bones in the latter are higher and the face narrower. Fifteen statuettes of the king had been left unfinished and even the group-statue of the king and Queen Khamerernebty II had not been entirely polished – a fact which can be explained by the king's untimely death and the parsimony of his successor. While the abandonment of these sculptures before completion must be deplored on aesthetic grounds, they throw more light in their present condition on the technical processes employed by Egyptian sculptors than if they had been preserved as finished works. Reisner, who conducted a minute examination of the figures, was able to detect eight distinct stages of development, some of which corresponded with the different stages illustrated by unfinished statues in scenes of sculptors' workshops represented in the wall decorations of private tombs.

The pyramid of Mycerinus occupies less than a quarter of the area covered by the Great Pyramid. Each side measures 356½ feet at the base. Its vertical height is now 204 feet; when complete, it was 14 feet higher. The upper portion is cased, in the normal manner, with dressed Tura limestone, but the lower sixteen courses have an outer facing of red granite, some of which has been left in the rough. It is possible that Mycerinus intended to case the whole pyramid with granite; the change of material may therefore indicate the stage reached at the time of his death. On the other hand, the combination of limestone and granite may have been deliberate, so that the only evidence of untimely death would be the undressed granite at the base. Removal of the sand from around the entrance has shown that the granite in that section of the north face was smoothed down to the ground. It has also brought to light an inscription which Diodorus saw.[11] He thought that it merely recorded that Mycerinus built the pyramid, whereas it also says that he died on the 23rd day of the 4th month of summer without mentioning the year of his reign, but adding that he was buried with very rich funerary equipment. It is later than the pyramid; it may date from the time of Khaemuas, son of Ramesses II, who left other inscriptions at Giza. Possibly the smoothing of the stone was also done at the same time.

Internally, at least one and probably two changes of plan are apparent. The first design consisted of a sloping corridor of the usual kind (fig. 32: 1) tunnelled through the rock and leading to a rectangular burial-chamber, the longer axis of which ran from east to west. When this design was abandoned the floor of the burial-chamber (fig. 32: 2) was deepened and a second sloping corridor cut beneath the first (fig. 32: 3). The only reason for this change of plan seems to have been a decision to enlarge the superstructure of the pyramid and the consequent necessity for constructing the corridor at a lower level in order to preserve the position of the entrance in the new north face at about the same height above the ground. As far as the point where it enters the rock, the new corridor is lined with granite. At the foot of the slope, the horizontal continuation of the corridor is enlarged into an antechamber, the rock walls of which are decorated with carved

11. *Diodorus*, Book I, 64, 9.

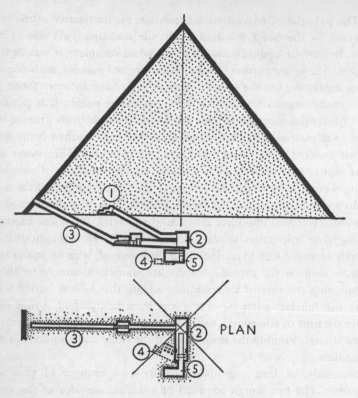

Figure 32. The pyramid of Mycerinus, section looking east and plan

panelling. Three granite portcullises, which fitted into vertical slots in
the walls, blocked the corridor between the antechamber and the
burial-chamber. According to Ricke they were constructed, like the
portcullises in the Great Pyramid, so that they could be lowered into
position by means of ropes which passed over roller-shaped timbers at
the top of each slot.

The third and last design did not involve any alteration of the earlier
plan, but only the addition of two chambers at a greater depth and an
approach ramp sloping westwards from the middle of the floor of the
original burial-chamber and terminating in a short, horizontal passage.

The first chamber, which lies on the right side of the passage, is entered by a flight of steps (fig. 32: 4). It is a rectangular room with four deep cells in the east wall and two in the north, the entire room being hollowed out of the rock. Both in number and in arrangement the cells correspond with the two groups of cells near the entrance to Chephren's mortuary temple and, in spite of the difference of their location, it seems likely that they served the same purpose. The second chamber, designed to take the place of the original burial-chamber, is situated at the far end of the passage (fig. 32: 5). Its walls, floor and roof are composed entirely of granite. The underside of its pointed roof has been rounded, thus giving it the appearance of a barrel-vault. Within this chamber, Colonel Howard Vyse found a rectangular basalt sarcophagus, the outer faces of which were carved with a panel decoration. Unfortunately, this fine sarcophagus, which must originally have contained the body of Mycerinus, was lost when the *Beatrice*, a merchant-ship which was transporting it to England, sank in the Mediterranean somewhere between Malta, whence it sailed on 30 October 1838, and the Spanish port of Cartagena. In the original burial-chamber, Colonel Vyse had discovered some human bones and the lid of a wooden anthropoid coffin inscribed with the name of Mycerinus. This lid, which is now in the British Museum, cannot have been made in the time of Mycerinus, for it is of a pattern not used before the Saite Period. Radio-carbon tests have shown that the bones date from early Christian times. Borchardt, possibly influenced by the dating of the lid, believed that the whole of the third design was the work of Saite restorers who, on entering the pyramid, found the upper burial-chamber in complete disorder, and the remains of the body lying exposed. Since Borchardt expressed this view, however, excavation of the tomb of Shepseskaf has revealed that it contained both a magazine and a burial-chamber resembling in style those of this pyramid. With this knowledge there can be no reason to doubt that the third design dates from the time of Mycerinus. How the human remains and the lid of the coffin came to be in the pyramid cannot be explained.

South of the pyramid of Mycerinus lies a row of three subsidiary pyramids, none of which appears to have been completed. The largest and most advanced stands at the eastern end of the row. Like the main pyramid, it was cased, in part at least, with granite. Neither of the other two pyramids had progressed beyond the construction of its inner core when the work was abandoned. Adjoining the east face of each pyramid stood a small mortuary temple composed mainly of crude brick, and therefore probably built by Shepseskaf after the death of Mycerinus.

No evidence of their owners' identity was discovered during Reisner's excavation of these pyramids, but the size of the first would suggest that it belonged to Khamerernebty II, the principal queen. In the second, Colonel Vyse discovered a small granite sarcophagus and some human bones, which he judged to be those of a young woman. This pyramid may therefore have been the tomb of a younger queen or a princess. The ownership of the westernmost pyramid in the row remains completely obscure.

Apart from the three major pyramids at Giza, the pyramid of Meidum and the two stone pyramids at Dahshur, only one pyramid of a IVth Dynasty king has been identified with certainty. Its builder was Djedefrē, who ruled between Cheops and Chephren. The site which he chose was a commanding eminence at Abu Roash, some five miles to the north of the Giza plateau. Apart from a nucleus of rock, very little of the superstructure has survived and it is impossible to be certain that it was ever completed. Petrie was told in 1880-81 that stone was being taken from it during the high Nile at a rate of three hundred camel-loads a day. Large heaps of granite chips lie all around the pyramid, showing that it must have been cased, at least partly, with granite. No exact calculation of its size is possible, but it has been estimated that its base covered an area about 328 feet square and the angle of its slope, to judge from fragments of casing, was 60°, in contrast with the usual pyramid angle of about 52°.

The substructure consists of an open trench, which slopes downwards, at an angle of 22° 35', to the floor of a perpendicular shaft measuring about 30 feet in depth, 30 feet from north to south and 70 feet from east to west. It is surprising that Djedefrē should have reverted to a design of substructure which was discarded when the true pyramid superseded the step pyramid in the reign of Seneferu. While it is not impossible that it was due to the poor quality of the rock and the architect's unwillingness to trust that a tunnel would not cave in, the size of the trench, which varies in width from 18 to 23 feet, seems unnecessarily large to contain a constructed corridor, at least of normal dimensions. No pyramid surveyed by Petrie had a corridor which was wider than 3 feet 4 inches; such a corridor in this trench would require more than 7 feet of packing on each side. The walls of the corridor and the rooms in the pit were lined partly with granite and partly with limestone. A suggestion made by Howard Vyse more than a century ago that the shaft, above the subterranean rooms, was divided into compartments, like those above the King's Chamber in the Great Pyramid, has not been confirmed by later investigation, but it cannot be ignored.

Owing to the configuration of the ground, the causeway, instead of running from east to west, approaches the pyramid enclosure from the north. By following that line, it was possible to utilize a ridge of rock and thus reduce the amount of building necessary for raising it to the required level. Petrie, who surveyed this causeway, estimated that it was nearly a mile in length and, in places, 40 feet high.

Not enough of the temple, on the east side of the pyramid, has survived for its plan to be traced in detail, but it is evident that it was far from finished when the king died. Much of it was hurriedly built in brick. On its south side there is a boat-pit measuring about 121 feet in length. Nothing remained of the boat, but inside the pit and close to it were countless fragments of statues which had been deliberately smashed. Among the pieces which had not been completely destroyed were three fine heads of figures of the king, two of which are in the Louvre (Plate 38) and one in Cairo.

In view of the immense size of the northern court - more than 100 yards in length - Maragioglio and Rinaldi suggested that the mortuary temple would have been built there, if indeed work on it had not already begun at the time of the king's death. The building on the east side of the pyramid, insofar as its plan can be understood, does not conform in its design with that of any known mortuary temple. In their opinion, it may have been built for some other, but unidentified, purpose. Without moving large heaps of rubble, their conjecture cannot be verified, but if it should prove to be correct it would be hard to avoid the conclusion that Djedefrē's pyramid was not a true pyramid but a step pyramid.

Although it cannot be dated with certainty, the so-called Unfinished Pyramid at Zawiyet el-Aryan, excavated in 1904-5 by A. Barsanti, may also have been constructed for a king of the IVth Dynasty. Some blocks bore, in red ink, a name written in cursive hieroglyphs which is capable of more than one interpretation. It has been read Nebka, but an alternative reading, Bikka, now seems more probable. Manetho includes among the kings of the second half of the IVth Dynasty a certain Bicheris, with whom Bikka can be identified. He was probably Chephren's successor and the predecessor of Mycerinus. His father may have been Djedefrē, whose name was inscribed on a schist plaque found by Barsanti near the Unfinished Pyramid. The surviving remains of that pyramid and the pyramid of Djedefrē are essentially alike in plan, even though the Unfinished Pyramid would have covered an area about twice as large as the pyramid of Djedefrē.

The main features of the Unfinished Pyramid are an open trench with sloping floor which enters the north side of a rock-hewn vertical shaft, 85 feet in depth and measuring 82 feet from east to west and 38 feet from north to south. The slope of the trench is broken by level stretches at two points, the first roughly half-way along its course and the second near the lower end. Between these level sections two parallel

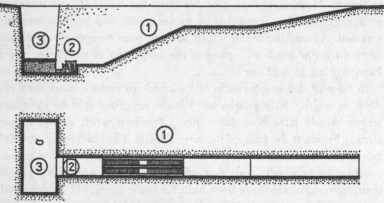

Figure 33. The Unfinished Pyramid of Zawiyet el-Aryan, section looking west and plan

flights of steps, separated by a broad raised ramp and bounded on each side by similar ramps, are cut in the rock floor (fig. 33: 1). At the lower end of the trench a pit has been cut and partly filled with limestone blocks rising to a somewhat greater height than the level section which immediately precedes it (fig. 33: 2). The floor of the shaft has also been built up and paved with red granite in the centre (fig. 33: 3). An oval granite sarcophagus was sunk in the floor, west of the centre, but was raised from its pit by the excavator. Its shape has no demonstrable parallel, but Petrie found in the pit of Djedefrē's pyramid some granite fragments which were curved and, in his opinion, they belonged to the king's sarcophagus. If he was right, the two sarcophagi must have been very similar. The sarcophagus in the Unfinished Pyramid was found with its lid attached with mortar to the base, but nevertheless empty. It had been covered with a thick layer of clay and blocks of limestone had been laid around and above it as a protection.

Shepseskaf, who completed the pyramid complex of Mycerinus, did not himself build a pyramid. His tomb, which is situated at Saqqara, was examined in 1858 by Mariette, who wrongly identified its owner first as Unas, the last king of the Vth Dynasty, and subsequently as Ity, a successor of Unas. In 1924 the Service des Antiquités conducted a thorough excavation of the site under the direction of Gustave Jéquier, and the real ownership of the tomb was established. Known to the Arabs as the *Mastabat Fara'un*, this tomb was built in the form of a huge rectangular sarcophagus resting possibly on a low platform (fig. 34). The sides of the sarcophagus inclined inwards at an angle of about 65°, and the square ends projected vertically above the level of the vaulted roof. Only the inner core of local stone is now visible, but originally it was cased with Tura limestone and given a skirting of granite. On the east side of the building stood a small mortuary temple, from the south-east corner of which a long causeway, with walls of crude brick, led down to the valley building.

A female contemporary of Shepseskaf named Khentkaues built, on an open space lying between the causeways of Chephren and Mycerinus, a tomb which was essentially similar to the *Mastabat Fara'un* (Plate 24). At one time it was thought to be an unfinished pyramid, but the

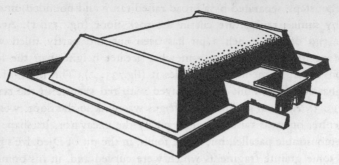

Figure 34. The Mastabat Fara'un

excavations of Selim Bey Hassan on behalf of Cairo University in 1932–3 proved that, in reality, the superstructure was in the form of a sarcophagus mounted on a high, almost square podium. The 'sarcophagus' was built of blocks of coarse limestone and the podium was formed from an outcrop of rock. Originally the sides of the podium were carved with the same kind of panel decoration as the sarcophagus of Mycerinus, and it can still be seen on the south face, but eventually both parts of the superstructure were overlaid with slabs of fine limestone. A small mortuary temple consisting of two rooms was hewn in the south-eastern part of the podium. The walls of the rooms were cased with fine limestone and were decorated with reliefs, of which very few fragments have survived. In the west wall of the second room there were two granite false doors, both of which are now badly damaged. The burial-chamber and its antechamber, which have six large magazines in the south and east walls, lie at a lower level than the mortuary temple. They are approached by a sloping corridor, lined with granite, which opens in the floor of the second room by the northern false door. In the south-west corner of the burial-chamber there is a small recess which may have been intended for the Canopic chest. A causeway, directed first towards the east and then turning abruptly southwards, links the tomb with its valley building, which extends along the full length of the valley building of the pyramid of Mycerinus.

Outside the enclosure wall of the tomb at the south-west corner lay a pit for a boat, nothing of which is preserved. In a similar position at the north-east corner there was a rectangular pool to which eleven steps descended. The suggestion has been made that the water was used for purification purposes when the body was being prepared for burial.

Much uncertainty surrounds the genealogical affiliations of Khent-kaues. Her most significant title has generally been translated 'Mother of the Two Kings of Upper and Lower Egypt', but the kings are not named. Most writers identify them with Sahurē and Neferirkarē, the second and third kings of the Vth Dynasty, about whom more will be said in the next chapter. Until 1976 it was generally supposed that the mastaba at Giza, which has just been described, was her only tomb, but between 1976 and 1978 an expedition of the Czechoslovak Institute of Egyptology in Cairo, under the directorship of Miroslav Verner, explored a small pyramid on the south side of the pyramid of Nefer-irkarē at Abu Sir, which has also been attributed to Khentkaues as her second tomb. Its superstructure is now reduced to about a quarter of its original height of about 53 feet. The entrance is at ground-level on the north side and from it a downward-sloping corridor, which is not absolutely straight, leads to a small burial-chamber only 6 feet 6 inches below the level of the entrance. It was empty when the Czechoslovak archaeologists entered it.

Khentkaues's ruined mortuary temple lies on the east side of the pyramid. It was built in two stages, the first in limestone and the second in sun-baked brick. At the end nearest to the pyramid there was a cult chapel preceded by an open court surrounded by a cloister, the square pillars of which were made of limestone painted red and stippled with black in imitation of granite. The walls of both the chapel and the court were decorated with scenes carved in relief, only frag-ments of which have survived. The pillars were probably all inscribed with the name and titles of Khentkaues. In the second stage of con-struction a limestone wall on the south side of the complex was dis-mantled and the blocks were used to build a small subsidiary pyramid. About two hundred papyrus fragments were found in the south-eastern part of the temple. In every probability they are temple records of the same kind as those which were found by illicit diggers at the end of the last century in the pyramid complex of Neferirkarē and are now known as the Abu Sir papyri.

If it were not for the title borne by Khentkaues in both tombs, the tomb at Abu Sir, chiefly by reason of its proximity to the pyramid of Neferirkarē, would probably have been ascribed to a different Khent-kaues, about whom nothing is known, but who would be assumed to have been the wife of the king. On balance, however, it seems more likely that an otherwise unknown title and two tombs should have belonged to one woman than that two women should have borne such a title. Any attempt to explain how the construction of a second tomb came about is bound to be conjectural, but it is not difficult to imagine that Neferirkarē believed his mother would receive magical benefits from a pyramid, which she would be denied if she were buried in a mastaba.

Viewing the pyramids of the IVth Dynasty as a whole, it is undeni-able that they are characterized chiefly by the employment of mega-lithic masonry. Reisner estimated that some of the blocks of local stone embodied in the walls of the mortuary temple of Mycerinus weighed as much as 220 tons, while the heaviest of the granite ashlars, all of which were transported 500 miles from Aswan, might exceed 30 tons. The use of such massive blocks offered two main advantages: greater stability was attained and the number of joints to be fitted was reduced. Cheops, who may have been a megalomaniac, could never, during a reign of about twenty-three years, have erected a building of the size and durability of the Great Pyramid if technical advances had not enabled his masons to handle stones of very considerable weight and dimensions. How completely they had mastered this art may be gauged from Petrie's observation that the joints in the casing of the Great Pyramid measured only one-fiftieth of an inch in thickness.

A parallel development to the handling of heavy blocks was the progress made in the art of cutting hard stones. Even as early as the Ist Dynasty, there is an instance of the use of granite for paving a chamber, while the small burial-chambers in Zoser's Step Pyramid and South Mastaba are composed entirely of this material. It was, however, only in the IVth Dynasty that structures of the size of Chephren's valley building and mortuary temple were faced completely or mainly with

Plate 1. Tutankhamun as the sun–god emerging from a lotus growing from the primeval mound

Plate 2. *Model heads of cattle on the terrace of a Ist Dynasty mastaba. Saqqara*

Plate 3. *Subsidiary brick mastaba of the Ist Dynasty. Saqqara*

Plate 4. Stepped mound in a Ist Dynasty brick mastaba. Saqqara

Plate 5. Mereruka represented emerging from the false door in his tomb-chapel.
Saqqara

Plate 6 (top opposite). Wall-relief from the tomb of Mereruka.
Above: a fish seized by an otter; below: forepart of a crocodile and a harpooned fish.
Saqqara

Plate 7 (bottom opposite). Reserve head of Seneferu-senb. Cairo Museum

Plate 8. Gateway to the Step Pyramid enclosure. Saqqara

Plate 9 (opposite). Limestone relief of Zoser performing a religious ceremony. Step Pyramid, Saqqara

Plate 11. *Papyrus-stem engaged columns. Saqqara*

Plate 10. *Limestone statue of Zoser. Cairo Museum*

Plate 12. Entrance colonnade of the Step Pyramid – a reconstruction by J.-P. Lauer

Plate 13. Tiled panelling in the South Mastaba of Zoser –
a reconstruction by Mrs C.M. Firth

Plate 14. *The Layer Pyramid. View from the north. Zawiyet el-Aryan*

Plate 15. *The Layer Pyramid – accretion coatings. Zawiyet el-Aryan*

Plate 16. *Pyramid of Seila. East side*

Plate 17. *Pyramid of Meidum. View from the east*

Plate 18. Seneferu's pyramids at Dahshur. View from the north-west

*Plate 19. Upper corridor of the Bent
Pyramid. Dahshur*

*Plate 20. Upper part of a stela of
Seneferu. Dahshur*

Plate 21. *Cedarwood framework in the upper chamber of the Bent Pyramid. Dahshur*

Plate 22. *Female offering-bearers personifying Seneferu's estates. Dahshur*

Plate 23. *Ivory figure of Cheops. Cairo Museum*
from Abydos   Ht. c. 7 cm / 3 inches

Plate 24. The pyramids of Cheops and Chephren.
In the foreground are the tomb of Queen Khentkaues and the head of the Sphinx.
Giza. Lithograph of drawing by David Roberts, c. 1838

Plate 25. The pyramids of Giza

Plate 26. Entrance to the Great Pyramid. Drawing by E.W. Lane, c. 1826

Plate 27. *Underground chamber in the Great Pyramid. Giza. Drawing by E.W. Lane, c. 1826*

Plate 28. *Granite plug-blocks in the Ascending Corridor of the Great Pyramid. Giza.*
Drawing by E.W. Lane, c. 1826

Plate 29. Boat of Cheops. Giza

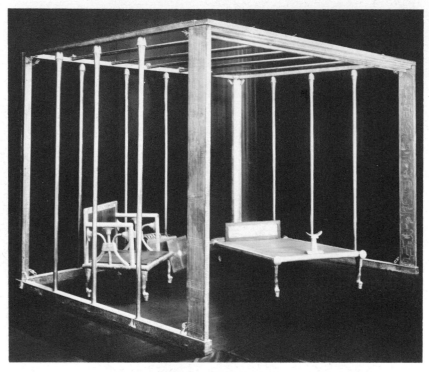

Plate 30. Gilded canopy and furniture of Hetepheres. Cairo Museum

Plate 31. The Giant Sphinx of Chephren. Giza

Plate 32. The Giant Sphinx of Chephren largely engulfed in sand.
Giza. Drawing by E.W. Lane, c. 1826

Plate 33. The valley building of Chephren. Giza

Plate 34. Diorite statue of Chephren. Cairo Museum

Plate 35. Pyramid and mortuary temple of Chephren. Giza

Plate 36. Schist triad: Mycerinus, Hathor and the goddess of the jackal-nome.
Cairo Museum

Plate 37. Schist group-statue of Mycerinus and Queen Khamerernebty II.
Boston Museum

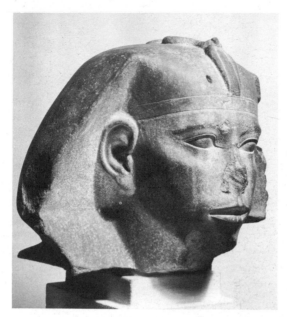

Plate 38. *Quartzite head of Djedefrē. Louvre Museum*

Plate 39. *Podium of obelisk and alabaster altar in the sun-temple of Niuserrē.*
Abu Gurab

Plate 40. Schist head from the sun-temple of Userkaf. Abu Gurab

Plate 41. Head of a colossal granite statue of Userkaf. Cairo Museum

Plate 42. *The pyramid of Neferirkarē showing the inner stepped formation. View from the north–north–east. In the foreground is part of the mortuary temple of Sahurē. Abu Sir*

Plate 43. *Causeway of the pyramid of Unas. Saqqara*

Plate 44. Burial-chamber of Merenrē, showing Pyramid Texts, and his granite sarcophagus and Canopic chest. Saqqara

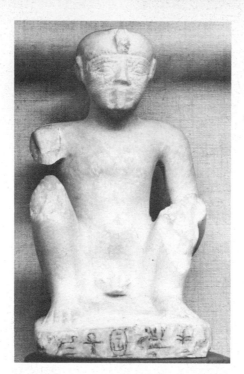

Plate 45. Alabaster figure of Pepi II as a child. Cairo Museum

Plate 46. Ruined funerary temple of Neb–hepet–Rē Mentuhotep. Deir el–Bahri, Thebes

Plate 47. Limestone statue of Sesostris I. Cairo Museum

Plate 48. Limestone panel inscribed with the name of Sesostris I.
Metropolitan Museum of Art

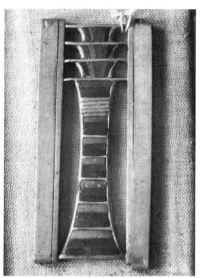

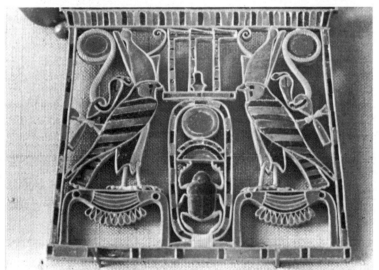

Plate 49a. Gold cloisonné tie and Hathor-pendant of a necklace inlaid with lapis lazuli, feldspar and carnelian from the tomb of Sat-Hathor at Dahshur. Cairo Museum

Plate 49b. Gold cloisonné clasp of a bracelet inlaid with lapis lazuli, feldspar and carnelian from the tomb of Sat-Hathor at Dahshur. Cairo Museum

Plate 49c. Gold cloisonné pectoral with the name of Sesostris II and inlaid with lapis lazuli, feldspar and carnelian from the tomb of Sat-Hathor at Dahshur. Cairo Museum

Plate 50a, b. Gold cloisonné pectorals with the names of Sesostris III and Ammenemes II and inlaid with lapis lazuli, carnelian and feldspar from the tomb of Merit at Dahshur. Cairo Museum

Plate 51. *The pyramid of Ammenemes III. In the foreground are the remains of brick residences of priests on the north side of the causeway. Dahshur*

Plate 52. *Tomb-chamber and sarcophagus of Ammenemes III. Dahshur*

Plate 53. Upper part of a granite statuette of Khendjer. Cairo Museum

Plate 54. *Natural pyramid dominating the Valley of the Kings, Luxor.*
In the foreground is a modern wall protecting the approach to
the tomb of Tutankhamun

Plate 55. *The pyramid of Tirhaqa. Nuri*

Plate 56. Pyramids in the northern cemetery. Meroe

Plate 57. Trenches cut in the rock for levelling. Giza

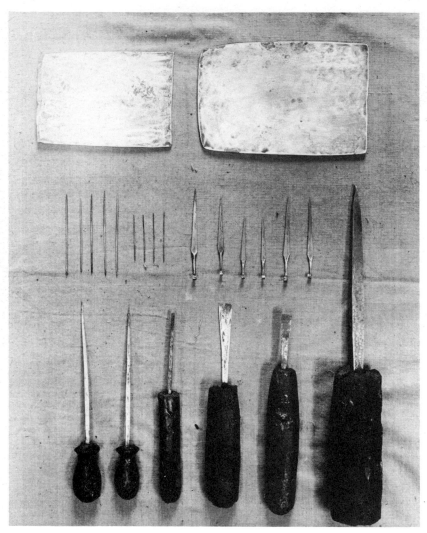

Plate 58. Copper implements of the Ist Dynasty. Cairo Museum

Plate 59. Quarrymen's wedge-slots. Aswan

Plate 60. Limestone model of a step pyramid. Petrie Museum

Plate 61. Limestone model of the Hawara pyramid. Petrie Museum

*Plate 62. Relics of brick retaining walls of a building-ramp at the First Pylon
of the temple of Karnak*

Plate 63. Tomb-chapel of Tia, a sister of Ramesses II, and her husband (also named Tia). The lower part of a pyramid can be seen in the foreground. Saqqara

granite. Basalt also occurs sporadically long before the IVth Dynasty, but not in the quantity employed in the pavement of Cheops's mortuary temple or the lost sarcophagus of Mycerinus. Petrie even expressed the opinion that one of the subsidiary pyramids of the Great Pyramid had arris lines of basalt extending down each corner to prevent wear and weathering.

Statuary during the IVth Dynasty made a very big advance both in quantity and in quality. Reisner, after examining all the fragments of sculpture discovered in Chephren's valley building and mortuary temple, calculated that the Second Pyramid complex alone contained between one hundred and two hundred separate statues. A similar number may well have been made for the Great Pyramid and the pyramid of Mycerinus, so that the aggregate of statues in the three complexes possibly reached a figure not far short of five hundred. The full effect of the stimulus to the sculptor's art given by the interest of these kings only becomes apparent in the two following dynasties, when nearly every private tomb in Giza and Saqqara included a statue of its owner. Artistically, the relatively few specimens which have survived from the three Giza pyramids bear testimony of a greater experience in portraying the human features than any earlier statues.

Until recently it was supposed that the temples and causeways of the IVth Dynasty pyramids were not decorated with reliefs. Now, however, it is known that they were employed on a large scale in the valley building, if such it be, of the Bent Pyramid (Plate 22) and there is evidence of their employment in the mortuary temple of Cheops, in the chapel of the second of his subsidiary pyramids and in Chephren's mortuary temple. In addition to the fragments found at Giza, other fragments which are believed to have come from the temples of Cheops and Chephren have been recovered from buildings of the Middle Kingdom at Lisht whither they had been taken for re-use. All these pieces show that the art of carving in low relief, so exquisitely illustrated in the galleries of the Step Pyramid and South Mastaba, was not lost during the IVth Dynasty, but, on the contrary, continued to develop and the range of subjects represented was greatly extended.

CHAPTER FIVE

PYRAMIDS OF THE Vth AND VIth DYNASTIES

Although documentary records are lacking, the character of the political events which attended the close of the IVth Dynasty may be conjectured from a number of indirect indications. The three successors of Cheops – Djedefrē, Chephren (Khaef-Rē), and Mycerinus (Menkau-Rē) – had proclaimed their recognition of the sun-god Rē by forming their names of compounds with his name. There is some evidence also that Chephren and Mycerinus had adopted the title 'Son of Rē' – a royal title which figures regularly from the Vth Dynasty onwards. It seems therefore reasonable to infer that the cult of Rē was already in the time of these kings superseding the more primitive cult of Atum in Heliopolis. At the end of the IVth Dynasty, however, Shepseskaf not only departed from the type of tomb built by his predecessors, but, so far as is known, did not follow their precedent by acknowledging unequivocally, either in name or title, his association with Rē. Whether he was guided by motives of religious principle or political expediency cannot be deduced from the evidence available, but, in view of the caution and conservatism shown by the Egyptians at all times in matters appertaining to religion and the after-life, it is difficult to believe that Shepseskaf would have introduced such fundamental changes if he had not thought that the increasing power of the priesthood of Rē directly menaced the authority and independence of the throne. Shepseskaf's struggle, which was perhaps passive and not waged with destructive bitterness, failed to achieve any permanent success, for his death, after a reign of little more than four years, led to the accession of a line of kings who raised the cult of Rē to the position of the official state religion.

A papyrus in the Berlin Museum, known as the Papyrus Westcar, has preserved a legend concerning the origin of the Vth Dynasty which may embody a kernel of truth. The papyrus itself probably dates from the Second Intermediate Period, but it was certainly a copy of an older document. According to this legend, a magician at the court of Cheops prophesied that the first three kings of the dynasty would be triplets, begotten of Rē and born of the wife of a priest of Rē. Userkaf, Sahurē and Neferirkarē were the first three kings, but their parentage – especially that of Userkaf – is still debatable. At the heart of the genealogical problem lies the uncertainty, mentioned in the last chapter, concerning the family connections of Khentkaues. Some authorities have regarded her as a daughter of Mycerinus, but Hartwig Altenmüller, in a new interpretation of the legend in the Papyrus Westcar, maintains that her father was Hordjedef, a son of Cheops. The identity of her husband is equally disputed, two of the possible consorts being Shepseskaf and Userkaf, the latter of whom may have been a son of Neferhetepes, daughter of Djedefrē. In one respect only is there general agreement among writers, namely that Sahurē and Neferirkarē were brothers, possibly twins, and sons of Khentkaues.

Each of the first three kings and three of their successors built special sun-temples. Contemporary inscriptions mention all six temples by their names, but only those of Niuserrē and Userkaf have hitherto been found (fig. 35: 1 and 2). Incomparably the better preserved, because it was built entirely of limestone, was Niuserrē's temple at Abu Gurab, about a mile north of Abu Sir, where Niuserrē built his pyramid. It was excavated in 1898–1901 by Ludwig Borchardt and Heinrich Schaefer on behalf of Baron von Bissing and the Deutsche Orient-Gesellschaft. In order that it should stand above the level of the desert, it was erected on an artificial mound faced on all four sides with a revetment of limestone. A causeway surmounted by a covered corridor led up to the terrace from a large pavilion on the eastern edge of the desert. At its upper end, a gateway opened on to a paved court, 330 feet long and 250 feet broad, which is still recognizable. Its principal feature is a rectangular podium, with sides sloping inwards, built of limestone on a platform of granite (fig. 36). In every probability it was intended to represent the primordial mound of sand – the so-called high sand – in the temple of Rē at Heliopolis. Mounted on the podium was a squat obelisk, the sacred symbol of the sun-god, which was also built

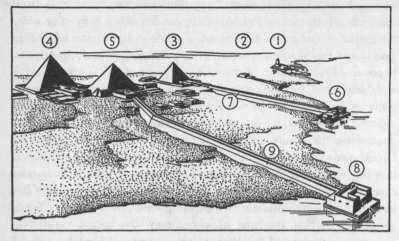

Figure 35. The pyramids of Abu Sir – a reconstruction

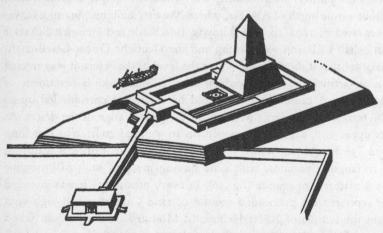

Figure 36. The sun-temple of Niuserrē

of limestone blocks, the core being yellow and the outer layer white (Plate 39). In its composite construction it differed from obelisks of the Middle Kingdom and later, which were monolithic. At the foot of the podium, on the east side, stands a low sacrificial altar composed of five massive slabs of alabaster. Outside the court, to the south, lay a hundred-foot-long model of the boat in which the sun-god made his daily journey across the sky. The hull, built of brick, had been covered with a layer of plaster and painted. All the other parts of the boat were made of wood. Below the eastern limit of the terrace, on both sides of the causeway, were buildings which had been occupied by craftsmen and priests who were employed in the service of this temple and the king's mortuary temple.

Temples and mortuary buildings of the Vth Dynasty were lavishly decorated with painted wall reliefs of the highest artistic quality. In Niuserrē's sun-temple the reliefs, later transferred to the museums of Cairo and Berlin, were found in the corridor of the causeway, in its continuation around the east and south sides of the court and in a chapel situated between the end of the corridor and the obelisk. A wide variety of subjects was represented in these reliefs, ranging from the flora and fauna created by the sun-god to the ceremonies connected with the foundation of the temple and the *heb-sed* of the king. The representation of the *heb-sed*, if it is to be regarded as a record of an historical event, would suggest that this temple was not built until many years – possibly thirty – after the king had ascended the throne. Since it is unlikely that Niuserrē would have delayed the construction of a sun-temple until so late in his life, the stone building may have replaced an earlier temple of brick, perhaps with the intention that it should be available for his use and for the celebration of his *heb-sed* festivals in the after-life.

Borchardt's work at the sun-temple of Niuserrē shed an immense amount of light on its lay-out and general character, but rather less on the actual purposes for which it was built. The scenes carved on the walls of the temple were not indicative enough to show what particular aspect of the sun-cult that temple and the other temples of its kind were intended to serve. The sun-god, according to the beliefs of the ancient Egyptians, possessed many aspects or identities which were sometimes reflected in his epithets, such as 'Rē on the Roof' (of the temple of Heliopolis), who is mentioned in the records of Sahurē on the Palermo Stone, together with three other forms of Rē. Another of these identities was the one in which a king existed before his incarnation and to which he returned after his death. Erich Winter, the Austrian Egyptologist, has suggested that this was the particular aspect of Rē to which the sun-temples were dedicated. The cult, as he points out, continued to be celebrated in the temples for many generations after the kings for whom they were built had died.

According to another view, it was the power derived from the communion of god and king in the sun-temple which enabled the king to guarantee the welfare of the whole land and the proper functioning of everything connected with it.

Besides fulfilling a religious function, the sun-temples were, at least partly, responsible for provisioning the mortuary temples in the pyramid complexes of their respective kings. Paule Posener, the Directrice of the French Institute of Archaeology in Cairo, has been able to show that the fragmentary Abu Sir papyri record deliveries of provisions to the mortuary temple of Neferirkarē from his sun-temple. These deliveries were made twice a day by a boat on a canal. At least one ox each day was killed in the slaughterhouse on the north side of the court of the sun-temple and the joints of meat were sent to the king's mortuary temple. Outside the slaughterhouse there were ten large alabaster basins sunk in the pavement of the court for the blood of the animals. Somewhere in the complex of buildings around the causeway of the sun-temple of Niuserrē there were probably granaries, a bakehouse and a brewery, because beer and three kinds of bread are among the provisions mentioned in the papyri. Doubtless many other commodities were also sent from the sun-temple to be laid on the altar of the deceased king before being divided among the temple staff; the record is incomplete, but it is sufficient to show that the sun-temples served a practical as well as a religious purpose.

Although Userkaf's sun-temple was located and partly explored by Borchardt at the beginning of this century, its site was not systematically excavated until 1955-7 when the work was carried out by a joint expedition of the Swiss and the German Institutes of Archaeology in

Cairo under the direction of H. Ricke. The buildings, composed partly of limestone and partly of Nile mud and limestone chips, were set out according to the same general plan as those of Niuserrē. Complete excavation of the pavilion on the fringe of the cultivation proved impossible owing to the rise in the water-level since ancient times, and no trace was found of either a boat-pit or wall-reliefs. A fine example of sculpture in the round came to light in the form of a head of a life-size schist statue (Plate 40) perhaps representing Neith, the goddess of Saïs, who was regularly portrayed wearing the crown of Lower Egypt. Alternatively, it may represent the king himself, but if so the absence of the royal beard is strange.

According to the Palermo Stone, Userkaf, one of the last kings named on the stone, built his sun-temple either in the fifth or in the sixth year of his short reign of seven years. The hieroglyphic sign which represents the temple, both in the entry on the Palermo Stone and in some other inscriptions dating from the beginning of the Vth Dynasty, seems to show only a podium without an obelisk, whereas inscriptions of the time of Neferirkarē and of later times show both these features. In every probability therefore the obelisk was a later addition, perhaps a gift by Neferirkarē. Discoveries made in the course of excavation seem to support the evidence of the inscriptions, at least to the extent of indicating that the original plan of the enclosure was altered three times and also that the later designs included an obelisk, built of blocks of granite, which stood on a podium of limestone mounted on a platform of quartzite or granite. On the altar in front of his monument, Userkaf, so the Palermo Stone records, sacrificed two oxen and two geese daily.

The practice of building pyramids, discarded by Shepseskaf, was resumed by the kings of the Vth Dynasty. In quality, however, these pyramids were inferior to their predecessors, being composed merely of a core of small stones within a casing of Tura limestone. As a result of their poor construction, all the pyramids of this period have suffered severely, and some have been reduced to little more than mounds of sand and rubble.

Userkaf built his pyramid at Saqqara, close to the north-east corner of the Step Pyramid enclosure. By the time of the Vth Dynasty,

Zoser's tomb may have acquired a particular sanctity and burial in its vicinity may have been thought to confer special benefits. Such an explanation would account for Userkaf's choice of a site which in other respects seems to have been unsuitable for a pyramid. Immediately to the east, where the mortuary temple would normally have been constructed, the ground rises steeply; only the sanctuary was therefore built against the eastern face of the pyramid, while the main temple stood exceptionally on the southern side. C.M. Firth's excavations on behalf of the Service des Antiquités in 1928-9 revealed that the temple had been destroyed in antiquity and that its site had been re-used in the Saite Period for building tombs, the superstructures of which were actually composed of stone taken from Userkaf's temple and from the neighbouring pyramids.

J.-P. Lauer, working intermittently between 1948 and 1955, succeeded in tracing the ground-plan of the whole enclosure with the exception of the valley building and the causeway, which still remain to be explored. The sanctuary (fig. 37: 1) was composed of a small hall flanked by two narrow chambers, the hall paved with basalt and the chambers with limestone. It was not possible to determine whether two emplacements in the floor of the hall were intended for rectangular granite columns or for stelae of the same material, but some fragments of quartzite found in the rubble were recognizable as having belonged to an altar. The walls of the hall, above a granite dado, were made of limestone and may have been decorated with sculptures carved in relief.

In addition to its exceptional orientation in relation to the pyramid, the main temple was abnormal in plan. The entrance lay at the upper end of the causeway near the southern corner of the eastern enclosure wall (fig. 37: 2). Two oblong chambers, both partly destroyed when a large Saite tomb (fig. 37: 3) was constructed, stood between the entrance and the open court (fig. 37: 4). A cloister with rectangular columns of granite was built on three sides of the court, no doubt for the protection of sculptured scenes on the walls, some fragments of which, showing the king fowling in the marshes of the Delta, were discovered in the course of excavation. Against the middle of the south wall, which was probably bare of decoration, stood a colossal red

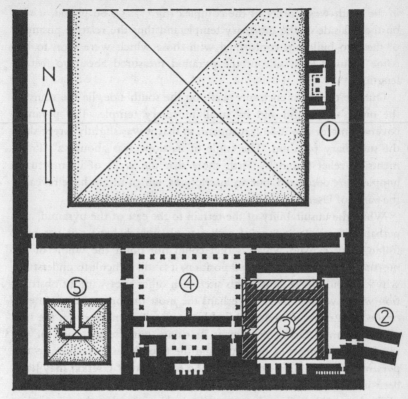

Figure 37. The pyramid enclosure of Userkaf

granite seated statue of the king facing the pyramid and giving the impression that he was gazing at it. The head of this statue, which measures about 2 feet 6 inches in height, was found by Firth and is now in the Cairo Museum (Plate 41). South of the court, and therefore farther from the pyramid, lay a small hypostyle hall and the customary five niches with which the five magazines situated near the entrance to the temple were probably associated. In that position, the statues in the niches, like the statue in the court, would have faced the pyramid. The subsidiary pyramid, which in subsequent enclosures generally stood on the valley side of the main pyramid, at the south-east corner, was built in the south-west corner of the complex (fig. 37: 5). So placed, it was on the left side of the mortuary temple and thus the relative positions of the two buildings conformed with those which were soon to become regular. Each side of the pyramid measured about 70 feet in length.

Outside the main enclosure wall, on the south side, lie the ruins of the queen's pyramid and its small mortuary temple. The pyramid covered an area about 86 feet square, so that it was slightly larger than the subsidiary pyramid. The angle of its slope was about 52°. Fragments of relief found by Firth show that the walls of its mortuary temple were decorated, but no inscriptions, which might have revealed the name of Userkaf's principal queen, were recovered.

While the unsuitability of the terrain to the east of the pyramid, and perhaps also the existence of earlier tombs which have not yet been found, may explain why Userkaf could not build the whole of his mortuary temple in the normal position, it is still difficult to understand why he should have chosen this site when other sites without obstruction were available nearby. Perhaps the most important requirements of the mortuary cult were satisfied by having the sanctuary on the side of the pyramid facing the sun at its rising, but the inversion of the regular arrangement of the court and the five niches in relation to the pyramid seems to defy explanation. To some extent Userkaf may have been influenced by a desire not to copy too slavishly the monuments of the kings whose burial practices he had re-introduced; nevertheless architecture and religious belief in Egypt were generally complementary and it would be strange if the peculiarities of this complex did not reflect some change, albeit short-lived, in the royal mortuary creed.

Sahurē, Neferirkarē, and Niuserrē chose for their pyramids a plateau on the desert edge near the modern village of Abu Sir (fig. 35: 3, 4, and 5). While conforming with the standard lay-out, the complexes of Sahurē and Niuserrē surpassed in artistic magnificence anything which had previously been attempted. Ludwig Borchardt, who excavated this group of pyramids on behalf of the Deutsche Orient-Gesellschaft in 1902-8, estimated that the area of wall-surface covered by reliefs in Sahurē's complex alone amounted to about 10,000 square metres. Unfortunately, later inhabitants of the neighbourhood discovered that the fine Tura limestone of the reliefs produced the best lime, with the result that of the original total only about 150 square metres, broken into innumerable fragments, survived their depredations. Niuserrē's complex had suffered even more severely than that of Sahurē. The complex of Neferirkarē was never finished, and it is probable that the work was abandoned before many of the intended reliefs had been executed.

The valley building of Sahurē was provided with two landing-stages, one facing towards the east and the other towards the south (fig. 35: 6; fig. 38: 1 and 2); ramps connected the landing-stages either with a canal or with the Nile, which, during its annual period of inundation, may well have spread so far beyond its normal bounds. Recessed in the east face of the building was a portico, the floor of which was composed of black polished basalt and the ceiling of limestone, painted blue to represent the sky and decorated with golden stars carved in relief; the eight monolithic columns were of granite and the walls, above a granite dado, were of limestone decorated with painted reliefs. In design, the columns were imitations of date-palms with their leaves tied vertically in a bunch to form the capitals (fig. 39). Somers Clarke and Engelbach, commenting on the great skill with which these columns were carved, wrote: 'It was found that on a portion 2 m 60 cm long, where the mean diameter tapers from 91.2 cm down to 79.8 cm, the error from the mean diameter was never greater than 8 millimetres.' This achievement becomes all the more remarkable when it is remembered that these are some of the earliest examples of the palm-tree column. A fragment of what may have been a similar column, inscribed with the name of Djedefrē, was found in the eastern temple of his pyramid complex at Abu Roash, but it lacked its capital and consequently its genre could not be determined. Palm-tree columns in wood, and relatively small in size, supported the roof of the deck-house on Cheops's boat. Each of Sahurē's columns bore, within a rectangular frame, the king's names and titles carved in hieroglyphs and inlaid with green paste.

A similar, though less deeply recessed, portico was constructed in the south face of the building; its floor, however, was of limestone and its columns were cylindrical, lacking any form of capital. Both the porticos were connected by passages with a small T-shaped hall, the

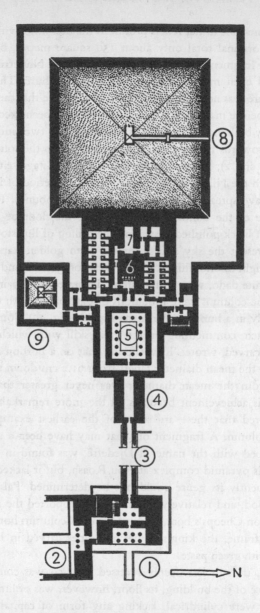

Figure 38. The pyramid complex of Sahurē

only apartment within the building. The reliefs in this hall probably showed the king, in the form of either a sphinx or a griffin, trampling underfoot Asiatics and Libyans, who were led to him bound as captives by the gods. This scene was repeated, possibly with slight variations, on the inner walls of the causeway at its lower end (fig. 35: 7; fig. 38: 3).

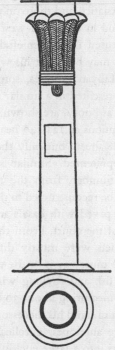

Figure 39. Date-palm column

Sahurē's mortuary temple consisted of the five main elements seen most clearly in the temple of Chephren – an entrance hall, an open court, five niches for statues, magazines and a sanctuary. The entrance hall (fig. 38: 4) is too badly damaged to allow all the details of its construction to be determined with certainty, but its floor was of limestone and its walls, above a granite dado, were probably of the same material decorated with painted reliefs. The open court (fig. 38: 5) was paved with polished basalt; apart from an alabaster altar standing in the north-west corner, it was completely bare. Around its four sides ran a cloister which resembled in construction the eastern portico of the valley building, except that its star-decorated roof was supported by only one row of palm-tree columns. The walls of the cloister were covered with reliefs of the king triumphing over his enemies, those on the northern side being Asiatics, and those on the southern side Libyans. One of these reliefs, found in the south-west corner, shows Sahurē in the act of slaying a captured Libyan chieftain; two of the chieftain's sons and a woman, who may be either his wife or his daughter, stand by imploringly. Other Libyan captives, some of whom are women and children, are also represented in a similar attitude. Elsewhere in the scene live animals, taken as booty, are shown; their number is given in the accompanying inscriptions as 123,440 head of cattle, 223,400 asses, 232,413 deer, and 243,688 sheep, but only the smallest fraction of this vast total is actually represented. Similar scenes, which may have amounted to eleven in number, from the remainder of the cloister were too fragmentary to be reconstructed in detail.

A wide corridor, also paved with basalt and decorated with reliefs, surrounded the outside of the court. From the surviving fragments, it is evident that these reliefs were mostly different in character from those of the court or the causeway. On the northern side were scenes of the king harpooning fish and fowling with a throw-stick. On the southern side, in a relief measuring about 30 feet in length, the king is shown hunting. Behind him stand his successor Neferirkarē and a group of courtiers. In front are antelopes, gazelles, deer and other horned animals, driven by beaters into a large enclosure where the king shoots them with arrows from his bow. Hounds seize some of the wounded beasts by the throat and dispatch them. Here and there the sculptor has varied the regularity of the scene with such lively touches as a jerboa and a hedgehog about to disappear into their holes and a hyena seizing a wounded antelope as its private quarry. The preservation of this remarkably fine piece of sculpture was due to the mere chance that this part of the corridor became in later times a sanctuary which housed a much-venerated figure of the fire-goddess Sakhmet.

Some of the most interesting reliefs in the whole temple were carved on the east wall of the western corridor. North of the door leading from the open court, the king, accompanied by his courtiers, was represented witnessing the departure of twelve sea-going ships to a land which is not specified, but which was probably Palestine or Syria. In the corresponding position on the south side of the door, the king and his retinue watched the return of the ships laden with cargo and carrying a number of Asiatics. Nothing in their appearance suggests that the Asiatics were prisoners; the ships may therefore have been employed on a commercial or perhaps a diplomatic errand. Even in the reign of Seneferu, the Egyptians had procured timber from Syria, so that if the cargo was merchandise this expedition represented no fresh enterprise initiated by Sahurē.

Access to every part of the complex could be gained directly or indirectly from the western corridor. By way of a door at the northern end, it was possible to reach either the pyramid enclosure or a staircase leading to the roof of the temple; a similar door at the opposite end of the corridor also led to the pyramid enclosure and, in addition, to the subsidiary pyramid court (fig. 38: 9) and a side entrance into the complex. In the middle of the corridor, on the west side, a passage followed by a short flight of steps opened into a small chamber containing the five statue-niches (fig. 38: 6). A door in the southern wall of this chamber provided the only means of access to the sanctuary (fig. 38: 7) and five rooms lying beyond, of which at least two were used for the performance of some kind of ceremony in the temple ritual. The sanctuary measured about 45 feet in length and about 15 feet in breadth. Its floor may have been paved with alabaster - a material which was certainly used for the low altar standing at the foot of the granite false door in the west wall. Above a dado of granite, the north, south, and east walls were composed of limestone and were decorated with reliefs of gods bringing gifts of provisions to the king. The gods personified their gifts.

The magazines, arranged in two rows, were approached by way of passages leading from two deep recesses in the west wall of the western corridor, seventeen from the southern recess and ten from the northern recess. Supporting the roof of each recess was a granite column, 12 feet

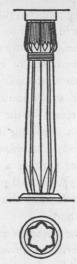

Figure 40. Papyrus-cluster column

in height and shaped like a cluster of six papyrus stems tied together, the capital being formed of their buds (fig. 40). The magazines were constructed in blocks of two storeys, each consisting of one room, and every block had its own staircase. It seems likely that the smaller group of magazines was intended for the storage of particularly valuable objects, such as decorated vases and gilded statues, used by the mortuary priests on special occasions. Some fragments of relief from the walls of one of the rooms showed the king holding an investiture; perhaps this room contained specimens of the gold decorations awarded by the king to his officials in recognition of distinguished service. The magazines in the larger group were probably used for storing stone vessels and provisions.

Through Paule Posener's recognition, in the Abu Sir papyri, of the names of rooms and architectural elements in the mortuary temple of Neferirkarē, it is possible to identify by name the corresponding elements in the temple of Sahurē. Beginning from the entrance to the temple, the first apartment is a long vestibule (fig. 38: 4) which was called the 'House of the Great Ones' (*per weru*), perhaps because nobles and high officials assembled there to form a guard of honour at the king's funeral and on occasions when an image of a god was brought to the temple. Immediately beyond lies the open court (fig. 38: 5) where the ceremony of the 'Royal Offering of the "Court"' (*weskhet*) was performed. The separate compartments in the chamber with the five statue-niches (fig. 38: 6) seem to have been called 'caverns' (*tjephet*); reference is made to one of the niches as the 'middle cavern'. The sanctuary (fig. 38: 7), in which the false door was situated and also the altar on which daily offerings to the deceased king were placed, was called the 'booth' (*seh*), a word which is commonly combined with the word for 'god' with the meaning 'sanctuary', literally 'god's booth'. In the case of magazines, specific names do not seem to have been given, merely indications of their locality. Thus, one group in the southern part of the temple was called the 'magazines which are in the midst of the temple' and a group near the pyramid was described as the 'magazines lying to the north of the road which the mortuary priest takes when he goes around the pyramid'.

In one respect, the subsidiary pyramid, which covered an area about $52\frac{1}{2}$ feet square, displayed a new architectural feature which was to be repeated in subsequent pyramids of its kind: its four faces inclined inwards at a steeper angle than those of any major pyramid. The slope of this subsidiary pyramid was $56°$ and was appreciably less than that of some of its successors.

An interesting feature in Sahurē's complex was its very elaborate drainage system. Rain falling on the roof escaped through stone spouts in the form of lions' heads which projected from the top of the outer walls. This type of gargoyle may have been chosen because rain was sometimes regarded as a manifestation of Seth and other hostile gods, who were thus consumed and expectorated, after being rendered harmless, by the lion, the protector of sacred places. In the unroofed parts of the complex, the rain-water flowed through apertures at the base of the outer walls, to which it was conducted by channels cut in the paving. A different method of drainage was, however, employed for removing water and other liquids used during the temple ceremonies, some of which may have become ritually impure and would therefore be dangerous to touch. Five stone basins, lined with copper and provided with lead plugs to fit the vents, stood in different parts of the inner temple, two in the rooms beyond the sanctuary, one in the sanctuary itself, another in the corridor leading to the sanctuary and the last in the smaller group of magazines. Pipes made of copper connected these basins with an underground drainage system consisting of a line of copper pipes which ran beneath the paving of the inner temple, the open court, the entrance hall and the causeway as far as the lower end, where it terminated in an outlet in the southern side. All the metal for this piping must have been mined in Sinai or in the eastern desert; it is more than 1,000 feet in length, and the use of such a quantity of this valuable metal provides eloquent testimony of the importance attributed to its presence by Sahurē.

Both externally and internally Sahurē's pyramid has suffered severely. When complete, its sides measured about 258 feet at the base and its vertical height was about 162 feet. Only a few fragments of the original Tura limestone casing have been preserved, but a considerable part of the rough inner core remains intact. The corridor leading to the burial-chamber is almost completely choked with fallen masonry so that it is virtually impassable. From its entrance in the north face (fig. 38: 8), at a point a little to the east of the middle and on a level with the surrounding court, it sloped downwards at an angle of 27° for a distance of about 14 feet to continue horizontally for 27 feet, where it was blocked by a granite portcullis; from there it ascended at a gentle gradient until it entered the oblong burial-chamber. Blocks of Tura limestone lined the whole corridor, with the exception of the entrance slope, a few feet on each side of the portcullis and a short section at the end, where it was lined with granite. The burial-chamber was built entirely of Tura limestone; its pointed roof consisted of three superimposed layers of masonry. Perring, who was able to examine the roof, estimated that its largest blocks measured 35 feet in length, 9 feet in width, and 12 feet in thickness. In spite of their size and weight, however, only two of these blocks remain unbroken.

Neferirkarē, whose reign probably lasted for more than ten years, planned a pyramid complex closely resembling that of Sahurē, but on a larger scale (fig. 35: 4). He was not, however, destined to see it completed. At the time of his death, the foundations of the valley building may have been laid, the causeway – but not the corridor above it – had been constructed, and work on the five statue-niches and sanctuary of the inner temple had reached an advanced stage. The pyramid, although nearer completion than the buildings in the remainder of the complex, was also unfinished (Plate 42); it measured 360 feet square at the base and rose to a height of 228 feet, so that it was slightly bigger than the pyramid of Mycerinus. The few fragments surviving from the outer casing show that the lowest course at least was composed of granite, the surface of which had not been dressed. Neferefrē, the second of Neferirkarē's short-lived successors, who had begun to build a pyramid of his own at a short distance to the south-west, and Niuserrē continued the construction of both the pyramid and the mortuary temple after Neferirkarē's death, but not in stone. Brick and timber were used for the entrance hall and cloistered court, the roofs being supported by wooden columns standing on limestone bases. Each column was carved in imitation of a bound cluster of lotus stems and buds. The valley building and causeway were left unfinished, and were subsequently appropriated by Niuserrē. As a consequence, Neferirkarē's mortuary priests, who would otherwise, no doubt, have followed the normal practice of building their pyramid city in the vicinity of the valley building, grouped their houses of crude brick against the walls of the mortuary temple. These were the priests who compiled the administrative records now known as the Abu Sir papyri which, in spite of their fragmentary condition, provide an invaluable insight into the duties of the men who looked after the property of the temple and maintained the mortuary cult of the king who was buried beneath its pyramid.

In order to use the causeway of Neferirkarē without any alteration, it would have been necessary for Niuserrē to build his pyramid complex immediately to the east of Neferirkarē's mortuary temple. He chose, however, a site lying to the north-east, so that the lower half of the causeway could be used as it stood. The upper half was dismantled and a large part of it rebuilt at the required angle towards the north-east (fig. 35: 9). This angle was somewhat lessened by the exceptional placing of the entrance hall and cloistered court of the temple opposite the southern half of the east face of the pyramid. Unless this position was deliberately selected with a view to shortening the distance between the temple and the older causeway, the decision to depart from the normal practice of constructing the temple in line with the main east-west axis of the pyramid must have been dictated either by the presence in that area of an obstruction – possibly a tomb – or by the unsuitable configuration of the ground.

Niuserrē's complex differed from that of Sahurē in detail only, but it provides a good illustration of the extent to which the standard plan could be adapted to fit the physical requirements of any particular site. The valley building (fig. 35: 8) had two porticos, the larger facing eastwards and the smaller westwards; instead, however, of the palm columns found in Sahurē's valley building, these porticos were furnished with papyrus-cluster columns of red granite. Tura limestone, red granite, and black polished basalt were again used in combination for the ceilings, walls and floors of the apartments. Basalt was also employed in the construction of a dado for the walls of the corridor of the causeway. Above this dado the walls were faced with Tura limestone and decorated with reliefs showing various scenes, which included the representation of the king as a lion or a griffin trampling his enemies underfoot. In the mortuary temple, papyrus-cluster columns supported the roof of the ambulatory surrounding the cloistered court. The magazines, owing to lack of space in the inner temple, were mostly built outside the north and south walls of the entrance hall. The sanctuary occupied its normal position due east of the burial-chamber, and therefore considerably north of the east–west axis of the temple. South-east of the main pyramid lay the usual subsidiary pyramid.

Some exploratory work by the Czechoslovak Archaeological Institute in Cairo, under the directorship of M. Verner, has brought to light the surviving remains of another pyramid at Abu Sir. If it had been completed, it would have been the largest pyramid in the group. It is situated between the pyramid of Sahurē and the sun-temple of Userkaf. The owner has not been identified, but it may be Shepseskarē, Neferirkarē's immediate successor. The only other king of the Vth Dynasty to whom no pyramid at either Abu Sir or Saqqara has been assigned is Menkauhor. He may have been buried at Saqqara in a pyramid lying north-east of the pyramid of Teti which is now in ruins. The evidence in support of this attribution is, however, rather slender. Another possibility, which depends largely on the interpretation given to a passage in a decree issued by Pepi I, is that Menkauhor's pyramid was built at Dahshur.

A successor of Niuserrē, Djedkarē Isesi, built his pyramid due west of the village of Saqqara. This pyramid, known formerly by its Arabic name 'Haram esh-Shauwaf' - the Pyramid of the Sentinel - was excavated in 1945 by the Service des Antiquités under the direction of Abdessalam Hussein assisted by Alexandre Varille, both of whom died before the results of their work had been prepared for publication. The superstructure is in ruins, but an examination of the subterranean burial-chamber revealed that the basalt sarcophagus, of which only small fragments had survived, had been embedded in the floor to a depth of about 5 inches. The lid, until it was required, had been placed on a block of limestone between the sarcophagus and the west wall. A small rectangular pit in front of the sarcophagus was intended for the Canopic chest. After the burial it would have been covered by a paving slab. Outside the pyramid, near the entrance, traces were discovered of a small offering-chapel of a kind already known from the Bent Pyramid and not uncommon in later pyramids.

One architectural element which made its first recognizable appearance was a subsidiary pyramid belonging to the queen's pyramid. Each side measured no more than about 13 feet at the base. The sides of both the queen's pyramid and the subsidiary pyramid in the south-east corner of the king's pyramid enclosure sloped at the steep angle of 63°.

Among the hundreds of pieces of architectural elements and sculpture found in the mortuary temple were broken palm-tree columns of red granite, fragments of limestone figures of calves and of captive foreigners with the arms tied at the elbows behind their backs, a figure which appears to be a sphinx and part of a relief showing the god Seth with eyelids inlaid with copper. An unexpected discovery at the entrance to the temple was a number of graffiti scratched on the floors of two rooms, giving the names of members of the personnel of the temple who lived in the late Vth and early VIth Dynasties, as well as some other people, both male and female, who were connected with them. Most of the graffiti included the standard offering formula, from which it seems evident that the place was chosen on account of the sanctity ascribed to the king's tomb.

The last king of the dynasty, Unas, erected his pyramid close to the south-west corner of the Step Pyramid enclosure wall and almost diagonally opposite the pyramid of Userkaf, the founder of the dynasty. Excavations by the Service des Antiquités under the direction first of Selim Bey Hassan in 1937-8 and subsequently of Abdessalam Hussein, revealed that the causeway had been preserved more completely in this monument than in any other known pyramid (Plate 43). It does not follow a straight line for its entire length of nearly 750 yards, but changes its direction twice in order to use the natural features to their best advantage. In spite of these adjustments, however, it was still necessary to bridge deep depressions in the ground. Some of the blocks employed in the bridging embankments were taken from the buildings of the Step Pyramid enclosure – a fact which proves that Zoser's famous monument was already falling into disrepair at the end of the Vth Dynasty. The sides of the embankment were built with a steep batter, which reduced its width at the top to about 22 feet. On this massive foundation the usual covered corridor was laid; its walls, possibly 13 feet in height, were about 6 feet 8 inches in thickness, and the central passage was approximately 8 feet 8 inches in width. The flat roof was made of slabs measuring 1 foot 6 inches in depth which projected inwards from each side, leaving in the middle a gap of about 8 inches in width to admit light. South of the causeway lie two boat-pits side by side, each about 148 feet in length and lined entirely with Tura limestone.

Scenes covering a wide range of subjects were delicately carved in low relief on the inner walls of the corridor. One group of reliefs illustrated the transport by ship from Aswan of the granite date-palm columns and architraves used in the construction of the mortuary temple. Another series represented craftsmen hammering gold, casting copper objects, and polishing vessels made of gold and stone. Elsewhere, labourers on the royal estates were shown gathering figs, harvesting corn, and collecting honey. Long trains of servants were depicted bringing provisions of every kind to the tomb. Hunting scenes included specimens of every horned animal known to the Egyptians, as well as a giraffe, a lion, leopards, foxes, hyenas, jerboas, and hedgehogs. Possibly the most graphic scene of all illustrated the victims of a famine, whose bodies were so emaciated that they were reduced to little more than skin and bone. Unfortunately this unique scene is incomplete and it is difficult to imagine its context; even the nationality of the people cannot be identified with certainty. Since, however, tomb reliefs depicted only incidents or events which the dead owner wished to perpetuate, it must be supposed that the starving people were not Egyptians and that the missing portion contained scenes of provisions being sent to them by Unas. All these reliefs were painted in bright colours, traces of which are still clearly visible. The ceiling also was painted with golden stars carved in relief on a sky-blue background.

Unas's mortuary temple was partly excavated by Alessandro Barsanti on behalf of the Service des Antiquités in 1900. A second and more complete excavation was undertaken by the Service des Antiquités in 1929 under the direction of C.M. Firth. Further explorations were conducted by J.-P. Lauer (1936-7 and 1939), by Selim Bey Hassan and Abdessalam Hussein (1937-49) and finally by members of the French Archaeological Mission at Saqqara (1974-6). In plan and construction it resembled very closely the mortuary temple of Sahurē, though the lay-out of the corridors and magazines in the inner temple was somewhat different. Its floors also were different, alabaster having been used as paving where basalt had been employed by Sahurē. In contrast with the large number of reliefs surviving from the causeway, only a few fragments showing servants bearing offerings have been preserved from the temple.

Externally, the chief interest in the pyramid of Unas lies in a damaged inscription by Khaemuas, son of Ramesses II (c. 1250 B.C.), at the bottom of the south face. It records that he perpetuated the name of Unas, when he failed to find his name on the face of the pyramid, because he (Prince Khaemuas) took pleasure in restoring the monuments of the (ancient) kings of Upper and Lower Egypt when they had fallen into ruin. Parts of similar inscriptions by Khaemuas had already been found in the pyramids of Sahurē and Niuserrē, and particularly at the *Mastabat Fara'un*, but they were too fragmentary to reveal what they had recorded. Khaemuas's interest in the monuments of the Memphite necropolis has long been known. This inscription, which was found by J.-P. Lauer in 1957, provides further evidence of it.

Unas's pyramid is the smallest of the main pyramids dating from the Old Kingdom. When built it measured at the base no more than 220 feet on each side and 62 feet in perpendicular height. Nevertheless, it included some important innovations. The entrance, although on the north side, is not in the face of the pyramid, but under the pavement.

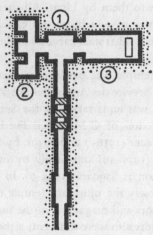

Figure 41. Chambers and corridors of the pyramid of Unas

Three portcullises of granite formerly blocked the corridor leading from the entrance to a square vestibule (fig. 41: 1). On the east side of this vestibule lies a long, narrow room, in the east wall of which are three statue-niches (fig. 41: 2). The burial-chamber occupies a corresponding position west of the vestibule (fig. 41: 3). At the far end of the chamber stands a rectangular stone sarcophagus which, although undamaged, had been robbed of its contents long before 1881, when it was found by Sir Gaston Maspero, the first archaeologist to clear a way into the pyramid. All the apartments are built of Tura limestone, with the exception of the west wall of the burial-chamber and the western halves of its north and south walls, opposite the ends of the sarcophagus, where the limestone is replaced by alabaster on which an elaborate panel design and a false door have been carved and painted.

More notable, however, than the structural innovations of this pyramid are the vertical columns of hieroglyphic inscription which entirely cover the walls of the vestibule and the limestone portions of the walls of the burial-chamber. Every hieroglyph has been filled with a blue pigment, so that it stands out clearly against the white background. These inscriptions are known as the Pyramid Texts. They are found not only in this pyramid but also in the VIth Dynasty pyramids of Teti, Pepi I, Merenrē (Plate 44), and Pepi II, in the pyramid of a king named Ibi, whose date is uncertain, and in the pyramids of Pepi II's three queens. They do not form a continuous narrative, but consist of a collection of spells assembled in no fixed order. Although most of the spells occur in more than one pyramid, very few are repeated in all the pyramids in which the texts are found; in the pyramid of Unas, for instance, only two hundred and twenty-eight spells are included out of a known total exceeding seven hundred.

The purpose of the Pyramid Texts, like that of every other element in the pyramid complex, was to secure for the king or queen a happy after-life. So powerful was the magic of the written word that its presence alone provided a sufficient guarantee that the thought expressed would be realized. Doubtless the spoken word, if delivered by a qualified person, possessed at least equal virtue, but its utterance was dependent on the goodwill or diligence of other people. A text which is generally inscribed on the north wall of the burial-chamber reproduces the ritual which the priests used to recite every day in the mortuary temple when laying the provisions on the altar in front of the false door. By having this ritual in writing and supplies of provisions in the magazines of his temple, the king believed that he would eliminate the risk of suffering hunger and thirst, even if the priests should neglect to perform their duties. Many of the texts describe the journey of the king to the other world, situated in the sky beyond the eastern horizon, and his activities on arrival. It is clear that the king could count on little assistance from the gods when making this journey, but, armed with the magic power of the texts, he might expect to overcome successfully its many hazards. With their help, moreover, his association with the sun-god in his daily voyage across the sky was assured. Among the texts were also collections of hymns to the gods and prayers on behalf of the dead king.

An interesting theory, which was advanced by Siegfried Schott, was that the Pyramid Texts as a whole represented the spells recited at the time of the funeral in the various chambers, corridors and courts through which the procession passed on its way to the pyramid. While this theory does not affect the explanation of the ultimate purpose of the texts already given, it attributes to them an added importance of a practical kind as furnishing a key with which the significance of many of the architectural features may be more clearly understood. Nevertheless the identification of the physical surroundings in which a particular spell was recited is often not easy to establish from its content, but Schott and his colleague H. Ricke produced a reconstruction which, though not acceptable to all authorities, has not yet been shown to be fundamentally unsound. Some of the results of their work have already been mentioned in connection with pyramids described in the previous chapters.

For the most part, the Pyramid Texts were certainly not inventions of the Vth or VIth Dynasties, but had originated in earlier times; it is hardly surprising, therefore, that they sometimes contain allusions to conditions which no longer prevailed at the time of Unas and his successors. As an example, Spell 662 includes the words 'Cast the sand from thy face', which could only refer to the burial practices of pre-dynastic times when the king was interred in a grave dug in the sand. Another anachronism of a similar kind, but referring to the brick mastabas of the Early Dynastic Period, occurs in Spell 355: 'The bricks are removed for thee from the great tomb.' A relic of even more ancient times is contained in a passage (Spells 273-4) which describes the dead king as a hunter who catches and devours the gods so that he may appropriate their qualities unto himself. On the other hand, many of the texts expressly mention the pyramid and, in consequence, may not have originated before the IIIrd-IVth Dynasties; for instance, Spell 599 states: 'They [the gods] are those who will cause this work to be enduring and this pyramid to be enduring.' It seems certain, in view of the constant references to the solar cult, that the texts were compiled by the priests of Heliopolis. When making the compilation, probably in the Vth Dynasty, they used old religious and funerary spells and added some incantations of a later date to meet contemporary needs.

Although the Pyramid Texts were designed to help the dead king, their presence in his tomb introduced a new complication of a very serious kind. Being written in hieroglyphs, they included many images of living creatures. Such images not only possessed the value of a particular hieroglyphic sign, but also, through the power of magic, became actual embodiments of the creatures which they represented. The lion, for instance, was simultaneously both a phonogram with the value of *ru* and the living animal itself endowed with all its attributes. Images of human beings, which form some of the most common hieroglyphic signs, likewise fulfilled a dual function. To overcome the dangers to the dead king which would have resulted from the presence of a multitude of potentially hostile and destructive creatures in his close vicinity, the Egyptian priests and sculptors resorted to a number of different devices. Sometimes the dangerous signs were omitted or replaced by signs representing inanimate objects which possessed the same hieroglyphic value. Human beings were deprived of their legs and bodies so that they consisted of heads and arms alone. Animals could be rendered harmless by the simple expedient of mutilating their bodies and carving them in two separate halves. As variants on that method, in the pyramid of Pepi I the hindparts of animals were sometimes covered with a layer of plaster and in the pyramid of Merenrē a thin line might be drawn over an animal, dividing it into two parts. Serpents were represented intact, but the scorpion was deprived of its tail. One creature which, with a single exception, was never allowed to appear on the walls of the burial-chamber was the fish. This omission was not due to any fear lest the fish should molest the tomb's owner, but was the result of a belief that the fish, although innocuous to living people, would defile a dead body.

During the Middle Kingdom, the Pyramid Texts were retained in a modified form. The custom of inscribing the texts on the walls of the chambers and corridors of the tomb was, however, abandoned. Instead, they were written on the interior surfaces of the rectangular wooden coffins used in that period – a fact which has caused them to become known as the Coffin Texts. By that time also they had ceased to be the exclusive property of royalty and had been usurped by the nobility, thus following the same course of democratization as so many other practices which had been designed in the first instance as a royal prerogative. Under the New Kingdom, the texts, after undergoing still further modifications, were written on papyrus, and were called the Book of Coming Forth by Day, better known in modern times as the Book of the Dead.

Teti, Pepi I and Merenrē built their pyramids at Saqqara, Teti to the north-east of the Step Pyramid of Zoser and his two successors near the pyramid of Djedkarē Isesi, about 1½ miles to the south. The pyramid of Pepi I was the first in which Pyramid Texts were found. Before their discovery by Emile and Heinrich Brugsch in 1880–81, it was supposed that the walls of the chambers and corridors of the pyramids had been left bare and uninscribed. Internally, all three pyramids were designed according to the same plan as the pyramid of Unas (fig. 41). Their external dimensions were also uniform, each measuring approximately 259 feet in length on every side and 172½ feet in height. Deliberate destruction over centuries in order to obtain building materials had resulted in the inner apartments being blocked; granite roof-beams weighing as much as thirty to forty tons had collapsed or were lodged precariously against other beams. In the midst of all the chaos hundreds of fragments of limestone from the walls were lying on the floors.

In 1950 the French Archaeological Mission at Saqqara began to carry out the structural rehabilitation of the three pyramids and to restore the broken pieces of limestone with inscriptions to their proper places. J.-P. Lauer conducted the operation, assisted first by J. Sainte Fare Garnot and, after his death in 1963, by J. Leclant. It is not yet finished, although several complete walls have been reconstituted. Eventually it will be possible to publish a new edition of the Pyramid Texts which will include many hitherto unknown spells.

Two fine sarcophagi were preserved in these pyramids; one of grey basalt was made for Teti and the other of granite belonged to Merenrē. Pepi I's sarcophagus had been destroyed; only some fragments were found in his pyramid. The sarcophagi were placed close to the west wall of the burial-chamber. In front of each sarcophagus, near the south wall, there was a rectangular pit, about 3 feet deep, in which a Canopic chest containing the king's viscera had been buried (Plate 44). Pepi I's Canopic chest still retained one of the packages with his viscera wrapped in bandages of fine linen which had been stained brown with resin. Only fragments of the jar had survived. J.E. Quibell, when excavating Teti's mortuary temple in 1907–8, discovered a mould for a plaster mask which has generally been regarded as a death-mask of Teti, although there is nothing to prove it. The mould is now in the Cairo Museum.

Outside the entrance to each of the three pyramids, on the north side, there was a small chapel, the walls of which were decorated with scenes carved in relief. A false door stood in front of the actual entrance to the pyramid. These chapels and the mortuary temples on the east sides of the pyramids were all in a devastated state, but it was possible to see that, like their pyramids, they were uniform in plan, at least as regards their main elements. Many fragments of sculptures carved in relief from the walls of the temples were recovered, but only enough to show the character of the scenes represented. One surprising feature in the architecture of the temples was that stone columns representing palm-trees and plants were no longer employed. Instead, the columns were square, octagonal and polygonal, reminiscent of the rectangular columns of the IVth Dynasty but more slender.

Pepi II, who succeeded Merenrē, ascended the throne as a child (Plate 45) and died, according to Manetho, a centenarian. Later Egyptian historical records credit him with having ruled for ninety-four years, which, if correct, would mean that his reign was by far the longest in the whole course of Egyptian history. His pyramid complex, or what remains of it after centuries of depredation, is situated a short distance to the south of those of his two predecessors and within 300 yards of the north-west corner of Shepseskaf's mastaba. It was excavated between the years 1926 and 1936 by Gustave Jéquier, who succeeded in recovering the whole of its ground-plan and not a little of its structure. As a result of his work, it is possible to see the plan of the standard pyramid complex in its final and most highly developed form.

In front of the valley building, and projecting for a considerable distance beyond its northern and southern limits, lay a broad terrace (fig. 42: 1). To reach this terrace from the level of the valley, it was necessary to mount a short ramp at either end and continue by a longer ramp ascending at a right angle. A high limestone wall of great thickness bounded the terrace on its north, south and west sides. Narrow staircases built in the masonry at each end of the wall led up to a parapet which extended along the wall for the whole of its length. In the middle of the long west wall stood a door set in a granite frame, on which the names and titles of the king were carved in large hieroglyphs. Beyond the door was a passage running through the thickness of the walls to an elongated hypostyle hall with eight rectangular pillars, probably made of limestone. As in the rest of the building, only the floor and foundations of this hall have been preserved substantially intact, but the excavator found among the débris some fragments of delicately carved and painted low reliefs which had once adorned the walls. The scenes represented appear to have been of the conventional kind, showing the king slaying his enemies, fowling in the marshes, and associating with the gods. It was undoubtedly the most important apartment in the whole building, the remainder of which consisted of magazines and two subsidiary chambers, apparently with bare walls. No trace of any sculptures in the round was revealed during the excavations, but it is not improbable that the building once housed a number of statues of the king.

Although in a far poorer state of preservation, the causeway of Pepi II (fig. 42: 2) resembles that of Unas in many respects. Both causeways change their direction twice, either in order to make the best use of available natural features or possibly to lessen the angle of their gradient. In their dimensions also the corridors surmounting the two causeways were approximately alike. In contrast, however, with the very substantial portions of relief which have been preserved in the corridor of Unas, only scattered fragments have been recovered from that of Pepi II. From these fragments it seems evident that the scenes at the lower end of the corridor were similar to those occupying a corresponding position in the corridor of Sahurē: the king, represented both as a sphinx and as a griffin, was shown trampling underfoot the traditional enemies of Egypt, who were led to him as captives by the

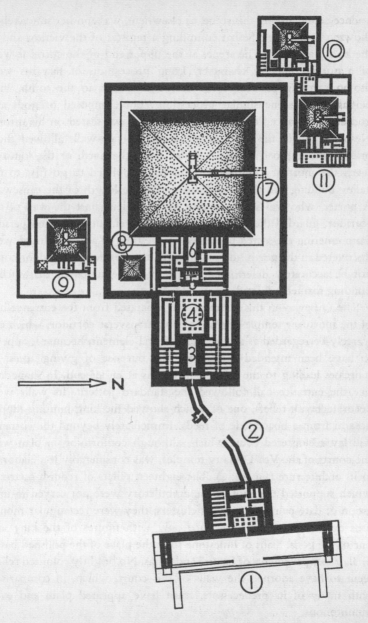

Figure 42. The pyramid complex of Pepi II

gods. Accompanying this scene, as elsewhere, was another set of reliefs showing the goddess Seshat compiling a register of the victims and of the booty acquired. The scenes at the upper end of the corridor were of a purely funerary character. Long processions of servants were shown carrying produce from the royal estates to the tomb. In a neighbouring scene similar processions, but composed of gods and goddesses, advanced towards the king, who was seated on his throne. Near the top of the corridor, doors in the side-walls allowed those priests who approached the complex from the north or the south to reach the mortuary temple without being obliged to go first to the valley building and then climb up the whole length of the causeway. A porter, who was stationed in a lodge built against the wall of the corridor, guarded the southern door to prevent unauthorized persons from entering the sacred precincts. No vestiges of a similar lodge were discovered in the north side, where even the position of the door could not be accurately determined, but it must be supposed that such a building formerly existed.

The causeway in this complex was separated from the entrance hall of the mortuary temple (fig. 42: 3) by a transverse corridor, which can scarcely be regarded as a new architectural element, because it appears to have been intended merely for the purpose of giving access to staircases leading to the roof from rooms at either end. In shape and size the entrance hall followed the standard pattern. Its walls were decorated with reliefs, one of which showed the king hunting hippopotami from a boat made of reeds. Immediately beyond the entrance hall lay a cloistered court which, although conforming in plan with the courts of the Vth Dynasty temples, was considerably less elaborate in its architecture (fig. 42: 4). The eighteen pillars of reddish quartzite which supported the roof of the ambulatory were not carved in imitation of date-palms or papyrus clusters; they were rectangular monoliths decorated on the outer face only with figures of the king and one of the gods. Slabs of limestone took the place of the polished basalt or alabaster pavements of Sahurē and Unas. No brightly coloured reliefs seem to have adorned the walls of this court, which, in comparison with many of its predecessors, must have appeared plain and even monotonous.

Beyond the cloistered court lay the central transverse corridor, which not only served to separate the inner apartments of the temple from those lying outside the enclosure wall of the pyramid, but constituted the focal point of the whole complex. Although developed architecturally from the western section of the corridor, which in earlier temples surrounded the outer walls of the cloistered courts, it had now become an independent element and the southern, eastern and western sections of the former corridor had been discarded. Doors at the northern and southern ends of this corridor gave access to the pyramid enclosure, in the south-east corner of which stood the subsidiary pyramid (fig. 42: 8). East of the corridor, flanking the northern and southern sides of the cloistered court and the entrance hall, lay extensive groups of magazines. Niuserrē, apparently owing to lack of space within his inner temple, had also constructed magazines on each side of the entrance hall, so that Pepi II can certainly not be credited with having introduced an architectural innovation in this respect. West of the corridor, and approached by way of a small court or hall containing the five statue-niches (fig. 42: 5), were the inner apartments and the remainder of the magazines.

Only fragments of the reliefs from the central transverse corridor have been preserved, but Jéquier's reconstructions have demonstrated that they were among the most interesting in the whole temple. At the southern end of the east wall the king was shown in the act of smiting a captured Libyan chieftain on the head with his mace. Behind the chieftain stood his wife and two sons, begging for mercy. The scene is not merely reminiscent of that in the temple of Sahurē, but is actually a replica of it, even the names of the wife and the two sons being repeated. This almost exact duplication of a scene in the temples of two kings whose reigns were separated by about two centuries furnishes conclusive proof that temple reliefs did not necessarily record historical episodes from the life of the king; all the evidence indeed goes to show that they were intended to depict the ideal life which the king wished to live in the next world. Elsewhere on the same wall the king, wearing the crown of Upper Egypt and carrying in his hands a flail and a small rectangular portfolio, was four times represented performing a ritual ceremony which involved running between some hoof-shaped boundary stones set at a distance apart. This ceremony, an earlier example of which occurs in the Step Pyramid (Plate 9), formed part of the *heb-sed* and seems to have been designed, at least originally, to restore fertility to the ground. Another scene on the wall, which may also be connected with a fertility rite, shows the king standing near a high pole supported by four wooden stays. Two men, one above the other, were represented in the act of climbing the stays, while attendants held ropes attached both to the stays and to the pole. Replicas of this scene, which is a little suggestive of the medieval maypole ceremonies, occur in later times on the walls of the temples of Karnak, Luxor, Dendereh, and Edfu; in the replicas, however, the god of fertility, Min, stands facing the king on the other side of the pole and receives his homage.

From a recess in the west wall of the central transverse corridor, a short staircase led upwards to the hall or court with five statue-niches (fig. 42: 5). Nothing now remains within the niches except one badly damaged pedestal, which serves to show that the statues were made of limestone. In accordance with the regular Egyptian custom, they were probably painted and each statue may have been inscribed with one of the king's five titles and with his name. Double doors of wood concealed the statues from view when they were not required for ritual purposes. A second group of statues may have been permanently hidden, if a hollow space lying in the masonry of the building behind the five niches has been correctly interpreted as a serdab.

Passages opened from each end of the statue-hall, the northern leading to a small group of magazines and the southern to a narrow chamber which, in turn, was connected with a larger series of magazines and with a square vestibule situated next to the sanctuary (fig. 42: 6). Among the reliefs which decorated the walls of the narrow chamber was one of the many examples in this temple of the king vanquishing his enemies. Only a few fragments were preserved, but they provided a clue to the reconstruction of the whole scene, for Jéquier recognized that it had survived in a copy made by Amenophis II in the temple of Karnak nearly a thousand years after the death of Pepi II. The central position in the scene was occupied by a gigantic figure of the king, who brandished a mace over the heads of a bunch of foreign captives. Behind the king was a small human figure representing his *ka*, presumably serving as his protector. Elsewhere in the scene the goddess Seshat was shown recording on a scroll the number of captives slaughtered and the amount of booty taken. The frequent occurrence of such scenes in mortuary temples suggests that periodic ceremonies were held to commemorate a victory gained in early times by the Egyptians over their foreign neighbours. A similar explanation may also account for the presence in both this temple and in certain of its predecessors of statues representing foreign captives in a kneeling position, with their arms bound. Of these statues not one has been discovered intact, and the majority bear every sign of having been mutilated deliberately. Possibly, therefore, they were used during the commemoration ceremonies as substitutes for live captives, whose slaughter in cold blood would have been alien to the Egyptian mentality.

A single pillar, which may have been octagonal in section, supported the roof of the square chamber. On each of its four walls, the king was shown being received by the deities of Egypt and by high sacerdotal and secular officials who had assembled to greet him as he entered the temple by way of the sanctuary from his tomb. The deities, who numbered about a hundred, stood erect, each carrying a sceptre in one hand and in the other the hieroglyph for 'life'. The officials, about forty-five in number, were bowed in an attitude of humble deference before their royal master. Butchers were shown slaughtering cattle in preparation for a feast. The scenes are reminiscent of episodes in the king's *heb-sed* and Dieter Arnold has compared the chamber with an apartment in the royal palace at Memphis which the king visited in the performance of the festival ceremonies. In the temple it was the functional equivalent of that apartment, and it was also a relic of the monumental buildings and court provided for the celebration of the festival in the Step Pyramid enclosure of Zoser.

The sanctuary (fig. 42: 6), which measured approximately 51 feet in length, 17 feet in width, and 24 feet in height, was the largest single apartment within the inner temple. Its vaulted ceiling was decorated in the regular style with golden stars on a sky-blue background. Nothing remains of either the false door, which covered the bottom half of the west wall, or the low altar placed at its foot. The painted reliefs of the north, south and east walls, although broken into hundreds of pieces, could be substantially reconstructed. On both the longer walls, the king was shown seated at a table laden with food. Behind him stood his *ka*. In front of each table was a procession of about a hundred and twenty-five offering-bearers consisting of priests, provincial officials, courtiers and other dignitaries who, by being included in these reliefs, were assured of an after-life in the service of the king. Among the offerings brought by the bearers were ducks, geese, wine, beer, fruit, bread and vegetables. Cattle, antelopes, gazelles and goats were led by ropes attached to their necks or front legs. Pigeons and quails were carried in cages. Above these reliefs was a deep frieze decorated with representations of provisions. This frieze was also continued on the east wall, where a scene of cattle being slaughtered took the place occupied on the north and south walls by offering-bearers.

In no other mortuary temple has it proved possible to reconstruct so much of the original decoration of the sanctuary or to see how completely it was devoted to the satisfaction of the physical requirements of the dead king. Every kind of sustenance was represented in the reliefs, so that if the priests omitted to provide daily supplies of fresh provisions on the altar he would not suffer from hunger or thirst; by the mere presence of the magic formula which accompanied the reliefs, the images would assume all the properties of their material counterparts. As a further precaution, wine and dried provisions may have been stored in a group of magazines lying to the north and connected by a passage with the sanctuary.

Before its excavation by Jéquier, a tumulus rising from the desert provided the only visible evidence of Pepi II's pyramid, which, like other pyramids of its time, had been built of small stones bonded with a mortar of Nile mud and held together by a heavy casing of Tura limestone. This method of construction had the great disadvantage that there was nothing to hinder the swift disintegration of the whole building when once a part of the outer casing had been removed. Originally, the pyramid measured about 259 feet square at the base, and its perpendicular height was approximately 172½ feet; it was the same size as its immediate predecessors. In one respect it was unique:

a square girdle composed of masonry and cased with Tura limestone had been built around its entire base, broken only on the east side where the temple joined the face of the pyramid. This girdle, which measured about 21 feet in breadth, rose to the level of the second or perhaps the third course of the pyramid casing. Since it was laid directly against the casing, it follows that the girdle must have been added to the pyramid after the lower part, at least, had been completed. There is indeed every reason to believe that it was an addition to the original plan, for Jéquier discovered that the north, south and west sides of the enclosure wall had been dismantled and subsequently rebuilt further from the pyramid, presumably in order to allow adequate space for the girdle. It is difficult to imagine why this addition was made, but it may have been necessitated by an earthquake, which had shaken the fabric of the building; the girdle would thus have been intended to increase its stability. A suggestion that the girdle might provide an explanation of the rectangular construction added to the base of the pyramid when it is used as a hieroglyph △ is hardly convincing, because the girdle is without any known parallel and its introduction in this instance seems to have been an afterthought, possibly dictated by an accident. It is far more probable that the hieroglyph represents a pyramid surrounded by its enclosure wall.

When dismantling a portion of the girdle lying outside the entrance to the pyramid, Jéquier discovered that some of the blocks in its structure were decorated with reliefs. As a rule, reliefs embodied in the inner cores of walls or buildings prove to be relics of earlier constructions which have been reused, often after a lapse of many centuries. These reliefs, however, were undoubtedly of the same date as those in the mortuary temple nearby, and the logical deduction seemed to be that they had once belonged to a building which had been pulled down when the girdle was added to the sides of the pyramid. The character of the building could be determined from the reliefs, which closely resembled those of the sanctuary in the inclusion of processions of officials bearing offerings to the king, seated at a table, and scenes of animals being slaughtered; the two buildings had evidently been designed for very similar purposes. Instances of offering-chapels standing at the entrance to the tomb have already been mentioned in connection with the pyramids of Djedkarē Isesi, Teti, Pepi I and Merenrē; other examples dating from later periods have been found elsewhere. There can be little room for doubt, therefore, that Jéquier was right in his explanation that a chapel of the same kind had also been built at the entrance to this pyramid (fig. 42: 7), but the addition of the girdle had necessitated its removal. Subsequently, it may have been replaced by an entirely new chapel, of which no trace has been preserved, or the plan may have been discarded.

All the pyramids of the VIth Dynasty were alike in the general design and arrangement of their internal apartments. The entrance corridor descended steeply for a short distance and then continued horizontally as far as a square vestibule lying between the serdab and the burial-chamber. At the beginning of the horizontal section, the corridor widened and also became higher, thus forming a kind of chamber. Within this chamber, in the pyramid of Pepi II, Jéquier found some fragments of alabaster and diorite vases inscribed with the king's name and with the names of some of his predecessors. From the examination of these fragments, Jéquier concluded that the vases, which may have may have contained perfume, had been deliberately broken in the performance of a funerary rite at the entrance to the tomb. The Pyramid Texts were carved on the walls of this chamber and on the whole of the remainder of the interior, with the exception of those parts of the corridor which were lined with granite, the serdab and the western end of the burial-chamber in the neighbourhood of the sarcophagus, where the walls were faced with alabaster decorated with the false door and panel design. Although less well preserved than the corresponding texts in the pyramid of Unas, they were both more numerous and more highly developed.

Outside the enclosure wall of the king's pyramid lay three small pyramids belonging to the queens Udjebten, Iput and Neit (fig. 42: 9, 10, and 11). A fourth queen named Ankhes-en-Pepi, whom he married in the latter part of his long reign and who survived him, was not buried in a pyramid. Each of the three pyramids possessed its own complex, which embodied in miniature the principal elements of the mortuary temple and pyramid enclosure of the king. The clearest example of their lay-out may be seen in the pyramid of Neit (fig. 42:

11). A narrow entrance in the south-east corner of the limestone enclosure wall gave access to a vestibule which in turn was connected with an open court surrounded on three sides by square columns. Both the vestibule and the court were decorated with reliefs which showed the queen either presenting offerings to various goddesses or receiving the homage of her family and attendants. A corridor led from the north-west corner of the court by way of a group of five magazines to the inner temple, which consisted of a long chamber or store-room, a small court with three statue-niches, and the sanctuary. Behind the long chamber and the niches lay a serdab constructed in the masonry of the building, and in that respect not unlike the serdab situated between the niches and the sanctuary in the king's temple.

Neit's pyramid, which measured approximately 79 feet square at the base and rose to a height of about 70 feet, was in all essential features only a replica of the king's pyramid on a reduced scale. In front of its entrance stood a small offering-chapel, the inner walls of which were partly adorned with reliefs showing the queen receiving provisions. An altar for the mortuary offerings rested at the foot of a false door, which formed the south wall of the chapel; since this door also covered the mouth of the pyramid corridor, it could not have been put into position until after the funeral. Inside the pyramid the side-walls of the corridor, beyond a single portcullis of granite, were decorated with Pyramid Texts, which were continued in the burial-chamber except at its western end where the walls were faced with alabaster and ornamented with the false door and panel design. The granite sarcophagus, when found, was empty and without a lid. By its side, sunk in the floor of the chamber, was a Canopic chest, carved of one block of the same material, which had once held four jars containing the viscera of the queen. At the opposite end of the burial-chamber, a short passage led directly to the serdab without the intervening vestibule of the king's pyramid.

Perhaps the most interesting feature in each of the three complexes of the queens was the subsidiary pyramid situated near the south-east corner of the main pyramid. Subsidiary pyramids of the same kind in the complexes of the Vth and VIth Dynasty kings had been regarded by some Egyptologists as tombs of the royal consorts, on account of their resemblance to the subsidiary pyramids erected by Cheops and Mycerinus, which certainly bear every appearance of being royal tombs. This conjecture was rendered improbable, however, by the discovery that Pepi II, although incorporating the usual subsidiary pyramid in his own complex, had also built separate pyramids with independent complexes for his queens; it was conclusively disproved when it became known that each of the queens' complexes contained its subsidiary pyramid. The discovery of the Canopic chest in the burial-chamber of Neit's pyramid, moreover, showed that her subsidiary pyramid had not been used as a sepulchre for the viscera; the entire floor of its square chamber was strewn with fragments of pottery vessels and with three alabaster vases, one of which was inscribed with her name. While the full explanation of the function of subsidiary pyramids has yet to be found, it seems to have been thought, in this instance at least, that the pyramid imparted some particular efficacy to the contents of these vessels, since they could otherwise have been stored in the magazines.

In the small court outside Neit's subsidiary pyramid, Jéquier found sixteen wooden models of boats buried side by side in a shallow pit. Although instances of such models in Old Kingdom tombs are comparatively rare, they were often included in tombs of the Second Intermediate Period and Middle Kingdom as part of the furniture of the burial-chamber and were placed on the lid of the sarcophagus. The difference between the position allotted to the models in the two periods was probably not accidental, but was the result of an important distinction in their purpose. In the Middle Kingdom they were certainly designed for use by the dead person in the after-life, and it was therefore necessary that they should be preserved with the same care as the rest of the tomb equipment. The boats lying beneath the ground in the complex of Neit, on the other hand, were reproductions in miniature of the fleet employed in the funerals of kings for conveying the body to the valley building. Neit's pyramid, although built at a considerable distance from the valley, possessed neither a valley building nor a causeway, so that an approach to its precincts by water was not practicable. Nevertheless, the ceremony of transporting the body by boat had acquired such a degree of sanctity that it was thought necessary to provide a substitute for it by means of model craft. With the arrival of the body at the tomb their function had been fulfilled and they were buried in a simple pit, exposed to the ravages of ants and other destructive forces.

Pepi II appears to have been the last king of the Old Kingdom to build a pyramid complex of classic dimensions, although one of his successors, named Ibi, left an unfinished pyramid, which was not very much larger than the pyramid of Neit and lacked the customary adjoining buildings. This decline did not result from any sudden change in religious ideas, but was the consequence of a cumulative loss of wealth and power on the part of the throne extending over a period of more than two hundred years. Even in the IVth Dynasty, kings had been accustomed to reward their courtiers not only with tombs, but with valuable tracts of land from the royal estates, the produce of which was intended to be used for supplying the tombs with provisions. Land so given was generally exempt from taxation, so that, in aggregate, the royal exchequer must have forfeited a very material part of its revenue. In the Vth and VIth Dynasties, moreover, the office of nomarch, which had previously been conferred by the king for a limited period or for the lifetime of its holder, became hereditary, with the result that there soon grew up a generation of provincial nobles who were no longer conscious of owing their position to royal favour, but considered it as a right obtained in virtue of their birth. It is likely, however, that the full consequences of these developments did not become apparent until the end of the long reign of Pepi II, when his senility may also have brought about a diminution in the personal prestige formerly enjoyed by the king. Within a short time after his death, the country, possibly harassed in the north by an invasion of Asiatics, had disintegrated internally and had again split into independent principalities resembling those which Menes had conquered when uniting the Two Lands in the beginning of historical times.

To survey briefly the most distinctive artistic features of the Vth and VIth Dynasty pyramid complexes, the outstanding innovations are the plant-shaped granite columns and the great increase in the use of wall-reliefs. Columns in the form of a single papyrus or lily flower had already been used by Zoser in the IIIrd Dynasty, but they were composed of limestone and were not free-standing. No comparable examples dating from the IVth Dynasty are known (with the exception of the relatively small wooden palm-tree columns of the boat of Cheops) and Chephren's complex, if it may be regarded as representative, shows that the columns of the period, although made of granite, were rectangular and entirely without decoration. By the time of Teti the rectangular column had again returned to favour; it was, however, neither plain nor made of granite. In execution, reliefs of the Vth Dynasty are perhaps not equal to those of the IVth Dynasty, but they cover a far wider range of subjects and are more lively in their expression. To that period belong some of the mastabas at Saqqara which are justly among the most celebrated for their reliefs, such as the tombs of Ti and Ptahhotep. The VIth Dynasty also produced many magnificent examples of carving in relief – those in the complex of Pepi II and in the mastabas near Teti's pyramid being probably the best (Plates 5 and 6) – but, in spite of possessing even greater liveliness and less regularity in form, the majority show an unmistakable deterioration in their technical qualities.

In contrast with the considerable quantity of reliefs found in the royal tombs of the Vth and VIth Dynasties, very few statues of the kings for whom the reliefs were made have come to light. There is no reason, however, to doubt that originally each temple housed at least the five statues in the niches, while other statues may have stood in the open courts. Those temples of the VIth Dynasty which were provided with serdabs seem also to have contained a number of statues hidden completely from view. The artistic quality of these lost sculptures may be conjectured not only from the few royal survivals, such as the colossal head of Userkaf discovered in his temple at Saqqara (Plate 41), but from the many statues of contemporary courtiers and officials which have been preserved in mastabas. Without doubt, the finest pieces date from the early part of the Vth Dynasty, when the lessons learnt from the sculptors who had carved the magnificent statues of Chephren and Mycerinus were still remembered. In the latter half of the Vth Dynasty and in the VIth Dynasty, the standard declined appreciably, but several pleasing specimens, including the alabaster figure of Pepi II as a child (Plate 45) were produced.

CHAPTER SIX

MIDDLE KINGDOM
PYRAMIDS

Following the close of the Old Kingdom, Egypt experienced one of the darkest periods in her long history. Not only was no attention paid to the development of arts and crafts, but most of the temples and tombs of the Pyramid Age, with their artistic masterpieces and untold treasures, were systematically pillaged and destroyed. According to Manetho, two dynasties of ephemeral rulers, namely the VIIth and VIIIth Dynasties, occupied the throne at Memphis, but their authority was only local, and complete anarchy prevailed throughout the greater part of the country. So great was the chaos that much of the land remained uncultivated; in a number of districts, at least, there was famine. At some time during the VIIIth Dynasty an attempt seems to have been made to restore order in the eight southernmost *nomes,* where a confederation was formed under the hegemony of the nomarch of Coptos. About forty years later, however, a nomarch of Herakleopolis Magna named Khety conquered the whole of Upper Egypt as far as the First Cataract at Aswan and became the founder of the IXth Dynasty (*c.* 2160). His kingdom extended northwards as far as Memphis, but may not have included the whole of the Delta, part of which was perhaps still under the control of Asiatic invaders.

Approximately a hundred years after Khety's conquest, Intef, the nomarch of Thebes, rebelled against the contemporary ruler in Herakleopolis and claimed for himself the title of King of Upper and Lower Egypt. A similar title was adopted by his two successors, both of whom were also named Intef, but it was an empty boast, for their dominion, although embracing the whole country as far as Aswan in the south, at no time extended beyond Abydos in the north. In spite of their limited realm, however, they were regarded in later times as the first three kings of the XIth Dynasty. Their tombs were constructed at Thebes, on the western side of the river opposite Karnak, in the district now called El-Tarif, near Dira Abu 'n-Naga. Known as *saff*-tombs (*saff* being an Arabic word meaning 'row'), they are all similar in their general plan. The central feature is a large trapezoidal court, which was sunk in the gravel of the plain. On three sides of the court are corridors with free-standing pillars hollowed out of the soft rock of the neighbouring foothills, those on the north and south sides being façades of tombs of courtiers and the corridor at the west end being the façade of the king's tomb. Viewed from a distance each ensemble, when complete, looked like a court with porticos on three sides.

Until the German Institute of Archaeology in Cairo, under the direction of Dieter Arnold, explored these tombs in 1970–74, it was thought that a brick pyramid was built either at the back of the court or on a ledge cut in the rock above each royal tomb. The chief reason for that belief was a statement in a papyrus in the British Museum known as the Abbott Papyrus. It is one of a group of papyri which report the findings of a commission appointed by a vizier in the reign of Ramesses IX (*c*. 1115 B.C.) to investigate certain allegations of neglect of duty, resulting in tomb robbery, laid by the Mayor of Thebes against the Mayor of the necropolis on the west bank. When describing the tomb of Intef II, the report says its 'pyramid is crushed down upon it; its stela is set up in front of it and the image of the king stands upon this stela with his hound, named Behka, between his feet'. The lower half of the stela was found at El-Tarif by Mariette in 1860, still *in situ*, where it had been seen by the investigating commission some three thousand years previously. The building in which it stood was not, however, the tomb of Intef II, surmounted by a pyramid, but a brick offering-chapel, situated about 265 yards to the east of the king's tomb. In the light of this discovery, there seems to be no justification for assuming that any of the tombs of the Intefs were provided with pyramids.

The three remaining kings of the XIth Dynasty were all named Mentuhotep, the first of whom, but the second to bear that name – Neb-hepet-Rē Mentuhotep – was one of Egypt's greatest kings. Early in his reign of fifty-one years he recaptured Abydos, which his predecessor had lost, and then drove northwards to overcome his weaker rival in Herakleopolis and established himself as the undisputed ruler over all Egypt. If some reliefs which once decorated a chapel built by Neb-hepet-Rē Mentuhotep at Gebelein may be regarded as a record of historical events, he also conducted successful campaigns against the Nubians, Libyans, and Asiatics; evidence of such a kind, however, is not always reliable. Unlike Menes, whose achievements of a thousand years earlier he had in some degree emulated, he did not transfer his residence northwards, but continued to live at Thebes, which thus became, for the first time, the seat of government. Little exact information is available regarding his provincial administration; it seems likely, however, that the nomarchs, with perhaps a few exceptions, were again appointed by the king and that the right of hereditary succession was suppressed. The arts, after two and a half centuries of neglect, began to revive; a sculptor of the period named Irtisen has left an inscription, now in the Louvre, in which he makes the following claims:

I was an artist skilled in my art, pre-eminent in my learning ... I knew [how to represent] the movements of the image of a man and the carriage of a woman ... the poising of the arm to bring the hippopotamus low and the movements of the runner ... No one succeeds in all this [task] but only I and the eldest son of my body.

Sculpture was not the only branch of the arts which prospered under Neb-hepet-Rē Mentuhotep. Architecture too made remarkable progress, as is demonstrated by the singularly impressive funerary temple which he built in a deep bay in the cliffs on the west bank of the river at Deir el-Bahri. It was first excavated by Edouard Naville and H. R. Hall on behalf of the Egypt Exploration Fund (1903–7) and subsequently by H. E. Winlock for the Metropolitan Museum of Art, New York (in fifteen seasons from 1911 to 1931). A further exploration was conducted by Dieter Arnold for the German Archaeological Institute in Cairo (1966–71) with results which differed, particularly in one important respect, from those obtained by the two earlier expeditions.

An unroofed causeway, nearly three-quarters of a mile in length and bounded at the sides by stone walls, led from the valley building at the edge of the cultivation across the desert to a large forecourt surrounded on all sides except the west by high walls. Sandstone statues of the king holding in his hands a crook and a flail, the emblems of the god Osiris, were set at intervals of about 30 feet against the inner walls of the causeway, those on the south side probably showing him wearing the crown of Upper Egypt and those on the north side wearing the crown of Lower Egypt. All the figures were clad in a short, close-fitting garment reaching to the knees, which resembled a cloak worn by kings when performing certain ceremonies in the *sed*-festival, but that cloak generally had a pointed collar.

From the entrance to the forecourt, an avenue led westwards to a colonnade with a double row of square pillars which masked the eastern revetment of the massive terrace on which a large part of the temple was built. It was certainly the architect's intention that the avenue - a processional way - should be lined for its whole length with sycomores (*Ficus sycomorus*), but, for reasons which are not apparent, only eight of the projected twenty-eight trees were planted, four on each side of the avenue at its western end, although prepara-tions were made for planting all except the last three at the eastern end. Fifty-three tamarisks (*Tamarix articulata*) flanked the sycomores in four rows of eight on the northern side of the avenue and in three rows of seven on the southern side. Two more tamarisks were planted beyond the westernmost sycomores by the ramp, which sloped up-wards from the court to the top of the terrace (fig. 43*a*; Plate 46).

Owing to the rocky character of the ground, it was necessary to make special preparations for the cultivation of the trees. Twenty-five circular pits were sunk to a depth of 30 feet for the sycomores, each pit measuring 18 feet across at its mouth and tapering inwards from top to bottom. Spiral steps were cut in the rock walls so that the workmen could go up and down without difficulty. The eight pits in which the sycomores were planted were filled with a mixture of Nile mud and sand. Near the top of the filling, sycomore poles, about 6 inches thick and 6 feet in length, were laid horizontally a few inches apart, but the purpose of this device is obscure; perhaps it was intended to prevent movement of the earth around the roots during irrigation. They must have been put there before they had dried, because they had sprouted and the shoots had been cut off. The seventeen pits which were dug but not used were re-filled with *tafl*. The pits for the tamarisks were much smaller than those for the sycomores. They measured only about 5 feet across and were not much more than about 4 feet deep. If a pit which Winlock cleared was typical of the rest, the filling of these pits consisted of broken mud-brick to a depth of 20 inches laid on a thick bed of *tafl*. Since large stumps of trees of both kinds have survived, it is evident that the trees grew and flourished for many years.

Broken sandstone statues of the king were found by Winlock in or near twelve of the pits for sycomores. From that discovery he concluded that statues had been placed under the trees in order to be shaded from the rays of the sun. Arnold, however, has expressed the view that the statues lined the avenue as far as the last two trees; further on they would have been concealed from view by the walls of the ramp.

The terrace, which was partly hewn out of rock and partly composed of masonry-filling, resembled an inverted T in shape, the crosspiece lying adjacent to the forecourt, and the stem being cut back into the face of the cliff. On the cross-piece stood a square building faced externally on all sides except the west by colonnades. Painted reliefs, of which only fragments have been preserved, adorned both the interior and exterior of its four walls. At its centre, spread over an area about 73 feet square, lay the ruins of a large edifice which had neither chambers nor corridors. Its inner core consisted of rubble enclosed within a revetment of heavy flint boulders and two outer layers of limestone casing no more than about 4 feet in thickness. When complete, it probably rose to a height of at least 30 feet, of which the uppermost 20 feet at least are now missing. Naville and Hall thought it was a monumental pedestal on which a pyramid had stood (fig. 43*a*). They suggested that some bricks which were lying at the top of the ramp from the forecourt had come from the core of the pyramid and that two fragments of slabs of alabaster, which were found in a pile of rubbish in the south-west corner of the temple, were relics of the pyramid's outer casing. Winlock also believed that the edifice was a pedestal which had supported a pyramid, but he did not agree that the alabaster fragments had belonged to its casing.

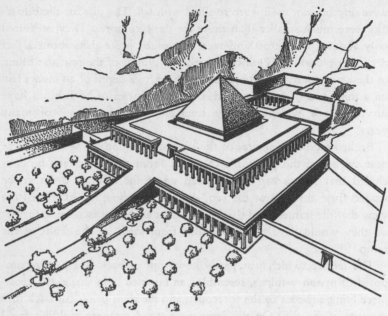

Figure 43a. The funerary temple of Neb-hepet-Rē Mentuhotep
– a reconstruction after E. Naville

Naville and Hall were greatly influenced by the report of the Ramesside commission in the Abbott Papyrus, which stated that the 'pyramid' of Neb-hepet-Rē had been found intact. There was no other known tomb of the king to which it could refer and they thought it resembled a type of funerary monument which was depicted in the Book of the Dead. Their reconstruction of the pyramid and pedestal remained unchallenged for more than half a century, but it has now been superseded by another explanation.

After his exhaustive survey of the temple, Dieter Arnold expressed the opinion that the loose filling and almost vertical walls of the so-called pedestal could not have withstood the outward pressure caused by the weight of a pyramid. Moreover, the tomb of Intef II at El-Tarif had also been described in the Abbott Papyrus by the same word as the term used to describe this tomb, but it had no pyramid and consequently there was nothing in the verbal description which implied

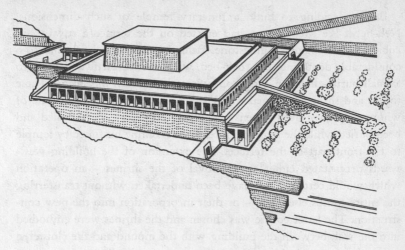

Figure 43b. The funerary temple of Neb-hepet-Rē Mentuhotep
– a reconstruction by D. Arnold

that the tomb of Neb-hepet-Rē embodied a pyramid. The word which in the Old Kingdom had been used with the meaning of 'pyramid' had acquired a wider significance by Ramesside times; it could mean royal funerary edifices in general, whether or not they were pyramidal. What had been accepted as a pedestal was in reality, Arnold believed, a representation of the primordial mound which had long been regarded as a powerful magical symbol (fig. 43b).

Between the mound-like structure and the walls of the building in which it stood was an ambulatory, the flat roof of which was supported by rows of octagonal columns, three rows on the north, south and east, and two rows on the west side. Farther west, on the narrow part of the terrace, were situated a cloistered court and a hypostyle hall. With its eighty octagonal columns, it is the earliest example of a large hypostyle hall now known; the small hypostyle hall in the valley building of Pepi II was merely an architectural development from the portico found in earlier pyramids. Inside the hall was a small chapel which housed an altar and a statue of the king placed in a niche carved in the face of the cliff.

Before deciding to build a funerary temple of such dimensions, Neb-hepet-Rē Mentuhotep had erected on the terrace a row of six cubical shrines made of limestone. Behind each shrine, and sunk to a considerable depth into the rock-bed, was a vertical shaft which led to a small burial-chamber lying approximately beneath the shrine. These tombs and shrines belonged to six ladies of the royal family, some of whom may have been queens and others princesses; all had died and been buried while the king still intended to confine his funerary temple to the front part of the terrace. The extension of the building westwards necessitated either the removal of the shrines – an operation which would certainly not have been undertaken without transferring the entire tombs elsewhere – or their incorporation into the new construction. The latter course was chosen and the shrines were embodied into the wall between the building with the mound and the cloistered court, three on each side of the doorway connecting these two parts of the temple. It was not an ideal solution because most of the reliefs decorating the exterior of the shrines were covered by the new wall, but, to the minds of the Egyptians, the existence of the reliefs was the first consideration; whether they were visible or invisible was less important. No disturbance of the tombs lying beneath the shrines was entailed by the extension of the temple; they had indeed gained in security, since the mouths of four out of the six shafts were now concealed beneath the paving, walls, or pillars of the cloistered court, while the two remaining shafts were also covered by a newly laid pavement. It must have been mainly due to the added protection and concealment thus afforded that all except two of these tombs had escaped being robbed more than once. Of their contents, the most valuable discoveries were undoubtedly the limestone outer sarcophagi of two of the queens named Kawit and Ashayet, both of which were decorated on their outer surfaces with beautifully carved reliefs. Among the scenes represented were incidents in the daily life of the queens, such as the performance of their toilet by a maid, drinking milk from cows which were shown accompanied by their calves, visiting a royal farm where peasants were engaged in filling the granaries with corn, and preparations for a banquet. Somewhat similar scenes were painted also on the interior of Ashayet's sarcophagus; but a band of painted inscription was the only decoration inside the sarcophagus of Kawit.

Neb-hepet-Rē Mentuhotep constructed within his temple enclosure two tombs, one of which is generally known as the Bab el-Husan, 'Door of the Horse'. Its entrance lies at the bottom of a large pit sunk in the floor of the forecourt. From the entrance, a passage was tunnelled for a distance of 155 yards through the subterranean rock to a point directly beneath the mound, where it terminates in a spacious chamber which, though it had never been opened before its excavation by Howard Carter in 1900, was found to contain nothing except the remains of offerings, some wooden implements and cord, a seated statue of the king wrapped in fine linen, and an empty wooden coffin. Under this chamber and connected with it by a vertical shaft was another room which yielded only a few pots and three roughly made wooden boats. To account for the existence of this tomb, it has been conjectured that it was a cenotaph used for a mock burial ceremony in the course of the *heb-sed*, which the king probably celebrated in the thirty-ninth year of his reign. Such an explanation would find support not only in the presence of the seated statue instead of the body of the king, but also in the attire of this statue, which represented the king wearing a short tunic which resembles the *heb-sed* garment, although it lacks the normal type of collar.

Another possibility is that the Bab el-Husan was the 'tomb' of the king as Osiris. A grove was a regular feature of tombs of Osiris and the trees in the forecourt may have been intended to fulfil that need; some of them were directly above the long entrance corridor. The location of the tomb under the mound may also be significant because the mound, although Heliopolitan in origin, had been adopted by the cult of Osiris as a magical symbol for both creation and renewal of life. Dieter Arnold has suggested that the shaft leading downwards from the upper chamber constituted a symbolical link with the Nile, which was such an important element in the Osirian creed. The model boats in the lower chamber may have been intended for the king to make his pilgrimage to Abydos.

If the Bab el-Husan was not a cenotaph of some kind, it may have been the original tomb which was constructed for the king before the plan of the temple had been changed. In that case it would probably belong to the same stage in the evolution of the building as the six tombs and shrines of the royal ladies. The real tomb lay at the end of a tunnel even longer than that of the cenotaph. Starting in the cloistered court, it descended in a straight line under the hypostyle hall to a burial-chamber situated far beneath the cliff. This chamber, which was lined with granite, contained a shrine made of alabaster and granite, within which, it must be supposed, a painted wooden coffin holding the mummy of the king was placed. When it was opened by the excavators, the only objects discovered in the chamber, apart from the shrine, were two small boats, some broken sceptres, canes, and bows. Neither the mummy nor the coffin was found.

While the tombs of the kings Intef I–III and the mortuary temple of Neb-hepet-Rē Mentuhotep were believed to include pyramids, they could, by a stretch of the imagination, be considered as links in the long chain of pyramid history. Arnold's discoveries have, however, shown that the earlier Egyptologists were mistaken in their architectural reconstructions and that, in reality, none of those monuments embodied a pyramid. The kings of the XIth Dynasty were Upper Egyptians, whose ideas of the nature of the after-life differed from those of their Memphite predecessors and also of their successors in the XIIth Dynasty. Whereas, in the Memphite pyramids and the buildings associated with them, the main intention had been to perpetuate, in his after-life, the concept of the dominant position which the king had occupied in this life, in the temple of Deir el-Bahri the king was represented as leading his after-life in company with the gods whose cults were celebrated in the temple.

Inscriptions on foundation-deposit tablets show that the temple was dedicated to Mentu-Rē, who was the Upper Egyptian counterpart of Rē-Harakhte in Heliopolis and Lower Egypt. In one respect alone does the temple of Deir el-Bahri reveal substantial borrowing from the Memphite temples, namely in the subjects chosen for representation in relief on its walls. Familiar scenes, such as the king as a sphinx trampling on his enemies, the hippopotamus hunt, fowling, fishing, sowing and reaping, were all depicted, with many others, in low relief and painted in bright colours. In view of what is now believed to be the character of the edifice in the centre of the front terrace, it is probably not by chance that scenes of processions of boats and of other aquatic activities were located at the base of the edifice – on the back wall of the colonnade – thereby suggesting to the mind the waters of chaos from which the primordial mound had risen.

No exact replica of the funerary temple of Neb-hepet-Rē Mentuhotep was ever built. His successor, Seankh-ka-Rē Mentuhotep, began to prepare a site for a similar building not far south of Deir el-Bahri, but, having ascended the throne at a ripe age, he died before the preparations for its construction had advanced beyond the initial stages, and further work was abandoned. Five hundred years later, however, a famous queen of the XVIIIth Dynasty named Hatshepsut instructed her architect, Senenmut, to build for her a mortuary temple embodying the chief architectural features of the temple of Neb-hepet-Rē Mentuhotep. In fulfilment of her command, Senenmut designed the larger and more magnificent terraced temple which stands on the north side of the ruins of Mentuhotep's building and which has justly become one of the most celebrated monuments of Egypt.

Very soon after the death of Seankh-ka-Rē Mentuhotep, the country was once again in confusion. Another Mentuhotep, who bore the name Neb-tawi-Rē, occupied the throne for part of the seven years which elapsed before order was restored, but, for reasons which are still obscure, later records do not credit him with having been a legitimate ruler. His successor was his Vizier and Commander-in-Chief Amenemhat, now generally called Ammenemes, the Greek form of his name, who thus became the founder of the XIIth Dynasty – a dynasty composed of four kings named Ammenemes, three kings named Sesostris and a queen named Sebek-neferu. It was one of the greatest dynasties in Egypt's history. The name of the founder, which means literally 'Amun-is-at-the-head', shows that he was born in Thebes where the god Amun was already established; his forebears, however, may have lived in El-Eshmunein, the earlier home of this god. He did not follow the example of the kings of the XIth Dynasty by making Thebes his capital, but, profiting from their experience and perhaps from his knowledge of the difficulty which they had found in maintaining control over Lower Egypt from such a distance, he transferred his seat of government northwards and established it at a place called It-tawi, 'Seizer of the Two Lands'. The exact location of It-tawi has not been determined with certainty, but it must have been situated in the vicinity of Lisht, where the tombs of both Ammenemes I and Sesostris I, his successor, have been found.

Influenced by the funerary monuments of the Old Kingdom, some of which could be seen from Lisht, Ammenemes I constructed his tomb on a plan conforming in its main features with the standard pyramid complex. In two respects, however, it resembled the mortuary temple of Neb-hepet-Rē Mentuhotep at Deir el-Bahri: its causeway was not roofed and it was erected on rising ground with its buildings on two different levels. On the upper terrace stood the pyramid, surrounded by a stone wall. West of the pyramid, also on the terrace but outside the stone wall, lay a row of tombs belonging to members of the royal family, all of which were found, when excavated in 1920 by an expedition of the Metropolitan Museum, to have been robbed in antiquity of their entire contents. On the lower and smaller terrace east of the pyramid stood a mortuary temple, near which, to the north and south, were the tombs of a few particularly favoured courtiers. Both the terraces and the adjacent tombs were enclosed by a rectangular wall of brick. Outside this wall lay a cemetery containing the mastabas of about a hundred nobles and officials.

When constructing the inner core of his pyramid and the walls of the mortuary temple, Ammenemes I employed a large number of limestone blocks taken from the Old Kingdom tombs at Dahshur, Saqqara and Giza. Many of these blocks had been decorated with reliefs or inscribed with texts and, since it is likely that the buildings to which they originally belonged were already falling into ruin when the blocks were removed, their re-use has preserved a number of interesting fragments of sculpture which might otherwise have been lost. In consequence, however, of the complete desolation to which this pyramid and its complex had been reduced by the time of their excavation, it was sometimes difficult to distinguish the re-used Old Kingdom blocks from those which had been prepared in the XIIth Dynasty for the decoration of this temple. The difference in style, which might have been expected between reliefs of the two periods, was not always very marked, because Ammenemes I deliberately reproduced some of the technical characteristics of Old Kingdom reliefs and occasionally made actual facsimiles of scenes from Old Kingdom tombs.

The entrance to this pyramid occupied its normal position on ground-level in the middle of the north face. In front stood an offering-chapel of the kind found as early as the Bent Pyramid and subsequently in the pyramids of Djedkarē Isesi, Teti, Pepi I, Merenrē and Pepi II, with a red granite false door, 11 feet 6 inches in height, built into the back wall. Behind the false door lay a granite-lined corridor leading towards the burial-chamber. Enormous plugs of granite were used for blocking this corridor after the king's funeral. Very little is known about the internal arrangement of the pyramid apart from the corridor because, owing to a considerable rise in the level of the Nile bed, the burial-chamber, which lies at the bottom of a vertical shaft, is now permanently flooded and the seepage of water is so rapid that all efforts to reach it have hitherto failed.

Sesostris I built his pyramid at a distance of about a mile to the south of the pyramid of his predecessor. Its ownership was first determined in 1882 by Sir Gaston Maspero, who found some fragments of alabaster objects bearing the name of Sesostris I inside the pyramid. Twelve years later, J.-E. Gautier and Gustave Jéquier excavated a considerable part of the site, and the remainder, together with the surrounding cemetery, was cleared by successive expeditions of the Metropolitan Museum, working intermittently from 1906 to 1934 under the direction of A.M. Lythgoe, A.C. Mace, and Ambrose Lansing. Fundamentally, it resembled closely the complex of Ammenemes I. Whereas only the general outline of the latter can be ascertained with certainty, however, the greater part of the original plan of Sesostris I's complex has been established, and the extent to which its mortuary temple was copied from the mortuary temples of the VIth Dynasty, as illustrated by that of Pepi II, is clearly evident (fig. 44).

A corridor with a flat roof, 8 feet wide, built on top of the causeway, linked the valley building - scarcely a trace of which was discovered - with the entrance hall of the mortuary temple. Above a dado stippled red and black in imitation of granite, the limestone walls were decorated with scenes of a conventional kind. At intervals of about 33 feet on both sides of the corridor were statues of the king represented as the god Osiris, each one standing in a recess. Similar statues, six of which were discovered in a pit near the pyramid, originally stood against the walls of the entrance hall (fig. 44: 1), thus emphasizing that

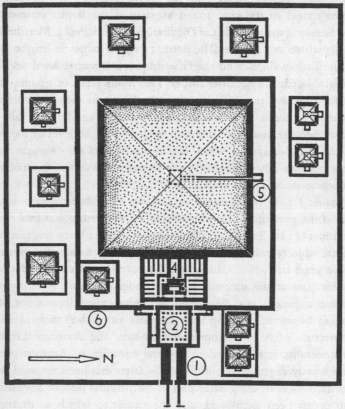

Figure 44. The pyramid enclosure of Sesostris I

this apartment was essentially a continuation of the corridor on the causeway. In the cloistered court (fig. 44: 2) there were also statues of the king, probably one against each of the twenty-four rectangular pillars supporting the roof of the ambulatory. Ten of the number, made of the finest Tura limestone, were found by Gautier and Jéquier lying side by side in a pit where they had been concealed in antiquity, like the Osiride figures, by someone who was anxious to preserve them from impending destruction. Although displaying slight differences in facial expression, they are really duplicates, each statue being a life-size representation of the king seated on his throne and wearing the customary regal attire (Plate 47). Other statues, no doubt representing the king standing, were placed behind the wooden doors of the five niches within the inner temple (fig. 44: 3). The remainder of the inner temple contained only the usual magazines, antechambers, and the sanctuary (fig. 44: 4); no serdab for a further group of statues seems to have been constructed in the masonry between the niches and the sanctuary.

Two remarkable wooden figures, each nearly 2 feet in height, were found in 1914, by the expedition of the Metropolitan Museum, concealed in a small chamber which had been constructed in the thickness of the enclosure wall of a mastaba lying north of the causeway and near to the east wall of the pyramid enclosure. The mastaba belonged to a high official named Imhotep, who, like his famous namesake, was high priest of Heliopolis.

Until recently the figures were regarded as contemporary portraits of Sesostris I, but if that were the case it would be hard to understand why they were not placed in the pyramid with the king's funerary equipment. Stylistically they resemble sculpture dating from the end of the XIIth Dynasty and the beginning of the XIIIth Dynasty. Perhaps they were cult-figures which had been used in the funeral of Imhotep, whose mastaba probably dates from about that time. Both the figures consist of sixteen pieces of cedar wood carefully joined. It can hardly be by chance that the number of pieces is the same in both figures and that it corresponds with the number of pieces into which, according to one version of the legend, Seth cut the body of Osiris. In each instance the figure is clad in a short kilt and in the left hand it holds a long sceptre in the shape of a shepherd's crook. The only significant difference between them is the white crown of Upper Egypt worn by one and the red crown of Lower Egypt worn by the other figure.

A wooden shrine placed in the same chamber as the figures contained the fetish of the god Anubis – a skin of a headless animal wrapped like a mummy and suspended on a rod mounted in an alabaster jar of ointment.

The arrangement of the enclosure walls in this complex was almost identical with the plan of the walls in the complex of Ammenemes I. An inner wall of stone, decorated at regular intervals with panels, about 14 feet in height, and inscribed with the king's names (Plate 48), enclosed the pyramid, the inner apartments of the mortuary temple and the subsidiary pyramid (fig. 44: 6). Between this wall and a mud-brick outer wall lay a wide court in which were situated the cloistered court and the entrance hall of the mortuary temple and nine small pyramids belonging to female members of the royal family. Both in its plan and in its decoration the mortuary temple was a copy of the temples of the VIth Dynasty. Inscriptions found in the easternmost small pyramid in the southern row and in its immediate neighbour to the west enabled their owners to be identified respectively as the principal queen, Neferu, and a princess named Itakayt. Each of these nine pyramids was provided with its own miniature mortuary temple, offering-chapel, and enclosure wall. Beneath the floor of the offering-chapel, a shaft was sunk vertically downwards to a considerable depth. A second shaft of the same kind was constructed, usually at a short distance to the east of the first, and was connected with it by a subterranean passage. It is not easy to account for the presence of the second shaft, but it may have been intended to enable the sarcophagus to be introduced at a stage in the construction of the tomb when the small offering-chapel had already been built. The body and probably the wooden inner coffin would be lowered down the first shaft and thence conveyed to the burial-chamber by way of a corridor which was subsequently blocked at intervals by portcullises sliding to the side.

In the burial-chamber of one of the small pyramids lying at the western end of the southern row, the excavators of the Metropolitan Museum found a fine, but empty, quartzite sarcophagus. So closely did it fit the chamber that the ancient plunderers, when searching for hidden treasure, had been compelled to break through its sides and floor in order to reach the walls of the chamber; their destructive work, however, appears to have yielded no reward. A Canopic chest, composed of the same material as the sarcophagus and made with equal care, lay in a niche in the south-east corner of the burial-chamber. Neither the sarcophagus nor the Canopic chest bore any inscription by which the name or title of the royal owner could be identified.

The king's pyramid occupied an area approximately 352 feet square and rose to a height of about 200 feet. Its superstructure consisted of a framework of eight massive stone walls radiating from the centre outwards to the four corners and to the middle of each side. The eight compartments so formed were further divided into two sections of unequal size by walls built parallel to the sides and about half-way between them and the centre. These sixteen compartments were filled with rough pieces of limestone laid in white sand, the whole mass being held together by a heavy casing of well-cut blocks of Tura limestone. The entrance was not in the face of the superstructure, but under the paving of the offering-chapel (fig. 44: 5). From there a corridor, which measured only 3 feet 1 inch square in section, sloped downwards in the direction of the burial-chamber. For a distance of about 36 feet it was lined with slabs of carefully dressed limestone, but beyond that point the lining was composed of granite. Although the body and the inner coffin were probably taken to the burial-chamber by way of this corridor, it seems unlikely, in view of its small dimensions, that the outer sarcophagus was similarly conveyed. Perhaps it was taken by a separate shaft which may still lie concealed beneath the ruins of the superstructure. Nothing is known about the burial-chamber, which, like its counterpart in the pyramid of Ammenemes I, is now under water.

Three of the four successors of Sesostris I built pyramid complexes at Dahshur, on the edge of the cultivation east of the two pyramids built during the Old Kingdom. The earliest of these complexes, which belonged to Ammenemes II, embodied no important innovations in design or in method of construction. It acquired, however, a particular distinction at the end of the last century as the provenance of part of the so-called Dahshur treasure – a remarkable collection of jewellery and personal accoutrements discovered by J. de Morgan and now preserved in the Cairo Museum. The owners of this part of the treasure were two princesses named Khnumet and Ita, whose graves were among a group of royal tombs lying close to the king's pyramid on the west side. In technical skill and artistic taste the whole treasure demonstrates the work of the Egyptian goldsmith and lapidary at the highest stage of its development.

Sesostris II, who succeeded Ammenemes II, discarded the most persistent of all the conventions of pyramid architecture, namely the location of the entrance on the north side. The supposed advantages of an entrance corridor oriented towards the circumpolar stars must therefore have counted for less in his eyes than the increased security likely to result from an approach starting in a more unexpected quarter. It certainly added to the difficulties of the archaeologist, for Petrie, who excavated his pyramid – situated at Illahun on the edge of the Faiyum – worked for some months in 1887-8 without being able to find a way inside. After a considerable expenditure of time and labour in the following year, he succeeded in discovering to the south of the pyramid a shaft which descended vertically to a passage tunnelled at a depth of 40 feet below the ground and leading by a devious course to a burial-chamber built entirely of granite. Subsequently he found, still further south, a second and larger shaft which also descended to the passage. By this shaft, as Petrie observed, the magnificent red granite sarcophagus found in the burial-chamber must have been lowered to the passage, because the first shaft was about 1 foot 7 inches narrower than the width of the sarcophagus. Commenting on the workmanship of this sarcophagus, Petrie declared that it was one of the finest pieces of mechanical work ever executed in such hard and difficult material. The parallelism, according to his calculations, was almost perfect, and the errors in regularity amounted to no more than one-hundredth of an inch in a cubit. Apart from the sarcophagus, the chamber contained an offering-table made of alabaster.

In its superstructure also, the pyramid of Sesostris II differed in many respects from its predecessors. To a height of 40 feet from the ground, the inner core consisted of a knoll of rock; above that level, in place of rock, there was a framework of retaining walls with the intervening spaces filled with mud-bricks. This core was cased in the normal manner with blocks of fine limestone, the lowest course being embedded in the rock foundation to counter the outward thrust of the structure. Around the base on each side lay a shallow trench filled with sand, the purpose of which was to absorb rain-water flowing off the face of the pyramid. Such a trench, Petrie estimated, could easily hold the volume of water resulting from the heaviest downpour likely to occur in Egypt. The pyramid was surrounded by a panelled wall, partly made of rock faced with stone and partly stone-built, and by an outer brick wall. At the north-east corner of the pyramid, outside the stone wall, there was a subsidiary pyramid, perhaps for a queen. Beyond the outer wall was a single row of trees planted in pits which had been sunk in the rock and filled with earth.

Between the two enclosure walls on the south side of the pyramid lay four shaft-tombs made for members of the royal family. When excavating the easternmost of these tombs in 1913, Petrie and his assistant, Guy Brunton, discovered a collection of jewellery and personal possessions belonging to a princess named Sat-Hathor-Iunut, the owner of the tomb. It was a collection which rivalled in every respect that previously found at Dahshur. Among the most important pieces were a magnificent gold diadem, two gold pectorals inlaid with glass and precious stones, one bearing the name of Sesostris II and the other the name of Ammenemes III, necklaces consisting of beads made of gold, amethyst, carnelian, lapis lazuli and feldspar, a gold collar composed of beads in the shape of double lion heads, bead girdles of gold and precious stones, bracelets and rings. Toilet objects included razors with copper blades and gold handles, alabaster vases for unguents and cosmetics, other vases designed for the same purpose but made of polished obsidian partly overlaid with gold, and a silver mirror with a handle of obsidian and gold. The whole collection had originally been placed in three ebony caskets, at least one of which was inlaid with gold, ivory, carnelian, and blue faience. All these objects, with the exception of a small number retained by the Cairo Museum, are now in the Metropolitan Museum of Art, New York.

Sesostris III and Ammenemes III, whose pyramids at Dahshur lie to the north and south respectively of the pyramid of Ammenemes II, followed the example set by Sesostris II, both in the employment of brick for the inner core of the superstructure and in the elaboration of the substructure into a kind of maze of chambers and corridors. In the same way also the entrance to the substructure was not placed on the north side, but at a point which could only be discovered either by chance or by exhaustive search, with the result that J. de Morgan, when excavating these pyramids in 1894-5, spent many months of fruitless labour before finding a way to the burial-chamber. Ultimately he located the entrance to Sesostris III's pyramid in the court on the west side of the building, and the entrance to the pyramid of Ammenemes III near the southern corner of the east face. In spite of this subterfuge, the architects of the pyramids had failed to defeat the ancient plunderer, and de Morgan reaped only a meagre reward for his efforts. He was, however, more fortunate when excavating the tombs of the royal family on the north side of each pyramid, finding in the tombs of the princesses Sat-Hathor and Merit (in the enclosure of Sesostris III) and in the tomb of yet another princess (in the enclosure of Ammenemes III) jewellery of the same character as the treasure buried with the princesses of Ammenemes II and Sesostris II (Plates 49, 50). Like the earlier treasures also, this jewellery had not been laid on the mummies of the princesses, but had been concealed in a separate place within the tomb - a fact which has given rise to the theory that a different, and possibly inferior, set of jewellery was prepared specifically for each mummy, while the jewellery found consisted of the objects actually worn by the princesses in their lifetime. Another interesting discovery by de Morgan, south of the enclosure wall of the pyramid of Sesostris III, was an underground chamber containing two wooden boats. No emblems of a solar nature were buried with the boats and consequently it seems more likely that they were used to convey the body of the king and some of his personal possessions to the pyramid than that they were intended to represent the day and night barques of the sun-god.

Two features in the pyramid enclosure of Sesostris III immediately strike the eye: first, its size - it covers about $14\frac{1}{2}$ acres and was, at the time it was constructed, the largest of the XIIth Dynasty complexes, although the pyramid itself is only about 350 feet square at the base - and secondly its orientation, with the longer axis from north to south. It conforms, therefore, with the orientation of the step pyramid enclosures of Zoser and Sekhemkhet, in contrast with the normal orientation of true pyramids, whose longer axis is directed from east to west.

In a number of other respects too the enclosure resembles Zoser's, notably in the design of the part of the outer face of the enclosure wall which de Morgan excavated and in having its main entrance located at the south corner of the east wall. Inside the entrance is a large paved court which corresponds with Zoser's south court. Until the site has been systematically explored, it will remain uncertain whether some brick-rubble and limestone chips near the south wall are the relics of a south tomb, but it seems a possibility. The pyramid itself resembles Zoser's in being asymmetrically located north of the centre of the enclosure. Even the decoration of the king's sarcophagus was copied from the design of the outer face of the enclosure wall of the Step Pyramid. The arrangement and number of the monumental gateways were the same as in the Step Pyramid, apart from the one which took the place of the actual entrance to Zoser's complex. Similar sarcophagi were placed in the Illahun pyramid and in the Dahshur pyramid of Ammenemes III.

Looking at the pyramid of Ammenemes III in its present eroded condition, it is difficult to imagine that it was once, like its western neighbour, a 'bent' pyramid with its upper part inclining at an angle of $55°$ and its lower part at $59°$ (Plate 51). Very probably the reason for altering the slope was the discovery, in the course of construction, that subsidences were taking place. Although the chambers and corridors were about 40 feet below ground, the thick limestone blocks which lined their walls, and on which their roof-blocks rested, had, in places, sunk 4 inches owing to pressure from the weight of the pyramid. Both de Morgan, at the end of the last century, and Arnold, who has directed the explorations of the German Archaeological Institute in Cairo at the pyramid since 1976, not only found it necessary to clear the corridors of fallen stones and rubble, but also to underpin the roofs before they could proceed with their work.

De Morgan, after discovering the entrance to the pyramid at the southern end of the east side (fig. 45: 1), proceeded to explore a corridor which ran westwards from the bottom of the entrance stairway before turning north. Of the fifteen rooms to which it gave access, not one had been used. One, however, was intended to be the king's burial-chamber (fig. 45: 2). Within it lay a fine red granite sarcophagus with a vaulted lid, a woven reed-mat decoration on the edges of its sides and ends, and a replica of the outer face of the Step Pyramid enclosure wall carved in bold relief at the base as a kind of skirting (Plate 52). Imitations of the fourteen larger bastions with representations of double doors were located in the same relative positions as in the Step Pyramid and the actual doorway to the enclosure in the

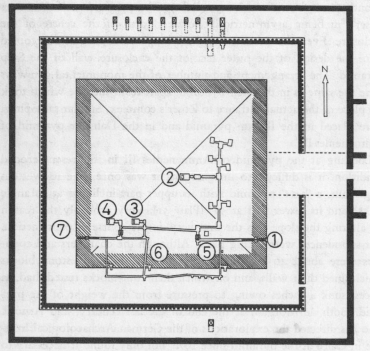

Figure 45. Plan of the pyramid of Ammenemes III at Dashur

south-east corner was reproduced distinctively by carving it so that it stood out beyond the line of the rest of the wall.

Arnold directed his exploratory work first towards the west, along a corridor which de Morgan had cleared, without, however, removing the blocking from the rooms connected with it. In two of these rooms Arnold found the bones of queens in granite sarcophagi. The first

queen, who died at the age of about twenty-five, could not be identified by name (fig. 45: 3). She had been robbed of all her funerary
equipment, apart from a few objects, which the thieves had overlooked, including an obsidian vase with gold bands, three alabaster
boxes in the shape of trussed ducks which contained meat and bones,
maceheads of granite and alabaster and some fragments of jewellery.
The queen in the second chamber, who died when she was about
thirty-five, was named Aat (fig. 45: 4). Her sarcophagus resembled that
of the king. Among the objects buried with her, which the thieves had
missed, were two maceheads, one made of rock-crystal and the other
of limestone, seven alabaster duck-boxes filled with meat and bones,
an alabaster unguent-jar and some relics of pieces of jewellery. In
addition, the queen's limestone Canopic chest, broken but reparable,
and one of her alabaster Canopic jars were also found. Not far from
the chamber of the first queen, some fragments of wood from a Canopic chest and some human-headed jars of the same material were
discovered. They were uninscribed and their owner could not be identified, but they probably belonged to the burial equipment of a third
queen. The evidence now available indicates that at least five members
of the royal family were buried in the pyramid.

After completing the clearance of these rooms, Arnold explored a
corridor which ran southwards from its mouth at a short distance
beyond the bottom of the entrance staircase (fig. 45: 5). Tunnelled at
a greater depth, it led to a series of small chambers, the first of which
was completely walled up. All the other chambers were filled with
bricks and their shrine-shaped entrances were blocked with slabs of
limestone. The eighth chamber, which stood on its own almost under
the centre of the south face of the pyramid (fig. 45: 6), contained two
objects: a very fine alabaster Canopic chest, with four cavities instead
of jars to hold the viscera, and an inlaid shrine with an elaborate
locking system, the whole of which had been smashed to pieces. Some
traces of a black substance in the cavities of the Canopic chest showed
that it had been used. The purpose of this room is still uncertain, but
Arnold has pointed out that it occupies a position suggestive of the
south tombs in the step pyramids of Zoser and Sekhemkhet.

One of the many interesting features of this pyramid is the existence within it of the tombs of members of the royal family. The last pyramid which included such tombs was Zoser's Step Pyramid, under the east side of which lay eleven tombs for the king's close relations. The tombs in the pyramid of Ammenemes III were part of the original plan; they were not an after-thought when the king decided to build a second pyramid for himself. They were linked by corridors with the king's burial-chamber, but they also had an entrance of their own at the southern end of the west side of the pyramid (fig. 45: 7).

The pyramid lay within an inner brick enclosure wall designed with alternate projections and recesses like the stone enclosure wall of Sesostris II's pyramid. Between the northern section of the wall and the pyramid lay ten shaft-tombs, only two of which had been occupied – the easternmost by a king of the XIIIth Dynasty named Hor and its immediate neighbour by a princess named Nubheteptikhred. A mortuary temple, of which only traces have survived, lay on the east side of the pyramid and from it ran an unroofed causeway, 20 yards wide, to the valley building. Between the pyramid and the wall on the south side there was a single tomb, which had been robbed before de Morgan discovered it, and nothing on the west side.

Reigning for at least forty-six years, Ammenemes III ranks as one of the outstanding monarchs of Egyptian history. His fame rests not on military achievements or administrative prowess – though a more complete knowledge of the political and social conditions of his time might well reveal that in these respects also he deserved recognition from posterity – but on the works of art and monumental constructions, including two pyramids, with which his name has been associated. Undoubtedly, the surviving portraits of this king are among the finest pieces of sculpture ever produced by the ancient Egyptians; they mark the culmination of the renascence in the arts which originated in the time of Neb-hepet-Rē Mentuhotep and continued to develop without noticeable interruption until the end of the XIIth Dynasty. But long before excavation had brought to light any of these sculptural masterpieces, Ammenemes III had been immortalized by the classical historians as the constructor of Lake Moeris in the Faiyum and as the builder of a labyrinth in the neighbourhood of the lake, which was considered to bear comparison with the older labyrinth of Minos at Knossos in Crete. Diodorus, who visited Egypt in the middle of the first century before the Christian era, describes the lake in the following terms:

Moeris ... dug a lake of remarkable usefulness, though at the cost of incredible toil. Its circumference, they say, is 3,600 stades, its depth at most points fifty fathoms. Who, then, on estimating the greatness of the construction, would not reasonably ask how many tens of thousands of men must have been employed, and how many years they took to finish their work? No one can adequately commend the king's design, which brings such usefulness and advantage to all the dwellers in Egypt.

Since the Nile kept to no definite bounds in its rising, and the fruitfulness of the country depended upon the river's regularity, the king dug the lake to accommodate the superfluous water, so that the river should neither, with its strong current, flood the land unseasonably and form swamps and fens, nor, by rising less than was advantageous, damage the crops by lack of water. Between the river and the lake he constructed a canal 80 stades in length and 300 feet in breadth. Through this canal, at times he admitted the water of the river, at other times he excluded it, thus providing the farmers with water at fitting times by opening the inlet and again closing it scientifically and at great expense. No less than 50 talents had of necessity to be expended by anyone who wished to open or shut this sluice. The lake has continued to serve the needs of the Egyptians down to our own days, and it has its name from its constructor, being still called the Lake of Moeris.[1]

Although Ammenemes III may well have undertaken some irrigation or land reclamation schemes in the neighbourhood of this lake, Diodorus and the classical writers were probably mistaken in ascribing its actual creation to him, for it was almost certainly in existence before his time, and its name was undoubtedly derived not from his prenomen - possibly pronounced Nemare - which was known to the Greeks colloquially as Mares, but from a town on the lake called Mi-wer (possibly identical with the modern Ghurab) or from the canal linking the Nile with the lake, which was also called Mi-wer.

Happily, the connection of Ammenemes III with the labyrinth has been shown to have been based on a firmer foundation. As long ago

1. Diodorus Siculus, *The Historical Library*, Book I, LI and LII (W.G. Waddell's translation).

as 1843 its site at Hawara was identified and explored by Richard Lepsius, and Petrie made a further investigation in 1888-9. The destruction of the buildings had, however, been so thorough that it was difficult to recognize even the general plan of the enclosure. Such knowledge of architectural details as has been gained is largely due to the descriptions of classical writers, and in particular to Herodotus and Strabo, both of whom actually visited the labyrinth, but even their accounts are at variance in many respects. Strabo, who went to Egypt in the latter part of the first century B.C., wrote as follows:

We have here [besides Lake Moeris] also the labyrinth, a work equal to the pyramids, and adjoining to it the tomb of the king who constructed the labyrinth. After proceeding beyond the first entrance of the canal about 30 or 40 stadia, there is a table-shaped plain, with a village and a large palace composed of as many palaces as there were formerly *nomes*. There are an equal number of aulae, surrounded by pillars, and contiguous to one another, all in one line and forming one building, like a long wall having the aulae in front of it. The entrances into the aulae are opposite to the wall. In front of the entrances there are long and numerous covered ways, with winding passages communicating with each other, so that no stranger could find his way into the aulae or out of them without a guide. The [most] surprising circumstance is that the roofs of these dwellings consist of a single stone each, and that the covered ways through their whole range were roofed in the same manner with single slabs of stone of extraordinary size, without the intermixture of timber or of any other material. On ascending the roof - which is not of a great height, for it consists only of a single storey - there may be seen a stone-field, thus composed of stones. Descending again and looking into the aulae, these may be seen in a line supported by twenty-seven pillars, each consisting of a single stone. The walls also are constructed of stones not inferior in size to these. At the end of this building, which occupies more than a stadium, is the tomb, which is a quadrangular pyramid, each side of which is about four plethra in length and of equal height. The name of the person buried there is Imandes. They built, it is said, this number of aulae, because it was the custom for all the *nomes* to assemble there together according to their rank, with their own priests and priestesses, for the purpose of performing sacrifices and making offerings to the gods, and of administering justice in matters of great importance. Each of the *nomes* was conducted to the aula appointed for it.[2]

2. Strabo, *Geographica*, Book XVII, I, 37 (Bohn's Classical Library).

Petrie, in his report on his relatively fruitless investigation, wrote:

Almost every stone has long since been broken up and removed; but the extent of the area we can measure, as marked out by the immense bed of chips of fine white limestone which lies on the south of the pyramid. Wherever we dig down we find a bed of flat laid sand, or of beton made of chips of stone rammed down, on which to lay the pavement and walls of some enormous building, and over that lie thousands of tons of fragments of the destroyed walls; on tracing these signs to their limits it is found that they cover an area about 1,000 feet long and 800 feet broad.[3]

Arnold, however, estimated that the measurements were 1,264 feet long and 520 feet broad, but in either case the enclosure is the largest of the XIIth Dynasty pyramids. These measurements represent the area of the whole enclosure, including the ground at the northern end on which the pyramid stands. The dimensions of the labyrinth itself were about 585 feet in length and 520 feet in breadth.

In spite of the total destruction of the buildings, it is possible to see that their general lay-out bore some resemblance to that of Zoser's Step Pyramid at Saqqara. In both enclosures the main axis ran from north to south and the only entrance was at the southern end of the east wall. Inside each entrance lay an open forecourt. Herodotus says that the labyrinth had twelve roofed courts, six facing northwards and six facing southwards, while Strabo speaks of palaces which were equal in number to the *nomes* in former times. Both descriptions probably refer to *sed*-festival pavilions such as were built in Zoser's enclosure. In contrast with the lay-out of the Step Pyramid, the mortuary temple was not on the north side of the pyramid, but in the middle of the south side. Another difference was that the labyrinth had a valley building and a causeway, at least a quarter of a mile in length, neither of which seems to have been constructed for the step pyramids of Zoser and Sekhemkhet.

The superstructure of the pyramid, in keeping with the practice of its time, was composed mainly of mud-brick overlaid with a casing of limestone. In its substructure, the intricacies of design already embodied in its immediate precursors were further developed, with the result

3. W.M. Flinders Petrie, *Hawara, Biahmu, and Arsinoe*, p. 5.

that Petrie was able to force a way into its passages only after weeks of toil extending over two seasons. From the entrance, situated about 80 feet west of the middle of the south face, a flight of steps (fig. 46: 1) descended to a small chamber (fig. 46: 2), beyond which lay a short passage leading to a dead end. Concealed in the roof of this passage, however, was a block of stone twenty tons in weight which slid sideways, thus forming a trap-door through which access could be gained to a second chamber (fig. 46: 3) and to the passages lying beyond. One of these passages was intended solely to delude any plunderer who might succeed in penetrating past the first trap-door, for although it had been carefully blocked, it was blind. The other passage, which had been closed only by a wooden door, led by way of two

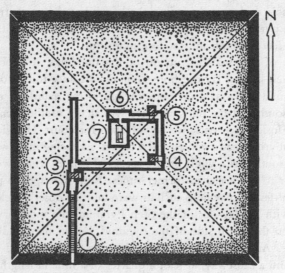

Figure 46. The pyramid of Ammenemes III at Hawara

right-angle turns and two further roof trap-doors (fig. 46: 4 and 5) – neither of which had been closed after the funeral – to a large antechamber (fig. 46: 6). At each end of the antechamber, a false well had been sunk into the floor and subsequently blocked with stone so that plunderers, labouring under the delusion that the entrance to the burial-chamber lay beneath, might be tricked into wasting time and effort in removing the filling. Another stratagem intended for the same purpose was the blocking of the entire northern half of the antechamber, although nothing but a solid wall was concealed behind.

An unexpected discovery in the antechamber was a small collection of alabaster objects, most of which bore the name of Ammenemes III's daughter Neferuptah. They consisted of an offering-table and some bowls shaped like halves of trussed ducks. The offering-table had representations of more than a hundred comestibles and vessels containing beverages carved in relief on its upper surface, their names being incised on them either individually or in groups. Hieroglyphic signs in the inscriptions on the table were mutilated, as in the Pyramid Texts, when they represented living creatures, birds being depicted without legs and reptiles without tails.

In order that the real way of approach to the burial-chamber (fig. 46: 7) should be intelligible, it is necessary first to describe the method by which this chamber was constructed. Before the superstructure was built, a large rectangular shaft was sunk into the rock at a point somewhat to the west of the centre of the area ultimately to be covered by the base of the pyramid. Into this shaft, after it had been lined with stone, the burial-chamber, composed of a single block of yellow quartzite and shaped like a box without a lid, was lowered. The length and breadth of this monolith, Petrie calculated, were about 22 feet and 8 feet respectively and the height was about 6 feet; its weight must have amounted to about 110 tons. Notwithstanding the hardness of the material, it was exquisitely cut and polished, while the inner corners were so sharp that, at first sight, Petrie supposed them to be jointed. The roof of the chamber consisted of three slabs of yellow quartzite lying side by side, each measuring about 4 feet in thickness (fig. 47: 1). These slabs did not rest directly on the walls of the monolith, but were laid on a course of stone blocks placed on top of the walls in order to heighten the ceiling of the room (fig. 47: 2). Above the burial-chamber were two relieving chambers, the lower with a flat roof (fig. 47: 3), and the upper with a pointed roof composed of limestone blocks, each weighing nearly 50 tons (fig. 47: 4). Lastly, an enormous arch of brick, 3 feet thick, was built over the pointed roof to support the core of the pyramid (fig. 47: 5).

Until the tomb had been finally closed, the roof-slab which lay nearest to the antechamber was propped up, leaving a gap between it and the course of blocks on which it was ultimately to rest. A cross-trench in the floor of the antechamber led directly to this gap. The king's mummy was therefore taken by way of this trench to the gap and then let down into the burial-chamber, where a large quartzite sarcophagus had already been placed in position before the roof-slabs were lowered into the shaft. A second, smaller sarcophagus, made of the same material and intended for the princess Neferuptah, had been

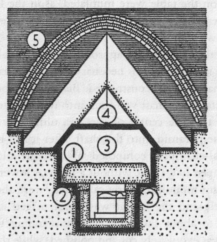

Figure 47. The burial-chamber of Ammenemes III at Hawara

built into the chamber, probably at the same time. Canopic chests, also made of quartzite, were included with the sarcophagi. After the funerary ceremonies had been completed, the raised roof-slab of the burial-chamber, weighing about forty-five tons, was lowered and the trench in the antechamber filled and covered with a pavement, so that no outward sign of its existence remained. In spite of all the precautions taken, however, this pyramid suffered the same fate as all its predecessors, and Petrie, when at length he succeeded in reaching the burial-chamber, found that all the movable objects had been plundered and the bodies, together with the wooden inner coffins, had been burnt.

In view of Petrie's discovery that there were two sarcophagi in the pyramid of Hawara, and particularly his statement that he had found 'bits of bone' within them, there appeared to be no reason to question that princess Neferuptah had been buried in the same chamber as her father, Ammenemes III. In 1956, however, two Egyptian archaeologists, Nagib Farag and Zaky Iskander, examined a site about 1¼ miles to the south-east of the pyramid of Hawara, where the exposed tops of seven massive limestone blocks could be seen lying edgewise side by side. Beneath the blocks they found a chamber, almost 17 feet in length, which had been hewn in the native rock; its walls and floor had been overlaid with limestone ashlars.

Much of the space inside the chamber was occupied by a red granite sarcophagus, which had a panel-work decoration at the base and a curved lid with rectangular ends. It is now in the Cairo Museum. Near the top of one side were carved two lines of inscription naming princess Neferuptah. At least it was clear that the sarcophagus had been made for her, but was it her tomb? There were several objects bearing her name in the chamber, the most outstanding being three handsome silver vases and a fine grey granite offering-table (a duplicate of the table found in the king's pyramid, but with no names on objects). When the water, which nearly filled the sarcophagus, had been pumped out, all that remained at the bottom was a sedimentary layer only about two inches thick. In addition to a substantial amount of jewellery and some gold leaf, it contained traces of decayed wood from two inner coffins, one rectangular and the other believed to be anthropoid, and some fragments of linen bandages to which minute particles of body-tissue had adhered and could be seen under a microscope.

Conditions in both the burial-chambers were similar, to the extent that, owing to changes in the water-table since antiquity, they were flooded each year at least for several months, and consequently not suitable for preserving organic material. In the case of the pyramid, it was not possible to remove the water while Petrie conducted his search, but it is difficult to imagine that he could have identified wrongly such objects as 'bones'. Microscopic identification of human tissue, when almost all other organic matter had completely decayed, is bound to arouse feelings of doubt in the mind. Nevertheless the fact that the sarcophagus contained a considerable number of amulets and other funerary accoutrements would seem to imply the existence of a body. The excavators explained the virtual disappearance of the body by assuming that, in the annual inundation, water entered the sarcophagus at the junction of the lid and the lower section; when the flood receded, some of the water came out bringing with it small quantities of decayed matter.

In order to account for a second tomb, it seems necessary to suppose that Ammenemes III died before Neferuptah, and that when she died it was decided not to undertake the difficult and laborious task of opening the Hawara pyramid. Ammenemes III had not constructed a second entrance for later burials at Hawara as he had done in the pyramid of Dahshur. If the decision to provide an independent tomb had been taken long before her death, arrangements would surely have been made to reach the burial-chamber from the outside and the way of approach would have been sealed after her funeral. In this tomb, however, once the roofing-blocks had been placed in position, access was impossible. Very little of the superstructure has survived, but it is evident that the brick core covered an area at least 115 feet square, to which must, in every probability, be added the thickness of a limestone casing.

While it is likely that structural weaknesses in his Dahshur pyramid played some part in Ammenemes III's decision to build a second pyramid, the architectural differences between the two complexes were radical enough to show that his ideas of sepulchral needs had undergone some fundamental changes in the course of his reign. The queens continued to be buried in the Dahshur pyramid and the king must still have regarded it as a place to which his spirit could return at will. Sesostris III may also have constructed, besides his pyramid at Dahshur, a cenotaph of mastaba form at Abydos, thus providing his soul with a second tomb, which it could occupy when so inclined, near the traditional tomb of Osiris. Religious motives could hardly have governed the choice of Hawara.

With the death of Ammenemes III, the Middle Kingdom virtually came to an end. A fourth Ammenemes and a queen named Sebekneferu (or Sebekneferurē) figure at the end of the XIIth Dynasty in the later historical records, but the evidence of contemporary inscriptions suggests that Ammenemes IV never reigned independently; he was probably co-regent with Ammenemes III – a position sometimes occupied by the heir apparent when the reigning king became advanced in years – and was deprived of his succession to the full title by premature death. Sebekneferu was subsequently appointed co-regent, and she may well have continued as the sole occupant of the throne for a short time after the demise of Ammenemes III. Neither Ammenemes IV nor Sebekneferu has left a pyramid which can be identified from written evidence, but E. Mackay, when working under Petrie in 1910-11, found at Mazghuna – about three miles south of Dahshur – the remains of two ruined pyramids which resembled more closely in plan the Hawara pyramid of Ammenemes III than any other pyramid at that time known. Some technical improvements in the devices for sealing the Mazghuna pyramids indicated that they were later than the pyramid of Hawara, and Mackay therefore ascribed one to Ammenemes IV and the other to Queen Sebekneferu, without attempting to identify the actual owner of each pyramid more precisely. If more recent discoveries have shown that Mackay failed to understand fully an important innovation in the method of closing the sarcophagus chamber, which is not otherwise known to have been employed before the next dynasty, it does not necessarily follow that his deduction regarding the ownership of the pyramids was incorrect. This innovation, which will be described in the next chapter, may have been introduced at the end of the XIIth Dynasty.

CHAPTER SEVEN

LATER
PYRAMIDS

During the two centuries occupied by the XIIIth-XVIIth Dynasties, Egypt passed through the second dark period in her dynastic history. Ruled by a succession of weak and ephemeral kings, the country gradually lapsed into a state of anarchy only comparable with the disorder which followed the end of the Old Kingdom. By an unfortunate chance, this period of chaos coincided with a vast ethnic movement which affected the whole of Western Asia and ultimately reached Egypt. At about the end of the XIIIth Dynasty or the beginning of the XIVth Dynasty, a host of Asiatics, the majority of whom were probably Semites, invaded the country, bringing with them a weapon of which the Egyptians had previously had no experience. These invaders were known as the Hyksos – a name which Manetho explained as meaning 'Shepherd Kings', but which probably means 'Rulers of Foreign Countries' – and their new weapon was the horse-drawn chariot. With the help of this weapon, their army gained not only in quality of arms, but also in power of manoeuvre. Having overcome whatever resistance they may have encountered, the Hyksos established their capital at Avaris, the site of which lay in the north-east of the Delta, very probably at Qantir, about fifteen miles south of Tanis – the Zoan of the Old Testament. From there they governed the whole of the Delta and Middle Egypt at least as far as Cusae, which lay about thirty miles north of Asyut. Further south, a native Egyptian dynasty continued to rule at Thebes, but probably only as vassals rendering tribute to their Hyksos overlords. At length, however, one of these vassals, named Kamose, the last of the kings of the XVIIth Dynasty, revolted and drove the Hyksos out of Middle Egypt, and may even have recovered Memphis. The complete expulsion of these foreign oppressors followed in the beginning of the sixteenth century B.C.

when Amosis I, the founder of the XVIIIth Dynasty, captured Avaris and pursued the invaders back into southern Palestine.

Royal funerary monuments dating from the so-called Second Intermediate Period (i.e. the XIIIth–XVIIth Dynasties) are rare – a fact which is no doubt partly to be explained by the unsettled political conditions of that time. Nevertheless, the ruined remains of three pyramids belonging to kings of the XIIIth Dynasty have been found. One of these pyramids, each side of which measured about 165 feet at the base, was partly excavated in 1957 at Dahshur. Its owner, whose sarcophagus and Canopic jars were found in the tomb-chamber, was a king named Amenyqemau (formerly read Amenyaamu). The two other pyramids, both of which were excavated by Jéquier between the years 1929 and 1931, are situated in the neighbourhood of the *Mastabat Faraʿun* at Saqqara. The builder of the earlier of these two pyramids bore the name Khendjer (Plate 53), but the owner of the second, which was probably never finished, has not been identified. Both pyramids demonstrate in plan and execution a further elaboration of the devices intended to render them impregnable, the development of which was certainly the main preoccupation of the architects of the pyramids of the Middle Kingdom.

Khendjer's pyramid, from which its neighbour differs only in detail, consisted of an inner core of brick measuring about 140 feet square at the base and an outer casing of Tura limestone, approximately 28 feet in thickness, of which almost nothing has been preserved. The entrance to the substructure lay beneath the outer casing on the west side. In order that sufficient space should be available for manoeuvring the coffin and other large pieces of funerary equipment, a rectangular well with walls of brick was constructed outside the entrance (fig. 48: 1). After the funeral the well was filled with rubble and paved with slabs of limestone so that, in appearance, the surface was indistinguishable from the rest of the corridor between the pyramid and the inner enclosure wall. From the entrance, a ramp with fourteen shallow steps leads downwards to a short horizontal passage ending in a blank wall (fig. 48: 2). At this point a large rectangular portcullis of quartzite still remains lodged in its recess on the south side of the passage. The floor of the recess slopes towards the passage, but apparently the angle of

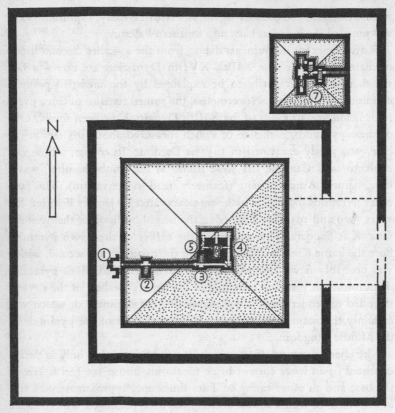

Figure 48. The pyramid of Khendjer, plan

incline was not sufficiently steep to enable the block to be moved into position. An opening in the end wall 5 feet above the floor of the passage, which the portcullis was intended to cover, gives access to a second ramp set on the same axis as the first but having thirty-nine steps. At the bottom of this ramp stood a wooden door with two leaves which, when open, fitted into recesses in the side-walls. Beyond the doorway, still resting in its recess, is another portcullis identical in design with the first (fig. 48: 3). The next section of the passage continues without change in direction and runs almost horizontally, but at a higher level than the bottom of the second ramp, to a rectangular pit, the floor of which was no doubt raised after the funeral to the level of the floor of the passage and thus concealed the entrance to the last section of the passage, which runs northwards to emerge in the floor at the eastern end of a wide antechamber lying north of the burial-chamber (fig. 48: 6).

Before describing the method of entry into the burial-chamber, it is necessary to explain that the whole of the substructure must have been completed before the lowest course of the superstructure could have been laid. The sequence of the operations probably corresponded with the order followed by the builders of the pyramid of Hawara. First, a rectangular pit measuring about 43 feet square and 36 feet deep was excavated, mostly south-east of the middle of the site on which the pyramid was to be built. In this pit the burial-chamber, its walls and floor carved of a single block of quartzite, was lowered by way of a trench with a temporary ramp which entered the pit at the south-west corner. The burial-chamber occupied only a small part of the whole area of the pit and as soon as it had been placed in position work was started on the construction of the antechamber and the passages in the pit, each at its proper level. While this work was in progress, the temporary ramp was dismantled and replaced by the two stepped ramps. Finally the portcullises were lowered into their recesses and the filling necessary to provide a level surface for the base of the pyramid was laid in the pit and in the trench of the stepped ramps, not however directly on the flat ceilings of the various constructions, but on brick vaults which had been built above them. Over the burial-chamber alone a pointed roof, composed of two pieces of limestone, was placed between the brick vault and the flat ceiling.

Entry into the burial-chamber at the time of the funeral would have been impossible if the two heavy ceiling-blocks of quartzite had already been laid on the walls. The block nearer to the antechamber was therefore propped up in the void between the ceiling and the pointed roof, leaving a gap above the northern wall to which a trench in the centre of the antechamber and a short corridor gave access. Two props of granite supported the block which projected on both sides about 1 foot 6 inches beyond the walls of the chamber. The props did not however stand on the floor of the pit but on deep beds of sand encased in vertical shafts built of stone, each shaft rising to the height of the walls and the upper part serving as a kind of socket for its prop. After the coffin, the Canopic chest and some of the king's personal possessions had been placed in the chamber, a stone at the base of each shaft was removed and the sand allowed to escape, no doubt gradually, until the props rested on the floor and the block on the walls. In order to enable this operation to be carried out, corridors leading to the shafts had been built in the pit, one from a trench in the east passage (figs. 48, 49 and 50: 4) and the other from a trench at the west end of the ante-chamber (figs. 48, 49 and 50: 5). When the ceiling-block, which measured about 5 feet in thickness, had been lowered the gap at the end of the corridor of approach to the burial-chamber was completely closed. Nevertheless as a further measure of protection the trench connecting this corridor with the antechamber and the two trenches of the corridors leading to the shafts were filled with masonry and paved.

Although this ingenious method of lowering a heavy block of stone in a confined space had not been recognized in any earlier pyramid, it may not have been an invention of the architect of this pyramid. Jéquier, to whom the credit for its discovery belongs, believed that it was employed by the builders of the pyramids of Mazghuna, but while the precise date of these monuments remains uncertain their chronological position in relation to the pyramid of Khendjer cannot be determined. It was not used in Khendjer's subsidiary pyramid, a building situated north-east of the king's pyramid (fig. 48: 7) and somewhat similar in plan, but exceptionally having two burial-chambers, each made of quartzite. These burial-chambers were, however, smaller than the burial-chamber of the king and the stone blocks supporting the raised portions of their lighter ceilings, which had never been lowered, could have been removed if the weight of the ceiling-slabs had been eased by means of levers while the blocks were being extracted. In every probability some unexpected turn of events prevented the execution of the plan for burying two queens in these chambers, but there is nothing to suggest that the king was not interred in his pyramid. How long his body remained undisturbed is not known, perhaps only

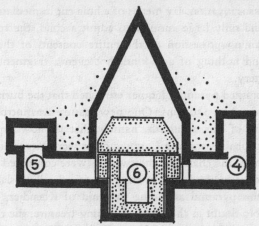

*Figure 49. The burial-chamber of the pyramid of Khendjer,
section looking north*

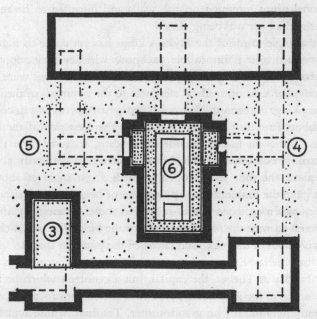

*Figure 50. The burial-chamber and surrounding passages of the pyramid of Khendjer,
plan*

until the Hyksos invasion. By means of a hole cut immediately beneath the ceiling and only large enough to admit a child, the robbers succeeded in gaining possession of the entire contents of the chamber, leaving behind nothing of any kind, not even a fragment of wood, stone, or pottery.

In the unfinished pyramid, Jéquier estimated that the burial-chamber weighed as much as 150 tons. One new feature was introduced into the fashioning of this monolith, namely that the lower portions of both the sarcophagus and the Canopic chest were carved in one piece with the floor of the chamber; the two lids were composed of separate pieces. The same method for lowering the raised ceiling-slab had been planned in this pyramid as in the pyramid of Khendjer, but it was never used. No doubt in the hope of finding treasure, the robbers had released the sand from the shafts, with the result that the quartzite props slid downwards; the ceiling-slab, however, still rests on four additional props mounted on the walls and intended to be removed when the chamber was being closed.

Not a single tomb of the Hyksos kings has yet come to light, and, in consequence, it is impossible to know whether they adopted the Egyptian practice of building pyramids or whether they were buried in some other kind of tomb. References to the pyramids of the XVIIth Dynasty kings occur in the Leopold–Amherst Papyrus and its congener the Abbott Papyrus. They were built on the west side of the Nile at Thebes. Although material evidence is scant, it seems clear that the superstructures, built of crude brick, covered an area only about 25 feet square; the four faces sloped inwards at an angle of about 65°, which gave the buildings the appearance of being tall and slender. At the apex was a capstone made, at least in some instances, of limestone and engraved with the name and titles of the king. The burial-chamber was carved out of the rock foundation of the pyramid chapel.

Perhaps the last Egyptian king to build a pyramid was Amosis I. His real tomb lay at Thebes, the capital, but a cenotaph which he built at Abydos was in the shape of a pyramid. He also constructed at Abydos a dummy pyramid for his grandmother, Tetisheri, whose actual tomb, although not yet found, is stated in an inscription discovered at Abydos to have been situated at Thebes. These two pyramids were, however, exceptional; the remaining kings of the XVIIIth Dynasty and their successors for many generations built neither tombs nor cenotaphs of pyramidal form. Experience must by that time have shown that the pyramid gave unnecessary prominence to the location of the tomb and that, even after the adoption of every stratagem which human ingenuity could devise, plunderers were ultimately able to force their way into the burial-chamber, and not only to despoil the contents but also to violate the body. A different method of countering these evils was now attempted. Instead of constructing their mortuary temples and tombs together in one place, the pharaohs of the New Kingdom built their temples in the Nile valley and hollowed out deep caverns in the western cliffs for tombs. By this method it was hoped that the knowledge of the actual location of the tomb would be shared only by those who had assisted in its construction, by a small number of officials and by members of the royal household. The architect of the first tomb of this kind to be constructed in the famous 'Valley of the Kings' - a valley running parallel with the Nile behind Deir el-Bahri which is dominated by a natural rock formation resembling a pyramid and rising to 1,000 feet (Plate 54) - describes the secrecy with which the work was carried out in the following words: 'I supervised the excavation of the cliff-tomb of His Majesty [Tuthmosis I] alone, no one seeing and no one hearing.' Neither Tuthmosis I nor his architect, however, could possibly have known that the lonely valley they had chosen was destined to become the regular burial-place of the pharaohs for many generations to come; inevitably the secret of the whereabouts of the royal tombs became common knowledge. Robbery was bound to follow sooner or later, and Tutankhamun alone of the sixty or more royal persons buried in this valley was left virtually undisturbed until modern times. His tomb was only spared by the fortunate chance which guided Ramesses VI to excavate his own tomb in the cliff immediately above the tomb of Tutankhamun, with the result that the entrance to the latter became deeply buried under rubble thrown out from the upper tomb, and must early have been forgotten. Fifty-three mummies from the other tombs in the valley, including those of such famous pharaohs as Tuthmosis III, Sethos I, and Ramesses II, were ultimately transferred to an unfinished tomb at Deir el-Bahri, and to the tomb of Amenophis II, where they remained without further disturbance until their discovery at the end of the last century.

Although scarcely meriting comparison with the royal pyramids, private tombs of pyramidal form or incorporating a pyramid in their architectural design were built at latest as early as the New Kingdom. In the past, some mud-brick pyramidal tombs found in 1858 by Mariette at Abydos were believed to date from the Middle Kingdom. They were certainly not royal tombs, and doubts about their supposed date had been expressed long before a study of similar tombs at Thebes conducted by the Austrian Archaeological Institute in Cairo in 1975-78 had proved that they dated from Saite times (c. 600 B.C.).

Early examples of these tombs, none of which was more than about twenty feet in height, consisted of a pyramid mounted on a rectangular base, both parts being coated with mud-plaster and painted white. An external stela was placed on the base with its back against the pyramid. Inside the pyramid lay a burial-chamber, conical in shape and corbelled in construction. The mummy was taken to the chamber through a hole in the front wall of the base which was subsequently closed with bricks. In later examples the burial-chamber was roofed and the void above it served as a relieving compartment. A two-storeyed building was attached to the pyramid. Each storey consisted of one room, the upper being a chapel with a stela set in a niche in one wall. At the funeral the mummy was let down through a hole in the floor of the chapel to the lower chamber and carried through a narrow passage to its wooden coffin in the burial-chamber. The passage was then blocked and the lower chamber filled with sand. Lastly the hole in the floor of the chapel was covered.

During the New Kingdom, a rather elaborate type of private tomb, outwardly resembling the upper-class dwelling-house of the time, came into fashion. Tombs of this kind were built in Thebes and at other places even as far away as Aniba, about 130 miles south of Aswan. Some of the best examples, however, were found by the excavators of the French Institute of Archaeology when digging at Deir el-Medina, near the Valley of the Queens (fig. 51). Their owners were the scribes, artists, and artisans who had been employed on the construction of the royal tombs of the XVIIIth-XXth Dynasties. Each tomb consisted of

Figure 51. Private tombs at Deir el-Medina – a reconstruction

two parts, a superstructure and a substructure. Above ground lay a court enclosed on three sides by a wall of brick or stone. On the fourth side of the court stood a chapel, usually masked by a colonnade. Internally, the chapel consisted of a single room decorated with painted scenes and having a stela recessed in the back wall. Mounted on the roof was a hollow brick pyramid, capped with a block of limestone. Figures of the owner adoring the sun-god, together with short inscriptions, were carved on all four sides of the capstone. A niche in the side of the pyramid facing the court contained a statuette of the owner, who was sometimes represented kneeling and holding a miniature stela. The burial-chamber, which lay deep in the rock, was a room with a vaulted ceiling of brick connected with either the court or the chapel by a shaft and an underground staircase. In the XVIIIth Dynasty only the owner and his wife were buried in the chamber. In the XIXth-XXth Dynasties, however, several generations of the same family regularly shared the same tomb and additional chambers were constructed when necessary. The walls of the chambers, after the XVIIIth Dynasty, were usually decorated with religious scenes and inscriptions.

More than eight hundred years after the last royal pyramid had been constructed in Egypt, pyramidal tombs suddenly made their appearance in the Sudan. The builders were a line of kings whose capital - known in ancient times as Napata - was situated on the banks of the Nile in the province of Dongola, a short distance downstream from the Fourth Cataract (fig. 52). Concerning the racial origin of these kings, very little information has yet come to light, but an inscription found by Reisner during his excavation of their tombs suggests that they were of South Libyan stock. Napata offered no rich pasturage to attract the settler; on the contrary, it lay in one of the most barren parts of the Nile Valley, and its importance was principally due to its geographical position on the main trade route between Central Africa and Egypt, which enabled its rulers to control the passage of slaves and supplies of ivory, ebony, myrrh, resin, incense, and other products required by the Egyptians. The rich gold-fields of the eastern desert were also included in their domain. To ensure an uninterrupted flow of these commodities, the kings of Egypt during the Middle Kingdom and again during the XVIIIth-XXth Dynasties had incorporated the Northern Sudan into their empire. In the latter period in particular, temples were built in honour of the Egyptian gods at many places between the First Cataract and the Fourth Cataract. The largest of these temples stood at Napata, where a high table-mountain, now called Gebel Barkal, acquired the reputation of being the dwelling of the god Amun. At the end of the XXth Dynasty (c. 1080 B.C.), internal weakness forced Egypt to relax her grip on the Northern Sudan and, little more than a century later, the ancestors of the kings who were to build the pyramids gained possession of the country, without, however, causing its people to discard the Egyptian religion or to abandon the fund of technical knowledge which they had learned from the Egyptians.

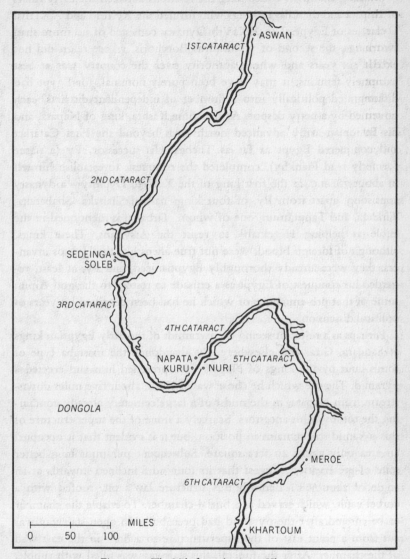

Figure 52. The Nile from Aswan to Khartoum

Nothing is known concerning the relations between the early rulers of Napata and the Libyan kings who formed the XXIInd and XXIIIrd Dynasties of Egypt. The XXIVth Dynasty consisted of no more than two kings, the second of whom was Bocchoris, whose reign did not exceed six years and whose authority over the country was at best extremely tenuous; it may have been purely nominal, for Egypt had disintegrated politically into a number of independent districts, each governed by a petty despot. At that time Kashta, king of Napata, and his Ethiopian army advanced northwards beyond the First Cataract and conquered Egypt as far as Thebes. His successor, Py (a name formerly read Piankhy), completed the conquest, to establish himself in about 721 B.C. as the first king of the XXVth Dynasty – a dynasty consisting, apart from Py, of four kings named Shabaka, Shabataka, Tirhaqa, and Tanutamun, one of whom, Tirhaqa, is mentioned in the Bible as helping Hezekiah[1] to resist the Assyrians. These kings, although of foreign blood, were not true aliens like the Hyksos invaders; they were already thoroughly Egyptianized, and Py, at least, regarded his conquest of Egypt as a crusade to restore to the god Amun some of that pre-eminence of which he had been deprived by years of political dissension.

Perhaps as a result of seeing the pyramids of the early Egyptian kings at Saqqara, Giza, and elsewhere, Py abandoned the mastaba type of tomb built by the kings of Napata who preceded him and erected a pyramid. The site which he chose was at Kuru, about five miles downstream from Napata, in the midst of a large cemetery already containing the tombs of his ancestors. Scarcely a stone of the superstructure of this pyramid still remains in position, but it is evident that it occupied an area only about 40 feet square. Subsequent pyramids in a better state of preservation suggest that its four sides inclined inwards at an angle of about 68°. Beneath this structure lay a pit, roofed with a corbel vault, which served as a burial-chamber. To enable the chamber to be entered after the pyramid had been built, an open stairway was cut from a point east of the superstructure to a door in the east wall of the chamber. After the funeral, this stairway was filled with rubble, and a mortuary chapel, consisting of a single room decorated with

1. II Kings xix, 9.

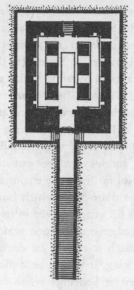

Figure 53. Pyramid of Tirhaqa

reliefs, was erected on top. Shabaka, when constructing his pyramid, added a short tunnel to the end of the stairway and cut his burial-chamber out of the rock. The mortuary chapel was built against the east side of the pyramid, directly above the tunnel, and the stairway – filled after the funeral like the trench of Py – lay outside the east wall. In this way, the chapel stood on a rock foundation, and its construction could be completed during the lifetime of the king. Tirhaqa, in his pyramid at Nuri on the opposite bank of the Nile to Kuru (Plate 55), developed the tunnel into a small antechamber and enlarged the burial-chamber into a hall divided by rock pillars into three aisles; he also cut a corridor which surrounded both apartments and gave access to the hall by a staircase at its western end (fig. 53). Some of his successors increased the number of underground chambers in their pyramids to three by interposing between the antechamber and the burial-chamber a room inscribed on its walls with the so-called 'Negative Confession' from the Book of the Dead. In spite of these modifications in matters of detail, however, the general pattern of the tomb as first developed by Shabaka was never radically changed.

Excavations conducted between 1963 and 1965 by Michela Schiff Giorgini and her collaborators at Sedeinga, thirteen miles north of Soleb, brought to light a small pyramid which the discoverers believed to be the real tomb of Tirhaqa. Its measurements at the base were about 32½ feet on each side. A core of rock and gravel was overlaid with a casing of schist, its lowest courses being about 6 feet thick. On the east side of the pyramid there was a small court to which access was gained through a gateway in the east side of the wall which surrounded the tomb. Not far from the enclosure the excavators found some pieces of sandstone door-posts which bore parts of two of Tirhaqa's names and part of his image carved in relief. The tomb-chamber contained innumerable fragments of bone which seemed to belong to a single skeleton. Although it cannot be denied that the bones may have been those of the king, it would be difficult to imagine why he should have been buried at Sedeinga when his Nubian predecessors had all been buried further south and the Nuri pyramid seems to have been provided with far more elaborate funerary equipment.

In addition to the kings' pyramids, Reisner found in the cemetery of Kuru a row of five pyramids built for the queens. Close to this row lay twenty-four graves of horses, four of which belonged to the horses of Py and four to those of Tanutamun, while the remainder were equally divided between the horses of Shabaka and Shabataka. Each horse was richly caparisoned with silver trappings and strings of beads. They were, without doubt, sacrificed at the time of the king's death, in order that they might accompany him to the Next World. Only one instance of a horse-burial is known from Egypt, although chariots were included in the tombs of royalty and some nobility during the New Kingdom. The sacrifice of the royal steeds was therefore probably an innovation by Py, whose affection for horses is witnessed by a passage in his famous Victory Stela. In this graphic account of his conquest of Egypt, he describes his indignation at the discovery that Namlat, the despot of El-Eshmunein, had allowed his horses to starve during the siege which he himself had laid to the city. Namlat was ultimately pardoned, but he came near to paying with his life for his neglect of the horses.

In about the year 661 B.C., the Assyrian king Ashurbanipal brought to an end a number of inconclusive encounters between Assyria and the kings of the XXVth Dynasty by defeating Tanutamun and conquering the whole of Egypt as far as Thebes. Tanutamun retreated to Napata, where he and his successors continued to rule without serious interference for about 350 years. Their kingdom was bounded on the north by the First Cataract and on the south by the swamps of the White Nile. With only two exceptions, these kings, of whom there were twenty-one including Tanutamun, were buried at Nuri in pyramids of the standard size and shape; the two exceptions were Tanutamun himself and a later king, both of whom erected their pyramids at Kuru. In addition to the kings' pyramids, the Nuri cemetery contained fifty-three smaller pyramids belonging to queens and princesses.

From about 300 B.C. until A.D. 350, when the kingdom was finally overwhelmed by the Abyssinians, the capital was situated at Meroe, a hundred and thirty miles north of Khartoum. Twice during this period rival claimants to the throne endeavoured, with some measure of success, to re-establish the capital at Napata, but on each occasion the dissident faction ultimately succumbed and the authority of Meroe remained unchallenged. Both the kings of Meroe and their rivals at Napata continued to be buried in pyramids, nearly fifty in Meroe (Plate 56) and eighteen in Napata; all these pyramids, like their predecessors, were of stone except those built at Meroe after A.D. 200, when brick coated with plaster was employed.

A barbarous custom, already practised during the Middle Kingdom in the Northern Sudan, was revived by the kings of Meroe. This custom was the burial of his servants with the king in his tomb, so that their spirits might continue to serve him in the next world. Whether they were actually buried alive or were put to death before burial is still open to conjecture. The queens were not subjected to this treatment, but were buried, also in pyramids, in a separate cemetery on the west side of the city. In this connection, Strabo makes the following statement: 'It is still the custom in Ethiopia that when the king, by accident or otherwise, has lost the use of a member, or a member itself, all his usual followers (those who are destined to die at the same time as himself) inflict on themselves a similar mutilation, and that explains the extreme care with which they watch over the person of the king.'[2] Strabo may have been misled in matters of detail, but the excavations of Reisner at Meroe suggest that the general accuracy of his assertion need not be doubted.

2. Strabo, *Geographica*, Book XVII, II, 3.

CHAPTER EIGHT

CONSTRUCTION
AND PURPOSE

Extant Egyptian records, whether written or pictorial, throw no light on the methods employed by the builders of the pyramids either in planning or in constructing their monumental works. Close study of the buildings, combined with an ever-increasing knowledge of the implements available to the builders, has, however, made it possible to determine many details of construction with certainty and the likely limits of practicability can often be deduced where positive evidence is lacking. Nevertheless, several problems remain to be solved, and in such cases it is only possible to suggest an answer without any pretence of support other than the belief that the means proposed would achieve the results which can be observed.

When choosing the site for a pyramid, it was necessary that certain overriding considerations should be borne in mind: it must be situated west of the river – the side of the setting sun; it must stand well above the level of the river, but not be too remote from its west bank; the rock substratum must be free from any defect or tendency to crack; it should be situated not far from the capital and possibly even closer to a palace which the king may have built as a residence outside the capital. Of the sites chosen by the kings of the Old Kingdom, Saqqara and Abu Sir lay in sight of Memphis, Abu Roash about seventeen miles distant to the north, and Dahshur only five miles away to the south. Thirty-three miles separated Memphis from Meidum, where one pyramid alone was built. Proximity to the river was an important factor, because much of the stone used for the pyramid and its adjacent buildings must be conveyed from the quarries by ship. Thus, during the season of the inundation, an expanse of desert only 250 yards in width lay between the river and the pyramid at Meidum, while at Giza the interval was about a quarter of a mile; at Dahshur and Abu

Roash, however, the most practical routes for hauling the building materials measured about a mile.

A suitable site having been found, the first task of the builders was to remove the thick surface layer of sand and gravel so that the buildings might stand on a firm foundation of rock. Levelling and smoothing of the rock were then begun, the pieces removed being either used to fill up depressions or placed on one side for subsequent employment. How accurately this operation could be performed is demonstrated by the Great Pyramid, in which the perimeter of the bed deviates from a truly level plane by only a little more than half an inch – the almost imperceptible amount by which the south-east corner stands higher than the north-west corner. Such a high degree of accuracy in the technique of levelling was undoubtedly the outcome of accumulated experience gained by generations of Egyptians, dating back to the pre-Pyramid Age, when preparing their lands for irrigation by means of water conducted through channels and canals from the river. To level an area like the bed of a pyramid it would have been necessary to surround it on all four sides with low banks of Nile mud, fill the enclosure so formed with water, and cut a network of trenches in the rock in such a manner that the floor of each trench lay at the same depth beneath the surface of the water; the intervening spaces could have been levelled after the water had been released. A grid of such trenches can still be seen at a short distance from the north side of the Second Pyramid, where levelling work was left unfinished (Plate 57). In actual practice the whole area to be covered by the pyramid was not always reduced to the same level as the perimeter; as the Great Pyramid shows, a mound of rock might be left in the centre and be incorporated in the pyramid.

The last of the preliminaries to be accomplished on the site was the execution of an accurate survey in order to ensure that the base of the pyramid should form as nearly as possible a perfect square, each side of which would be so oriented as to face directly one of the four cardinal points. The unit of measurement was the royal cubit (20.62 inches in length) consisting of seven *palms* or twenty-eight *digits*, one *palm* being equal to four *digits*. Measuring cords were made either of palm-fibre or flax-fibre, both of which would certainly have stretched when used; it is therefore hardly surprising that there should be a difference of 7.9 inches in length between the longest and shortest sides of the Great Pyramid – indeed, it seems remarkable that on sides exceeding 9,000 inches in length so small an error should have occurred, especially when it is remembered that the central mound of rock would have rendered impracticable any measurement of the diagonals to check the accuracy of the square.

An exact orientation of the pyramid on the four cardinal points could only have been achieved with the aid of one or more of the celestial bodies, since the magnetic compass was certainly unknown to the ancient Egyptians. The results of the method, as exemplified by the Great Pyramid and the pyramid of Chephren, left little to be desired, the errors in the four sides of the former being the following fractions of one degree:

> North side   2′ 28″ south of west
> South side   1′ 57″ south of west
> East side   5′ 30″ west of north
> West side   2′ 30″ west of north

According to Petrie's survey, the mean error of the east and west sides of Chephren's pyramid was about 5′ 26″ west of north.[1] Which or how many of the celestial bodies were employed to attain these results cannot be deduced with certainty, but it was clearly only necessary to fix one axis; the other axis could be determined by the use of a set-square; contemporary buildings with corners forming a perfect right angle prove that an accurate instrument for this purpose must have been available to the pyramid builders. East and west could have been discovered approximately by observing the rising and setting of the sun on the two equinoctial days every year, and north by an observation of the Pole Star, but in each case the resultant error (even after

---

1. Among other pyramids surveyed by Petrie were three in the orientation of the east and west sides of which he observed the following errors:

> Meidum pyramid: 24′ 25″ west of north.
> Bent Pyramid: 9′ 12″ west of north.
> Pyramid of Mycerinus: 14′ 3″ east of north.

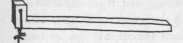

Figure 54. The merkhet

allowance has been made for a change in the position of the Pole in relation to the Pole Star in the course of about 4,500 years) would have been greater than the amount revealed by at least the two main pyramids of Giza. To judge from the instrumental and representational evidence so far found, it seems more likely that the high degree of accuracy was achieved by astral than by solar observations.

Egyptian texts giving information on the method of orienting buildings are few in number, late in date and formal in character. They refer invariably to the foundation ceremonies of temples performed by the king. According to the most instructive of these texts, which are inscribed on the walls of the Graeco-Roman temples of Dendereh and Edfu, the king marked out the line of the four outer walls after observing the position of the stars in the Great Bear. In conducting the observation he was assisted by a priest, impersonating the god Thoth, who was in charge of an instrument called the *merkhet*. As long ago as 1899 Borchardt was able to identify as a *merkhet* a bone object dating from Saite times in the Berlin Museum which consisted of a narrow horizontal bar with a small block at one end rising above the level of the bar; a transverse hole bored through the block and a perpendicular groove cut beneath each aperture of the boring were no doubt intended to hold the upper end of a plumb-line (fig. 54). The word *merkhet* means literally 'instrument of knowing' and may be translated 'indicator'. It was used, as the Czech Egyptologist Z. Žába was able to show, to express 'shadow-clock', 'water-clock', and 'astral-clock', an instrument for measuring nocturnal hours by determining the height of a star above the horizon. All three instruments also possessed individual names; the general term *merkhet* would refer to their common function as indicators of time by means of

measurement. The *merkhet* used in astral observations and the *merkhet* used in sunlight for registering the hours of the day by measuring the length of shadow cast by the block on the horizontal bar were, however, identical apart from the addition of a plumb-line to the former and the calibration of the bar in the latter.

As an astral gauge the *merkhet* was employed in conjunction with another instrument which the Egyptians called the *bay* (*en imy unut*), or 'palm-rib (of the observer of hours)'. Borchardt recognized an example of this instrument also in the Berlin collection and its inscription revealed that it had belonged to the same priest as the *merkhet* previously mentioned. It was a straight palm-rib with a V-shaped slot cut in the wider end (fig. 55). How these two instruments (neither of which is mentioned in Egyptian texts before the XVIIIth Dynasty) may have been used for purposes of surveying will shortly be described.

In spite of the relatively late date of the inscriptions referring to the episodes of the foundation ceremonies, there is no reason to doubt that they preserve an ancient tradition. Some indication that similar ceremonies were already current in the Pyramid Age is provided by a fragmentary relief found in the Vth Dynasty sun-temple of Niuserrē, which shows the king and a priestess impersonating the goddess Seshat, each holding a mallet and a stake to which a measuring cord is attached. The scene is in complete agreement with the text in the temple at Edfu which represents the king as saying: 'I take the stake and I hold the handle of the mallet. I hold the (measuring) cord with Seshat.' Nevertheless it is necessary to bear in mind that actions performed in a religious ceremony would be symbolical and would not reproduce fully the various measures laboriously taken beforehand to secure the desired results. Thus a text in the temple at Denderĕh which describes the king as 'looking at the sky, observing the stars

Figure 55. The bay

245

and turning his gaze towards the Great Bear' should not be regarded as more than a record of a formal ceremony in which the king was credited with having himself determined the orientation of the temple, although in reality he merely went through the motions, as is done at the present day in laying a foundation-stone.

A simple method of determining true north, which would have been consistent with the evidence of the later texts, was by sighting on a star in the northern heavens and bisecting the angle formed by its rising position, the position from which the observation was made, and its setting position. To achieve the degree of accuracy needed, it would have been necessary either to be able to see the true horizon at the points where the star rose and set or to create an artificial horizon at a uniform height above those two points.

Since an observation of the true horizon would be precluded any-where on land by irregularities, however slight, in the ground, an artificial horizon would be required. This end could have been secured by building a circular wall with a diameter of a few feet on the already levelled rock-bed of the pyramid. The height of the wall must be sufficient to prevent a person standing within the circle from seeing anything outside other than the sky, but, subject to this single reser-vation, it should not be higher than such a person could reach. For the whole of its circumference, the top of the wall must be on an absolutely even plane – a requirement which again could easily have been attained by means of water, temporary mud-banks on the inner and outer peripheries of the top surface providing the support necessary to pre-vent the water from flowing away. The observation would be made by one person sighting over a short perpendicular rod or through the slot of the *bay* at the centre of the circle (fig. 56: O); a second person standing within the circle would receive directions from the first and, at the moment when the star (fig. 56: P^1) appeared above the wall, would place a mark or the *merkhet* on the wall directly in line between the observer and the star. This operation would first be performed towards the east (fig. 56: P), and subsequently, some hours later, per-haps with a second *merkhet*, towards the west (fig. 56: Q^1 and Q), the same star being sighted on both occasions. If the *merkhet* had not been invented at this period a plumb-line (which the Egyptians of the Pyra-

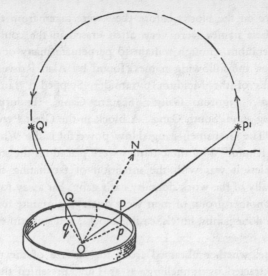

Figure 56. A method of discovering true north

mid Age are known to have possessed) would have been suspended
from the two marks on the wall and corresponding marks made on
the ground at points perpendicularly below (fig. 56: *p* and *q*). The first
of these two operations would have been unnecessary if the *merkhet*
with a plumb-line attached to the block were available to the pyramid
builders. By bisecting the angle *p*O*q*, true north would be obtained
and the bisecting line N–O would run due north and south. As a
check, the operation could have been repeated by sighting several
different stars in the same way before dismantling the wall in readiness
for the foundation ceremonies.

At the same time as the preliminary work was being conducted on
the pyramid site, other preparations for building were being made
elsewhere. The foundation of the causeway, composed of stone quarried in the locality, was being laid so that it could be used for the
passage of material when constructional work on the pyramid began.
Fine limestone blocks for the outer casing of the building were being
quarried on the east bank of the Nile at Tura and in the Muqattam
hills. The men employed on this work painted the names of their gangs

in red ochre on the blocks before they were taken from the quarry; although these names were very often erased in the course of subsequent operations, enough remain to perpetuate many of the gangs. As examples, the following names, found by Alan Rowe, occur on casing-blocks of the Meidum pyramid:[2] 'Stepped Pyramid Gang', 'Boat Gang', 'Vigorous Gang', 'Sceptre Gang', 'Enduring Gang', 'North Gang', and 'South Gang'. A block in the Great Pyramid bears the name: 'The Craftsmen-gang. How powerful is the White Crown of Khnum Khufu!' Why these names were placed on the stones is not evident, unless it was with the intention of facilitating the task of keeping a tally of the work done by each gang. Far away to the south, at Aswan, another group of men were quarrying granite for columns, architraves, door-jambs, lintels, casing-blocks, and sometimes the outer sarcophagus.

Limestone, whether obtained from the surface of the rock, as at Giza, or extracted by tunnelling, as at Tura, presented the pyramid builders with no serious difficulties in its quarrying. A discovery by W.B. Emery in the early dynastic cemetery of Saqqara has shown that even in the Ist Dynasty the Egyptians possessed excellent copper tools, including saws and chisels, which were capable of cutting any kind of limestone (Plate 58). As an aid to sawing, a wet abrasive material such as moistened quartz sand, which is plentiful in Egypt, may have been employed, but there is no positive evidence either of the material used or of the practice. Chisels and wedges were, however, the tools most favoured for quarrying limestone, the former for cutting the blocks away from the rock on every side except the bottom and the latter for detaching the blocks at the base. In a tunnel-quarry, for instance, a deep hollow resembling a shelf and extending across the whole breadth of the passage was first cut between the roof and the block to be detached. The purpose of this hollow was to allow a quarryman to crawl across the top of the block and separate it from the rock behind by chipping vertically downwards with a chisel struck by a wooden mallet. At the same time other quarrymen made similar vertical cuttings down the two sides. Finally, wedges were inserted into holes cut at the bottom in order to make a horizontal split in the rock, which

2. Alan Rowe, *The Museum Journal*, Philadelphia, Vol. XXII (1931), p. 21 (Pl. VI).

freed the block entirely. Sometimes the wedges were composed of wood, and the split was achieved by wetting the wood and so causing it to expand. The process was afterwards repeated on the rock below, without the necessity of cutting the initial hollow, until floor-level had been reached; a new series of cuttings, starting at roof-level, was then begun deeper in the tunnel.[3] Surface-quarrying was carried out by exactly the same method. It possessed a great advantage over tunnel-quarrying, in so far as the space for working was not so confined and a greater number of men could therefore be employed at one time. On the other hand, the finest limestone often lay in strata buried deeply beneath the surface, and tunnelling offered the only practical means of access.

The methods employed in the Pyramid Age for quarrying granite and other hard stones are still a subject of controversy. One authority even expressed the opinion that hard-stone quarrying was not attempted until the Middle Kingdom; before that time, the amount needed could have been obtained from large boulders lying loose on the surface of the ground.[4] It seems difficult, however, to believe that a people who possessed the degree of skill necessary for shaping the colossal monoliths built into the granite valley building of Chephren were not also able to hew rough blocks of this stone out of the quarry, particularly since tunnelling was never adopted. Furthermore, on the backs of the slabs roofing Mycerinus's burial-chamber marks made by the insertion of wedges may still be seen, and the natural inference appears to be that the operation denoted by these wedge-marks was the splitting of the slabs from the rock in the quarry. This method of quarrying was certainly practised in later times, as is demonstrated by the countless rows of wedge-slots still visible today in the Aswan quarries (Plate 59); there is nothing to suggest that quarrymen were not detaching blocks by the same device in the Old Kingdom. The slots may have been made either by rubbing an abrasive powder with

3. Many soft-stone quarries in the United Kingdom are worked at the present time in the way described above, the only important difference being the substitution of steel tools and the greater use made of the saw. The mason's pick, now used instead of chisels, may also have been known to the ancient Egyptians, but no specimen has yet been found.

4. A. Lucas, *Ancient Egyptian Materials and Industries* (1948), pp. 82–3.

stone or by a metal tool. Since copper was the only metal for tools which is known to have been available in Egypt before the Middle Kingdom, it has been supposed that the Egyptians had mastered a process, now lost, of giving copper a very high temper, but this surmise has not yet been proved.

An alternative and more laborious method of quarrying granite was by pounding the rock around the block to be detached with balls of dolerite – a hard greenish stone found over a wide area of the eastern desert near the Red Sea. An unfinished obelisk dating from the New Kingdom, which still lies at Aswan, was undoubtedly quarried by this method, and there is no inherent improbability in the supposition that quarrymen were already acquainted with the technique in pyramid times.

By whatever method of quarrying the granite blocks were obtained, the procedure for reaching stone of the quality required, if it were not available in the uppermost stratum, would have been similar. Granite, like many other stones, if heated to a high temperature and then suddenly cooled, will develop superficial cracks, and the face, when subjected to the slightest friction, will immediately crumble away. A fire lit on the rock to be pared down would soon raise its temperature to the requisite degree, and the application of cold water would cause the disintegration of the surface, which could then be rubbed away with the aid of a small stone scraper. If necessary, the process could be repeated many times until stone of the desired hardness had been reached.

By no means the least remarkable achievement of the pyramid build-ers was the transport of the blocks from their quarries to the site of the pyramid. Some of the heaviest pieces of local limestone embodied in the mortuary temple of Mycerinus, according to Reisner's estimate,[5] weigh about 200 tons. In comparison with this amount, the casing-blocks of the Great Pyramid, which average only about 2½ tons, and the 50-ton granite roof-slabs of the King's Chamber may seem trivial, but it must be remembered that the latter required not only to be loaded on barges and subsequently unloaded, but also, for the most part, to be raised at the end of their journey to a very considerable

5. G. A. Reisner, *Mycerinus*, p. 70.

height above ground-level. The navigation of these megaliths, probably undertaken in the main during the inundation season, may well have been the least formidable part of the whole task, though the control of heavily laden barges on a fast-flowing river must always have been a hazardous operation requiring great skill. Moreover, the journey from Aswan, although free from cataracts, involved negotiating the difficult waters and shifting sand-banks near Gebel Abu Foda, about ninety miles south of Saqqara.

For transport over land, the method employed was probably the same whether the weight to be moved was 200 tons or $2\frac{1}{2}$ tons, the number of men being regulated by the amount of the weight. What was this method? It is highly improbable that wheeled vehicles were used, because, although some of the carrying possibilities of the wheel had been realized at least as early as the Vth Dynasty,[6] scenes in tombs of the XVIIIth Dynasty demonstrate that, even after a lapse of a thousand years, statues and heavy blocks of stone were not moved by wheeled transport. Instead, sledges were employed, and there can be little doubt that the pyramid-builders also used this method. Each block was probably levered on the sledge either directly from the ground or by way of a low ramp composed of brick or stone. Both sledge and block, lashed together by ropes, may then have been raised again by means of levers, in order that wooden rollers might be placed underneath. The loaded sledge would subsequently be dragged over a way paved with baulks of timber by men pulling on ropes attached to the sledge. An illustration of the actual process of transport was included by Djehutihotep, a nobleman of the XIIth Dynasty, in his tomb at El-Bersheh (fig. 57). In this scene an alabaster statue of Djehutihotep, which probably weighed about 60 tons, is mounted on a sledge pulled by 172 men.[7] Water or some other liquid is poured on the ground to lessen the friction and thus facilitate haulage.

6. A relief in the Vth Dynasty tomb of Kaemheset at Saqqara shows a scaling-ladder mounted on wheels. (See Somers Clarke and R. Engelbach, *Ancient Egyptian Masonry*, Fig. 83.)

7. Reliefs from the Palace of Sennacherib at Nineveh, now in the British Museum, show that the Assyrians of the seventh century B.C. transported their sculptures by a very similar method.

Figure 57. The transport of a colossus

An experiment, which was carried out under the direction of Henri Chevrier, a French architect who worked for the Egyptian Antiquities Service, proved how easily a heavy weight could be moved over level territory. A track was prepared by putting a layer of earth on firm ground in the first court of the temple of Amun at Karnak. When the earth had been lightly trodden down until it had become well compacted, its surface was wetted and a sledge bearing a block of stone weighing about six tons was lowered on to one end of the track. Ropes, which were attached to the sledge, were pulled by two squads of men, one squad on each side of the track, and it was found that six men could drag the heavy load without difficulty.

With his material close at hand and the site prepared, two difficult problems still confronted the pyramid-builder: he must raise the stones to the height required and must lay them so that the monument gained internal cohesion and regularity of outward form. Before attempting to explain how these problems were overcome, it may be worth while to stop and consider the main internal and external features of the

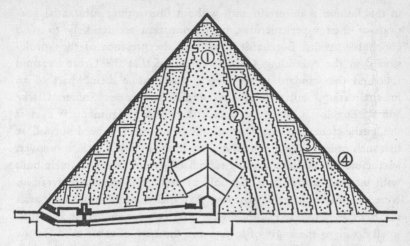

Figure 58. The pyramid of Sahurē, section looking east

structures to be built, disregarding, for the present, the chambers and corridors.

When describing the pyramid of Meidum it was stated that its core consisted of several coatings of masonry diminishing in height from the centre outwards and leaning on a central nucleus at an angle of about 75° (fig. 17). Each layer was cased from top to bottom with Tura limestone, and its outer surface dressed smooth. The step pyramid so formed was subsequently converted into a true pyramid by filling the steps with backing-blocks and adding an outer casing of dressed Tura limestone. Borchardt was able to show that the same method, modified only to the extent of leaving the faces of the internal casing-stones rough, was still practised by pyramid builders in the Vth Dynasty (Plate 42),[8] and it may well have continued until an even later date in the Old Kingdom. The pyramid of Sahurē at Abu Sir, for example, was composed of upright layers of core masonry (fig. 58: 1), internal casings of fine limestone (fig. 58: 2), backing-blocks of stone (fig. 58: 3), and lastly the usual smooth outer casing of Tura limestone (fig. 58: 4). Whether the three main pyramids at Giza were also built

8. L. Borchardt, *Das Grabdenkmal des Königs Sahure*, Vol. I, Pl. 7.

in this fashion is uncertain and, without dismantling substantial portions of their superstructures, no examination seems likely to yield conclusive results. Borchardt considered the presence of the 'girdle-stones' in the Ascending Corridor as proof that the Great Pyramid followed the standard pattern, each 'girdle-stone' being part of an internal casing,[9] but two equally eminent authorities, Somers Clarke and R. Engelbach, refused to accept Borchardt's arguments;[10] even if the 'girdle-stones' are not internal casings, however, it need not follow that such casings do not exist elsewhere in the pyramid. It is, moreover, irrefutable that all the surviving subsidiary pyramids at Giza were built with internal casings, and it would be strange if the main pyramids were constructed in a different way. Externally, all pyramids built after the Bent Pyramid at Dahshur were alike, except in size and in such small details as the angle of incline and the kind of stone used for the lower courses of the outer casing. The normal angle of incline was about 52° – a slope which, in the pyramid of Meidum and in the Great Pyramid, would have resulted if the height had been made to correspond with the radius of a circle the circumference of which was equal to the perimeter of the pyramid at ground-level. The northern stone pyramid at Dahshur, with its gradient of 43° 36′, provides the only striking exception to this rule.

By reason of their shape, pyramids required progressively less constructional material with each successive upward course. Mathematical calculation can show that in a pyramid with no interior corridors or chambers 70 per cent of its mass would be embodied in the lowest third and 80 per cent in the lower half. Not more than 4 per cent of all the stone in the pyramid would have had to be lifted to the uppermost third. Nevertheless, what must have been one of the most difficult operations in the whole process of building remained until every course had been laid; it was the raising and placing in position of the pyramidion or capstone.

No architectural plans dating from the Old Kingdom or the Middle Kingdom are known to have been preserved, but a rough sketch in

---

9. L. Borchardt, *Einiges zur dritten Bauperiode der grossen Pyramide bei Gise* (Cairo, 1932).

10. Somers Clarke and R. Engelbach, *Ancient Egyptian Masonry*, pp. 123–4.

red ink on a flake of limestone, which dates from the IIIrd Dynasty, suggests that such plans were produced (fig. 59). It shows a curved line and beneath it five upright lines of varying length which are spaced at approximately equal intervals apart. On the right-hand side of each line is written the measurement of the height of the point at which that line touches the curve above a base-line which is not shown. The measurements are given in cubits and fractions of a cubit, namely

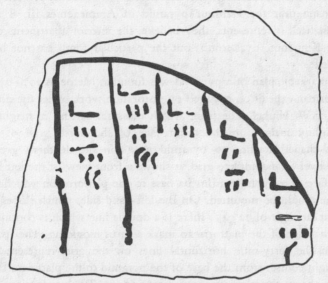

Figure 59. Sketch-plan of the saddle-back roof of a building in the Step Pyramid enclosure

palms and fingers. As the curve rises, the height increases from zero to 3 cubits, 3 palms and 2 fingers. The sketch was found on the west side of the northern building in the Step Pyramid enclosure and it seems likely that it was drawn for the guidance of masons engaged in constructing the saddle-back roof of one of the buildings in the same vicinity.

Two limestone models of pyramids may perhaps be placed in the category of architectural and planning aids (Plates 60, 61). The first was obtained (but not excavated) by Petrie at Memphis and he expressed the opinion that it was a model of Zoser's Step Pyramid. The second is a true pyramid which he found in his excavations at the labyrinth of Ammenemes III, and there is no reason to doubt that it represents the king's Hawara pyramid. It also shares with that pyramid its angle of inclination, which is flatter than was customary in the Middle Kingdom. There is, however, no certainty that these models were not made after their respective pyramids had been built. The purpose of another limestone model, which was found by Arnold and Stadelmann near the Dahshur pyramid of Ammenemes III, is also problematical. It represents, they believe, the interior apartments of a Middle Kingdom royal tomb, but the particular tomb has not been identified.

A remarkable plan of a pyramid was found at Meroe in 1979 by an East German expedition engaged on restoration work under the direction of F.W. Hinkel. The plan, which measures 1.70 m. in height, is very lightly incised on the outer face of the north wall of the offering-chapel attached to pyramid no. 8 in the northern group. Drawn over an incomplete grid, it shows a front view of the left half of the face of a pyramid from its base to the platform on which the capstone would be mounted. On the left-hand side, which slopes inwards at an angle of 72° 45', there is a double line which is continued along the edge of the platform to mark a torus moulding. The spaces between the forty-nine horizontal lines on the grid represent the forty-eight courses from the base of the pyramid to the platform, their total height on the plan amounting to 1.675 m. Twelve divisions are marked on the base-line, although only five of the vertical lines are actually drawn, in addition to the central bisecting line of the complete face of the pyramid. The eleven divisions thus indicated have a combined length of 0.578 m. for half the base of the pyramid. An examination of the other pyramids in the northern group showed that there was only one, no. 2 – the pyramid of Amanikhabale, a king who ruled in the second half of the first century B.C. – which fulfilled all the requirements of the plan and also showed that the plan had been produced at a scale of approximately 1:10. The actual dimensions of the base of pyramid no. 2 are 11.65 × 11.70 m., the angle of its slope is 72° 48' and its edges have a torus moulding. The very small discrepancies between the plan and these measurements are easily accounted for by the condition of the pyramid and the difficulty of drawing a perfectly exact plan on five courses of sandstone blocks.

Herodotus, who was presumably quoting the tradition current in Egypt during his time, makes the following assertions with regard to the building of the Great Pyramid:

The pyramid was built in tiers, battlementwise, as it is called, or, according to others, stepwise. When the pyramid was completed in this form, they raised the remaining stones to their places by means of machines formed of short beams of wood. The first machine raised them from the ground to the top of the first step. On this there was another machine, which received the stone upon its arrival, and conveyed it to the second step, whence a third machine advanced it still higher. Either they had as many machines as there were steps in the pyramid, or possibly they had but a single machine, which, being easily moved, was transferred from tier to tier as the stone rose – both accounts are given and therefore I mention both. The upper portion of the pyramid was finished first, then the middle, and finally the part which was lowest and nearest the ground.[11]

Archaeological discovery, while tending to confirm the concluding sentence, has so far revealed little evidence in support of Herodotus's statements as a whole, but it must be admitted that pyramid construction is a subject on which the last word has certainly not yet been written.

In the absence of the pulley – a device which does not seem to have been known in Egypt before Roman times – only one method of raising heavy weights was open to the ancient Egyptians, namely by means of ramps composed of brick and earth which sloped upwards from the level of the ground to whatever height was desired. If, for instance, a short wall were to be built, the stones for each course after the lowest would be taken to the required level on a ramp constructed against the wall for the whole of its length and projecting outwards at right angles to the line of the wall. With the addition of each successive course of masonry, the ramp would be raised and also extended so that the gradient remained unchanged. Finally, when the wall had been built to its full height, the ramp would be dismantled and the outer faces of the stones, which had not previously been made smooth,

11. *Herodotus*, II, 125 (Rawlinson's translation).

dressed course by course downwards as the level of the ramp was reduced. Relics of the brick retaining walls of individual compartments of such a ramp can still be seen on the inner (eastern) side of the base of the First Pylon of the temple of Karnak. In every probability the pylon was built in late times; it was never finished, as the roughness of the surface shows (Plate 62). What seems to be a clear indication that the same method was used in building the pyramids has been furnished by the discovery of the remains of ramps at the pyramid of Meidum, in the unfinished mortuary temple of Mycerinus, and at the pyramid of Ammenemes I at Lisht. The gradient of a ramp probably depended on the weight of the material to be conveyed. A papyrus in the British Museum dating from the XIXth Dynasty gives the following approximate measurements for a hypothetical ramp: length 415 yards, width 32 yards, and maximum height 35 yards. By arithmetical calculation it may be deduced that the gradient of this ramp would have been about 1 in 12. The gradient of the ramp in the mortuary temple of Mycerinus was about 1 in 8.

If it be conceded, as the evidence would appear to demand, that ramps were employed by the builders of the pyramids, how were these ramps set out? No difficulty would arise in the construction of a step pyramid, because each step could serve as a platform on which four ramps could be built sideways, one against each face of the monument. Narrow foothold embankments built of brick against the portions of the faces which were not partly or entirely covered by the ramps would enable the builders to manoeuvre more easily the stones of the outer casing. By a progressive reduction in the height of the embankments they could subsequently begin work on dressing the exposed surface of the casing while the upper part of the pyramid was still under construction. The operation could not have been completed until the last stone had been taken to the top and the ramps had been dismantled.

It has been suggested that a similar method, but without the addition of foothold embankments, was employed in building the true pyramid.[12] According to this suggestion one ramp would begin at each

12. Dows Dunham, 'Building an Egyptian Pyramid', in *Archaeology*, Vol. 9, No. 3 (1956), pp. 159-65.

corner of the monument and continue its upward course around all four faces until it reached the summit. Helicoidal ramps of this kind, built in tiers, would depend for their support, beyond the first stage, on the casing-blocks which, it is maintained, would be laid in steps and cut back to the correct angle after the work of building was finished. In order to demonstrate the feasibility of this method a model of a pyramid with tier ramps was constructed at the Museum of Science, Boston, Mass., in 1950, and no practical difficulties in putting the theory into effect were discovered. Nevertheless it is hard to believe that this was in reality the method employed by the ancient Egyptians for three reasons: it does not accord with the traces of ramps found at Meidum and elsewhere; undressed casing-blocks, such as may be seen at the base of the pyramid of Mycerinus, though rough, are not step-like and would not have provided support for a ramp; if, as observation suggests, the casing-stones were laid from in front it is questionable whether the widest possible step would have allowed sufficient space for blocks of the weight of those at Giza to be unloaded from their sledges and placed in position. It may perhaps be argued that the rough granite casing-blocks in the pyramid of Mycerinus represent an inter-mediate stage after the steps had been cut away, but support for the ramps would have been almost completely lacking in the Bent Pyra-mid, the casing-blocks of which, being laid on beds inclining down-wards towards the centre, required very little trimming and would have presented an almost unbroken surface at every stage in construc-tion.

A more plausible solution seems to be that a single supply-ramp was constructed to cover either the whole or a part of the pyramid. As the pyramid rose in height, so the ramp was increased both in height and in length; simultaneously the top surface would become progressively narrower to correspond with the constantly diminishing breadth of the pyramid face. If the angle of incline of the pyramid were 52°, the two side faces of the ramp would also slope at an angle of 52°, so that any risk of collapse would be eliminated. The sides of the pyramid which were not covered by the supply-ramp would have foothold embank-ments of sufficient width at the top to allow for the passage of men and building material, but, since they were not required for raising the stones from the ground, their gradient on the exposed outer surface could be as steep as would be compatible with firmness. Wooden baulks, some of which were actually found *in situ* by the American excavators at Lisht, would be placed on the top surface of both the supply-ramp and the foothold embankments in order to provide a firm roadway for the passage of sledges bearing the stone blocks.

As an illustration of the practical application of the method suggested, let it be imagined that a pyramid has been built to half its final height. Nothing of the stonework already laid would be visible from the ground, because three of the outer faces would be entirely covered by the foothold embankments and the fourth face would be screened either entirely by the supply-ramp or partly by the supply-ramp and partly by foothold embankments. The top surface of the pyramid would resemble a square platform and would be ready to receive the next course of masonry. The first stones to be hauled up to the platform would be core-blocks from the local quarries; their sides and top surfaces would be left rough, but the bottom surfaces – the so-called bedding joints – would be smooth. These stones would be taken to the centre of the platform and laid against each other, the gaps caused by the irregularities in their sides being often left unfilled. Care would be taken to extend the new course evenly in all four directions, so that it always remained approximately in the form of a square, and at regular intervals its sides would be made absolutely equal in length by the addition of an internal casing composed of Tura limestone laid directly above the corresponding casing in the floor of the platform; the outer face of the casing would be cut so as to incline inwards at an angle of about 75°, but it would not be dressed smooth. At length, the area of the course being laid would have been enlarged until only a narrow margin at the outer edges of the original platform remained uncovered. At that stage the backing-blocks of local limestone would be added and considerably greater attention would be given to securing close joints. In the Great Pyramid the backing-blocks were laid in such a way that they sloped slightly inwards towards the centre of each course, with the result that a noticeable depression runs down the middle of each face – a peculiarity shared, as far as is known, by no other pyramid.

The core having been completed, only the outer casing of Tura limestone remained to be added. It was a delicate operation and imperfections in the setting of the stones would not only mar the outward appearance of the monument, but, unless counteracted, would lead to irregularity in the pyramidal form. The joints, moreover, must be as close as possible. In order to save time and to achieve the highest possible degree of accuracy, the fitting of the rising joints – those between neighbouring blocks on the same course – was probably carried out by highly skilled masons working on ground-level. Only by such a method could the results to be observed in the so-called oblique rising joints – those cut either not at right angles to the bedding joint or not parallel with the central axes of the pyramid – have been attained. Possibly the joints between the backs of the casing-stones and the front faces of the backing-blocks were also fitted on the ground so that, when each block finally reached the men who were to lay it, only the upper surface and the front – already cut to the pyramid angle but not dressed – needed further attention from the masons.

Even after making such careful preparations, the laying of a casing-block was still a difficult task, especially if it were a large block weighing perhaps more than ten tons. Doubtless it would be carried on its sledge to the furthest possible point, namely on the embankment directly opposite the place in the structure which it was ultimately destined to occupy. The block would then be levered sideways off the sledge until it rested on battens placed ready to receive it on top of the casing-stone in the course below; in order to enable levers to be used, bosses were left by the masons on the outer face of every casing-block. While it stood in that position, a thin layer of mortar would be spread over both the bedding joint and the rising joint about to be formed. The main purpose of the mortar was to provide a kind of lubricant so that the casing-block, after being lowered to its bed, might be slid first into contact with the block of casing previously laid and then back against the backing-blocks. How this last operation was performed is not clear, but it is possible that it could have been achieved by pulling on ropes attached to a baulk of timber laid across the free outer corner of the casing-block and then pressing it back into line by levering from in front. The few remaining casing-blocks at the foot of the Great

Pyramid offer the best examples of such jointing hitherto discovered; the credit for being the first to bring their excellence to the notice of the modern world belongs to Petrie, who wrote of them:

Several measures were taken of the thickness of the joints in the casing-stones. The mean thickness of the joints of the north-eastern casing-stones is 0.02 inches, and therefore the mean variation of the cutting of the stone from the straight line and from a true square is but 0.01 on a length of 75 inches up the face, an amount of accuracy equal to the most modern opticians' straight-edges of such a length. Though the stones were brought as close as $\frac{1}{500}$ inch, or, in fact, in contact, the mean opening of the joint was but $\frac{1}{50}$ inch.[13]

When the casing-stones on all four sides of the course had been placed in position, it would be necessary to make a survey in order to ascertain whether the correct form had been retained. Small deviations were almost inevitable and, if detected in time, could be counteracted in the laying of the next course. While this work was in progress, the main supply-ramp and the foothold embankments would be raised to the new level of the pyramid and masons would be employed on the task of dressing the tops of the stones just laid – the bedding joints of the course about to be added. So the building would continue to grow course by course until lastly the capstone, often made of granite or basalt, would be placed on the apex. As a means of securing the stone firmly to its bed, a projection resembling a disk would be carved in the centre of the base to fit like a tenon into a mortice cut to receive it in the middle of the top course of masonry. It may therefore be deduced that the capstone, already shaped but still in the rough, was taken to the top of the pyramid on its sledge, and then supported on levers while the sledge was being removed. Battens would be inserted underneath and a thin layer of mortar be spread over the bed; finally, after the removal of the battens, it would be lowered by means of levers placed under the side-bosses. An inscription found by Jéquier at the pyramid of Queen Udjebten refers to the gilded capstone on her pyramid, which suggests that these stones were, at least sometimes, overlaid with gold. The earliest known example was discovered in

13. W.M.F. Petrie, *The Pyramids and Temples of Gizeh*, p. 44.

1982 by the excavators of the German Archaeological Institute in Cairo at the northern pyramid of Seneferu at Dahshur. Made of Tura limestone, it had no inscription or decoration and it showed no sign of having been overlaid with gold or any other metal. Its base was about 5 feet square and its height was between 3 and 4 feet, the precise size being uncertain until the pieces into which it was broken are re-assembled. Part of another Old Kingdom capstone, made of black granite, was found in the season 1978-9 by the Czechoslovak expedition under Miroslav Verner near the pyramid of Khentkaues at Abu Sir.

Undoubtedly the finest capstone yet known is one made of grey granite which is now in the Cairo Museum. It was found at the beginning of this century by chance on the east side of the pyramid of Ammenemes III at Dahshur. All four sides bear inscriptions in which are invoked deities associated with the geographical regions which the sides face. The first is the god of the rising sun, Harakhte, who is addressed in these words: 'May the face of the king be opened so that he may see the Lord of the Horizon [i.e. Harakhte] when he crosses the sky; may he cause the king to shine as a god, lord of eternity and indestructible.' Harakhte replies that he has 'given the beautiful horizon' to the king. Among the deities invoked on the other sides are Anubis, Osiris, Ptah, Neith and the constellation of Orion. So well preserved is this capstone that some doubt has been felt whether it was ever put in position and exposed to the effects of wind and sand erosion. Possibly the plan was discarded when the king decided to build another pyramid for himself. It has also been noted that the angle of its slope differs from that of the pyramid, but this feature can be paralleled by the capstone, now missing, which stood on a small pyramid at the west end of the tomb-chapel of the princess Tia, a sister of Ramesses II, and her husband of the same name (Plate 63). The tomb was excavated in 1982 by a joint expedition of the Egypt Exploration Society and the Leiden Museum under the direction of G.T. Martin.

The laborious process of assembling the pyramid was now finished, and work could be started on dressing the four outer faces, beginning with the capstone. As the work proceeded, the supply-ramp and the foothold embankments would be lowered, thus making fresh courses of casing-stones accessible for dressing. In order to complete the task more quickly, it is possible that the reduction of the ramp and embankments was not carried out gradually, but in layers of several feet; wooden scaffolding would then be erected in their place so that a large number of men could be employed on different levels at the same time. Scaffolding was certainly known to the Egyptians, and the time saved by its use when dressing the five acres of casing on each face of the Great Pyramid, for example, would have been very considerable. When at length the whole operation had been completed, the builders would be free and the ground clear for erecting the mortuary temple, the corridor of the causeway, and the valley building, some of which had certainly had their foundations laid before the construction of the pyramid had been begun.

No mention has yet been made of the method whereby corridors and chambers would have been incorporated into pyramids. In one respect, the task resembled that of building the internal casings; both operations necessitated the introduction of closely fitting stones into a core otherwise composed of rough masonry. Since, however, the corridors and chambers occupied so small a portion of the whole pyramid, they may have been built almost independently of the rest of the work. Subsidiary ramps, capable of being dismantled in a few hours, could have been erected at any stage convenient, so that blocks could be taken to a considerably greater height than the level of the course under construction. In this way, the men employed would have time to complete their work on the interior of the pyramid before the surrounding courses of core-masonry had risen to such a height that it would become necessary to roof the corridor and chambers; afterwards, access to the interior would not be possible until the foothold embankment or supply-ramp covering the northern face of the pyramid had been lowered to the level of the entrance. As a further aid, the stones would be carefully prepared before they were required by the builders; the roofing-slabs of the King's Chamber in the Great Pyramid, for instance, were fitted together on the ground and numbered so that, when they were taken to their final position, they could be reassembled with the minimum delay. The sarcophagus, portcullises and, in the Great Pyramid only, the plug-blocks, would be introduced before the walls of the chamber, slots or gallery in which they were to rest had been fully built.

It must be emphasized that the foregoing attempt to reconstruct the methods used by the pyramid builders differs in many important respects not only from the explanation previously mentioned but also from the views expressed by some other authorities.[14] The main divergence of opinion arises in connection with the number and arrangement of the ramps – a problem on which archaeological investigation has not yet revealed sufficiently conclusive evidence to enable positive deductions to be made. Petrie, in one of his last essays on this subject, stated his belief that the casing-stones of the Great Pyramid had been taken to their respective courses with their outer faces already dressed, and that they were laid in position from the inside. The casing would thus have been laid first in every course, and the core have been filled in afterwards. By such a method, as Petrie pointed out, only one ramp would have been required and three faces of the pyramid would have been finished as soon as their casing-stones had been laid. In support of his views Petrie wrote: 'There is a small difference of angle between the [casing-]blocks at their junction, proving that the faces have not been even smoothed since being built together.'[15] There is certainly no good reason for doubting the accuracy of Petrie's observations or his deductions in so far as they apply to the method adopted for laying the few casing-stones of the Great Pyramid which have survived to the present day, but his general conclusion that the same procedure would have been followed when laying all the casing-stones of the building is open to grave objections. All the stones in question stand on the lowest course; beneath them lies a smooth pavement of Tura limestone which also projects outwards beyond the pyramid to a width of about two feet. It would have been impossible to lay these stones from the outer side without damaging the fringe of the pavement which was to

14. Petrie, 'The Building of a Pyramid', in *Ancient Egypt*, 1930, Part II, pp. 33-9; N.F. Wheeler, 'Pyramids and their Purpose', in *Antiquity*, Vol. IX (1935), pp. 172-4; G. Goyon, *Le secret des bâtisseurs des grandes pyramides*, Khéops (1977), pp. 87-233; D. Arnold, 'Überlegungen zum Problem des Pyramidenbaues', in *M.D.A.I.K.*, Vol. 37 (1981), pp. 15-28.

15. Petrie, op. cit., p. 34.

remain exposed. Likewise, it would have been undesirable to dress the lower edge of stones after they had been placed in position: the surface of the pavement would inevitably have been chipped and scratched. Moreover, these particular casing-stones may well have been laid before the core in order to define the size and orientation of the pyramid base. Slight adjustments in the setting of the stones could so much more easily have been made if they were free at both back and front; any error at the base would result in the faulty orientation of the whole monument, and might destroy its regularity of form. If Petrie could have shown that casing-blocks on a higher level than the bottom course in any pyramid were laid at an angle to each other, his argument would have carried greater weight. Furthermore, the evidence in favour of the method of laying casing-stones from the front is very considerable. Several unfinished works testify that it was the technique employed by Egyptian builders from the inception of megalithic masonry until the latest times. An example exists even in a pyramid, namely the pyramid of Mycerinus, where the limestone which cased the upper portion was completely dressed, but the granite casing lower down was left partly in the rough, thus marking the point where work on the monument came to a premature end. Laying masonry from the front, however, necessitated both leaving the outer faces of the stones in the rough until they had been placed in position and the erection of embankments against the outer face of the course previously laid, which would have involved, in the case of a pyramid, building embankments against all four faces.

A theory which differs considerably from the theories suggested hitherto has been advanced by Dieter Arnold. Proceeding from the fact that, at the northern pyramid of Seneferu at Dahshur, the tracks along which the stone was brought from the local quarries ended within about 150 yards of the foot of the pyramid, he contends that the space between the tracks and the pyramid would not have allowed room for ramps of the ordinary kind. He also rejects, on technical grounds, theories which involve the use of helicoidal ramps. Instead, he suggests that the ramp was begun in the middle of one side of the pyramid and was directed inwards, leaving a chasm in the heart of the pyramid (fig. 60: 1). Its length was increased as each new course was

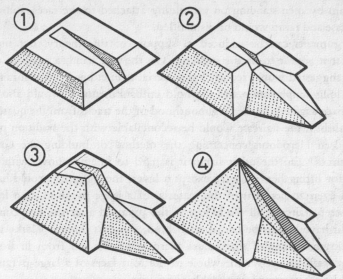

Figure 60. Pyramid construction by internal ramps and external stairs

laid, until it had reached a point near the opposite side of the pyramid. It could still be used for several more courses by making its gradient steeper, but a slope of about 10° was probably the limit. At that stage the ramp would be gradually lengthened outwards until it had reached a point in line with the nearer end of the tracks from the local quarries (fig. 60: 2). This ramp also would continue to be used until its gradient had risen to 10°. Two ramps would then be constructed at the top of the central ramp, one on each side of it, and both would be turned backwards in relation to it (fig. 60: 3). When those two ramps had served their purpose, only 20 per cent of the building material remained to be laid. The chasm in the pyramid was then filled with masonry and the outer part of the ramp became the base of a straight high staircase which ultimately reached the top of the pyramid (fig. 60: 4). In order to place the heavy capstone in position, it would be necessary to erect a temporary wooden platform at the summit on the three sides of the pyramid which were not covered by the staircase. Finally the four faces of the pyramid would be smoothed from top to bottom by men standing on scaffolding attached to the faces, and the staircase and ramp would be dismantled.

Arguments can be adduced in support of this theory, but those against it appear to be the stronger. On the one hand, a ramp of the kind suggested would require less material than either helicoidal ramps or a long supply-ramp and foothold embankments; it would also fit the space available in the neighbourhood of the tracks from the quarries at Dahshur; the staircase would be reconcilable with the tradition preserved in Herodotus concerning the method of building the Great Pyramid.[16] On the other hand, it is hard to imagine how, with no tool for lifting heavy blocks except a lever, the Egyptians could have lifted even 20 per cent of the material of a large pyramid up a long and steep staircase; all the blocks in the pyramid after the first course would have had to be laid from behind, whereas Somers Clarke and Engelbach concluded that stones were generally laid from in front; fixing scaffolding over the whole of the four faces of a large pyramid would have presented formidable difficulties.

The methods used by the ancient Egyptians will probably long remain a subject of debate, at least in matters of detail, and one reason is likely to be the conflicting nature of some of the evidence. The likelihood seems to be that there was less consistency in procedure than has sometimes been supposed. A simple instance of evidential conflict can be illustrated by two recent discoveries. It has already been mentioned that the pyramid of Mycerinus, in which parts of the granite casing at the base have not been smoothed, shows that, at least in that pyramid, the process of smoothing was carried out from the top downwards. In the northern pyramid at Dahshur, however, the German excavators found in 1983 that (a) the casing and the core-blocks had been laid at the same time, and (b) the smoothing process had followed from the bottom upwards. Similar instances of conflicting evidence in matters of technique have now become too numerous to be ignored.

A suggestion regarding the construction of pyramids which owes its origin to Richard Lepsius was that their size was determined by the length of their owner's reign – the so-called accretion theory. Undoubtedly some pyramids, notably the Step Pyramid of Zoser and the

16. See p.257, above.

Meidum pyramid, underwent successive enlargements and some, probably including the Great Pyramid and the pyramid of Mycerinus, were altered internally while under construction, but changes in the original design were, on the whole, exceptional. If length of reign had possessed any direct bearing on the dimensions of a pyramid, it might have been expected that Pepi II, who occupied the throne for about ninety-four years, would have built a pyramid several times larger than that of Mycerinus, who reigned only about eighteen years, or that Cheops in a reign of about twenty-three years would have failed to build a pyramid equal to that of Unas, who is believed to have ruled for thirty years. Clearly, therefore, the length of a king's reign did not necessarily affect the size of his pyramid; the determining considerations seem rather to have been his personal inclinations, his power, and the religious beliefs current in his time.

Divergent opinions have been expressed by chemists on the question whether the pyramids were painted. Tests carried out by A. Pochan on fragments of the outer casing of the Great Pyramid and of the pyramid of Chephren revealed traces of chemical elements which were not naturally present in the stone, but which he believed could be explained on the assumption that the monuments had been coated with a thin layer of siliceous gypsum plaster and painted with a pigment of red ochre. That the casing-stones of pyramids show coloration varying from brownish-red to greyish-black is not disputed. There is, however, disagreement on the cause of this coloration. A. Lucas, who accepted in the main Pochan's chemical analysis, maintained that no coating of plaster had been applied and that the colour was merely the result of desert patination brought about gradually by atmospheric conditions. Both these authorities have received independent support for their contentions, but a valuable piece of evidence which seems to have been overlooked is that the pyramid, when employed as a hieroglyphic sign on the painted walls of Old Kingdom mastabas, is usually represented white with a band of brownish-red stippled with black at the base and sometimes a blue or yellow capstone. The stippled band is clearly intended to indicate pink granite, as exemplified in the two lowest courses of the casing of the pyramid of Chephren, the blue signifies grey granite and the yellow must represent the gold overlay which was sometimes placed on the capstone. If the main body of the casing of pyramids had normally been painted, it would surely not have been depicted, when reproduced as a hieroglyph, in white, the natural colour of Tura limestone.

In the face of so many unknown or unconfirmed factors, speculations regarding the number of men required for building one of the larger pyramids and the time needed for the work may perhaps appear vain. Certainly, any estimate based on the evidence now available must lack precision and can only serve to convey an approximate idea. Herodotus claims to have been informed that the Great Pyramid was built in twenty years. Levies numbering one hundred thousand men, he says, were employed for 'periods of three months' on transporting the stones from the quarry to the pyramid.[17] Herodotus seems to have intended his readers to understand that the aggregate of men engaged annually was 400,000 – four separate groups of 100,000, each group being employed for three months in the year. Such a number would, however, have been unnecessarily large, as a simple mathematical calculation will demonstrate. If the estimated total of 2,300,000 separate blocks in the pyramid is approximately correct, the average number of blocks to be transported annually for twenty years would have been 115,000. The mean weight of the blocks is about $2\frac{1}{2}$ tons, a weight which Petrie believed could have been handled by a gang of eight men.[18] Assuming that Petrie was right and that only 100,000 men were employed in a year, each gang would have been required to move ten blocks in twelve weeks. Such a task would almost certainly have been within the ability of a gang, bearing in mind that the distance to be traversed, especially by the core-blocks, was not very great. Moreover, as Petrie pointed out, the work could have been done during the inundation season, between the end of July and the end of October, when the land could not be cultivated and the majority of the population would have been idle.

A possibility which cannot be ignored is that oxen were sometimes used in the Old Kingdom to draw sledges. In the tombs at Meidum of Nefermaat and Rehotep, both of whom lived in the time of Seneferu,

17. *Herodotus*, II, 124.
18. Petrie, *The Pyramids and Temples of Gizeh*, p. 210.

there are scenes of oxen drawing ploughs, but the earliest instance of oxen being depicted drawing a sledge loaded with a large block of limestone does not occur until the beginning of the XVIIIth Dynasty. Appropriately it is represented on the wall of a quarry at Tura. Oxen, Arnold asserts, could have been used not only on ground-level, but on an internal pyramid ramp to a height of about 65 feet.

There can be little doubt but that, in addition to the men levied annually for the special purpose of transporting the blocks of the Great Pyramid, a large number of whole-time workers must have been engaged in building the pyramid. These men, consisting of skilled masons and an attendant body of labourers, were continuously employed preparing and laying the blocks and erecting or dismantling the ramps and foothold embankments. They lived, it may be presumed, in the buildings found by Petrie lying west of the pyramid of Chephren. About 4,000 men, according to Petrie's estimate, could have been housed in these barracks, and that figure would therefore represent the total number of permanent workers. The chips of stone cast away by the masons were dumped over the side of the cliffs both north and south of the pyramid. Commenting on the size of the dumps, Petrie wrote: 'They are probably equal in bulk to more than half of the pyramid.'[19]

A complete solution to such problems as the methods used by the pyramid builders, the number of men employed and the time required for the task would undoubtedly shed a very valuable sidelight on technical development in ancient times, but it would hardly be likely to provide an answer to an even more interesting question, namely why the early Egyptian kings should have chosen to construct their tombs in the pyramidal form. Before this question is considered, however, the derivation of the name is worth examining. In Egyptian, this type of tomb, at least in the geometrically true form, was called *m(e)r*, a name which has not been suspected of concealing any descriptive significance. The word 'pyramid' owes its origin to the Greek *pyramis*, plural *pyramides*, for which a satisfactory Egyptian derivation has often been sought, but in vain. A geometrical term *per-em-us* (literally 'what goes [straight] up from the *us*' – a word of uncertain meaning), which

19. Petrie, op. cit., p. 213.

embodies the requisite consonants, is used to indicate the vertical height of a pyramid in an Egyptian mathematical treatise.[20] To suppose, however, that *pyramis* was derived from *per-em-us* would imply that the Greeks either mistook the meaning of the Egyptian term or, for reasons unknown, deliberately named the whole structure after a part, by the linguistic process known as synecdoche. In the absence of any more convincing explanation, it seems better to regard *pyramis* as a purely Greek word which had no etymological connection with the Egyptian language. An exactly similar word exists with the meaning 'wheaten cake', and the suggestion has been made that the early Greeks used this word humorously as a name for the Egyptian monuments,[21] possibly because, when seen from a distance, they resembled large cakes. The word *obeliskos*, which in addition to meaning an obelisk also means a 'little spit' or 'skewer', furnishes another example of the same kind of process of thought whereby the Greeks, instead of borrowing a foreign word, jocularly adapted a descriptive word of their own to name an object which had no exact parallel in their own country.

Two important factors, one constant and the other variable, which influenced the development of early Egyptian sepulchral architecture were the need to provide sufficient protection for the body and the belief that the tomb, in its general character, should supply the owner with the basic requirements of the after-life. Within the limits thus imposed the architect could exercise his artistic talents and introduce structural innovations. Although it follows as a corollary that a major change in the design of the tomb probably signified a change in the prevailing conception of the after-life, it does not also follow that previous architectural elements were immediately discarded; if possible the architect tried either to superimpose the new on the old or, alternatively, to combine the new with the old as separate constructions within one complex. The results of the two methods are seen most clearly in the brick mastabas of the Ist Dynasty at Saqqara which embodied the predynastic mound (figs. 3 and 4), the Step Pyramid of Zoser (figs. 5–7), and the pyramids of Meidum and Sahurē (figs. 17 and

20. The Rhind Mathematical Papyrus in the British Museum.
21. W.G. Waddell, *Herodotus*, II, p. 139.

58). It is true that the mastabas at Saqqara were not, at least exclusively, royal tombs and that the two examples chosen were the only mastabas in which at the time of excavation the mound could be recognized, but in the light of the knowledge gained by this discovery its presence has been suspected in other mastabas previously excavated. It must also be conceded that no account is taken of the Early Dynastic royal 'tombs' at Abydos, the superstructures of which were completely destroyed. Nevertheless the evidence available, though manifestly incomplete for the early period, is capable of interpretation as a connected sequence of architectural developments which reflected progressive changes in the nature and location of the royal after-life and in the apparatus considered necessary for its realization.

Burial customs in Upper and Lower Egypt before the unification under Menes were certainly not identical. One important difference concerned the type of grave. In Upper Egypt the dead were buried in cemeteries situated on the edge of the desert and separated from the settlements of the living. Their graves, though sometimes lined with brick and roofed with timber, were outwardly marked only by mounds of sand. In Lower Egypt, however, if the practice exemplified at Merimde Benisalame (about 30 miles north-west of Cairo) may be regarded as typical, the dead were buried within the settlement and occasionally under the floors of dwelling-houses. Perhaps the original intention of the house-burial was merely to give the dead greater protection than would have been possible in isolated cemeteries, but it can easily be imagined that in the course of time the belief would grow that the dead required houses as part of their burial equipment. It would certainly explain why the Upper Egyptian conquerors, who undoubtedly adopted other Lower Egyptian customs, should suddenly have begun to build tombs in the shape of houses (mastabas), made, moreover, of mud-brick, a material which had been used for houses in Lower Egypt for centuries, but not in Upper Egypt. Among the customs of their own people which they continued to observe were the separation of the cemeteries from the settlements and, at least in some instances, the construction of the mound above the actual grave. It is hardly conceivable that a feature so adventitious in origin as the mound should have been retained if it had not acquired some magico-religious significance which gave it too great an importance to permit of its general abandonment. Only one explanation suggests itself, namely that it had already come to be regarded as a symbol of the primeval mound which emerged from the waters of chaos, as patches of high ground emerged annually from the Nile when the waters of the inundation receded. On this mound Atum, the god of creation, was believed to have first manifested himself and to have created the universe. It was thus the symbol of existence, as opposed to non-existence, and consequently, when placed above the grave or embodied in the tomb, it was imagined that it could serve as a potent source of magic from which the dead might hope to receive a renewal of existence.

The suggestion has been made that the pyramid, in both its designs, was only a monumental representation of the primeval mound, but although this conception may have been present in the minds of the Egyptians it seems more probable that a different motive inspired its development. Just as the mastaba had been superimposed on the mound in the Ist Dynasty, so was Zoser's Step Pyramid, at the beginning of the IIIrd Dynasty, superimposed on a solid box-like structure which has generally been regarded as a mastaba. But was it really a mastaba? If so the squareness of its plan would be difficult to understand. Nothing, however, seems to rule out the possibility that the structure represents the mound which, in the simple form but not in the stepped form, was nearly square (34 feet 6 inches × 30 feet 3 inches) whereas the mastaba (123 feet 3 inches × 52 feet) was oblong. The existence of an independent mastaba (the South Mastaba) is not decisive. On the one hand it may be explained as a substitute for the central structure conceived as a mastaba, and, on the other hand, if the central structure be regarded as a mound, it may be considered as having no connection with an original plan to build a mastaba tomb which was superseded when it was decided to build a pyramid. Whichever explanation is correct, its position in the core of the southern enclosure wall would be in accord with the regular practice of concealing the older type of tomb.

If the step pyramid is not itself a monumental mound and not, as has sometimes been supposed, a mere architectural development achieved by superimposing one mastaba on another, how is its form to be explained and what was its purpose? The Pyramid Texts suggest an answer to these questions. One of the many different ways by which the deceased king, or more probably his spiritualized body, could approach the celestial heaven was by a staircase. Spell 267 reads: 'A staircase to heaven is laid for him [i.e. the king] so that he may mount up to heaven thereby.' The same thought is repeated almost verbatim in Spell 619. It is not difficult to imagine that the same process of imitative magic as had inspired the inclusion of the mound in the mastaba was again responsible for the choice of the step pyramid. As models, both were credited with embracing the magical properties ascribed to the objects which they represented. Through the possession of the pyramid the king would be able to mount up to heaven at will and to return to his tomb in order to enjoy the offerings brought to him by his priests and relations. One of the Pyramid Texts, Spell 717, makes it clear that the king had five meals in the course of a twenty-four-hour day, three in the sky and two on earth. It seems from the Abu Sir papyri that the terrestrial meals occurred one in the morning and the other in the evening.

Perhaps some support for the explanation of the step pyramid as a staircase may be seen in the writing of the Egyptian word ꜥr meaning 'to ascend'. It was the regular practice of the Egyptians to add a sign, the so-called determinative or sense-sign, to the consonantal spelling of a word, in order to define its meaning; vowels were never written. The determinative of the word ꜥr is ⌂, which has generally been regarded as a double staircase, but it could equally well have been a representation of a step pyramid, for the Egyptians, when depicting an object, always gave a full view, either from the front or from the side. The technique of drawing a three-quarter view was unknown to them. Thus the determinative of the word for a true pyramid – the word for a step pyramid has not yet been identified – is always written △ which represents the front view of a true pyramid and of one side of the surrounding wall. If ⌂ does represent a step pyramid it must have been chosen as the determinative of the word ꜥr because step pyramids were particularly associated with the idea of ascending.

Step pyramids (apart from a brief revival in the time of the XVIIIth Dynasty at Soleb in the Sudan) remained in favour for perhaps less than a century. At the beginning of the IVth Dynasty Seneferu built the Bent Pyramid at Dahshur, the first tomb planned from the beginning as a true pyramid. In doing so he made the task of the builders incomparably more difficult and laborious; the true pyramid required for its construction long and high embankments and at least one ramp of immense length and height, whereas a step pyramid needed only a small number of low ramps. Whether or not a step pyramid was embodied within the Bent Pyramid has never been ascertained, but if Seneferu had already built a step pyramid at Meidum he may not have thought it necessary to build a composite pyramid. His successors however certainly followed the practice of superimposing the new type of tomb on the old (fig. 58) and thereby no doubt hoped to profit from the magical properties ascribed to both types. What were the supposed advantages offered by the true pyramid at the cost of so much additional labour in comparison with the step pyramid?

J.H. Breasted, writing about the importance of the pyramid, stated:

The pyramidal form of the king's tomb was of the most sacred significance. The king was buried under the very symbol of the sun-god which stood in the holy of holies in the sun-temple at Heliopolis, a symbol upon which, from the day when he created the gods, he was accustomed to manifest himself in the form of a phoenix; and when in mountainous proportions the pyramid rose above the king's sepulchre, dominating the royal city below and the valley beyond for many miles, it was the loftiest object which greeted the sun-god in all the land and his morning rays glittered on its shining summit long before he scattered the shadows in the dwellings of humbler mortals below.[22]

Although it now seems probable that the stone symbol of the sun-god at Heliopolis, the *benben*, was conical and not pyramidal in shape, Breasted was undoubtedly right in associating it with the true pyramid. The construction of a conical building of pyramidal dimensions would surely have defeated the ancient Egyptian builders, and moreover it could not easily have been superimposed on a step pyramid. But what did the *benben* and its architectural derivative, the true pyramid, represent? Only one answer suggests itself: the rays of the sun shining down on earth. A remarkable spectacle may sometimes be seen in the late

22. J.H. Breasted, *The Development of Religion and Thought in Ancient Egypt*, p. 72.

afternoon of a cloudy winter day at Giza. When standing on the road to Saqqara and gazing westwards at the pyramid plateau, it is possible to see the sun's rays striking downwards through a gap in the clouds at about the same angle as the slope of the Great Pyramid. The impression made on the mind by the scene is that the immaterial prototype and the material replica are here ranged side by side.[23]

Is it necessary to suppose with Breasted that the true pyramid was intended merely as a copy of the solar symbol in the temple of Heliopolis? Could it not, like the step pyramid, also have possessed a supposed practical purpose? The Pyramid Texts often describe the king as mounting to heaven on the rays of the sun. Spell 508 of these texts, for instance, reads: 'I have trodden those thy rays as a ramp under my feet whereon I mount up to that my mother, the living Uraeus on the brow of Rē.' Again, Spell 523 reads: 'Heaven hath strengthened for thee the rays of the sun in order that thou mayest lift thyself to heaven as the eye of Rē.' The temptation to regard the true pyramid as a material representation of the sun's rays and consequently as a means whereby the dead king could ascend to heaven seems irresistible. Such an explanation would give the true pyramid a practical purpose in keeping not only with the step pyramid but also with the other elements in the royal mortuary complex. Moreover, the pyramid would not be the only material representation of an intangible object included in the king's funerary equipment; the wooden boats placed near the pyramid in pits lined with Tura limestone may, in some cases, have been representations of the immaterial boats in which the dead king would traverse the sky in company with the sun-god. The underlying conception in each case was the principle of creation by imitation: a model, whether it was a stone statue of a person or a scene carved in relief, was thought to possess all the virtues of the actual object which it represented. Size was not a matter of primary importance to the efficacy of the substitute, and herein may be one reason for the rapid

23. Alexandre Moret, *Le Nil*, p. 203, makes the following observation: 'These great triangles forming the sides of the pyramids seem to fall from the sky like the beams of the sun when its disk, though veiled by storm, pierces the clouds and lets down to earth a ladder of rays.'

decline in the dimensions of the pyramid after the time of Cheops and Chephren.

Although the two types of pyramid admit of interpretations which are similar, at least in their broad conception, it seems unlikely that the change in design occurred merely because doubts were felt about the efficacy of the staircase method of approach to heaven. The transition was accompanied by the construction of a complex of a very different kind in which the mortuary temple was placed not on the north side but on the east side facing the rising sun. This position would be natural in a solar cult, whereas a northern orientation would seem to be inexplicable. If the same principle governed the choice of position for the temple of the step pyramid it should be indicative of the cult with which it was associated.

Turning again to the Pyramid Texts, it may be seen that the dead king was frequently considered to have ascended to the stars, and particularly to the circumpolar stars, the so-called 'Indestructibles'. As an example, Spell 269 reads: 'He [Atum] assigns the king to those gods, who are clever and wise, the Indestructible Stars.' On the ground of internal evidence alone it has been deduced that the Pyramid Texts which refer to the stars had an independent origin from the solar spells and that eventually they were merged into the Heliopolitan doctrine. Imhotep's title 'Chief of the Observers', which became the regular title of the High Priest of Heliopolis, may itself suggest an occupation connected with astral, rather than solar, observation. Here therefore may be the difference between the underlying purpose of the true and the step pyramid, the latter being a product of the stellar cult and intended to enable the king to reach the astral heaven.

The consistency with which the entrances of pyramids were located on the northern sides would alone suggest that there was some significance in that position. As a rule, the entrance was at a higher level than the burial-chamber and the connecting passage sloped downwards, ending in a horizontal section which continued to the chamber. In origin, such corridors must have had a purely practical purpose: they gave access to the tomb after it had been built and the slope made it easier to block the corridor with massive plugs after the burial. In the course of time the Egyptians began to ascribe a magical purpose to the corridor, just as their ancestors had done in the case of the mound of sand above the predynastic grave. Seen from the burial-chamber, the entrance corridor would be sloping upwards; it would resemble a large ramp which pointed northwards towards the circumpolar stars. Through the action of imitative magic the ramp would provide the king with a way to ascend to the northern stars and to return at will to his tomb. Its function was similar to that of a step pyramid, but more specialized.

One of the consequences of changing the interior design of the Great Pyramid was that the burial-chamber was no longer under ground and approached by a downward-sloping corridor but in the superstructure, where it was approached by an upward-sloping corridor. The ramp for the king's ascent to the circumpolar stars was therefore lost. Nevertheless, a substitute for the ramp was devised in the form of the northern ventilation shaft, which was a replica, on a reduced scale, of the lower entrance corridor. From a narrow opening in the north wall of the chamber the shaft ran first, horizontally, for $6\frac{1}{2}$ feet and then rose through the masonry of the pyramid at an angle of $31°$ so that it pointed directly towards *Alpha Draconis*, which was the Pole Star in the time of Cheops.

While the northern ventilation shaft was simply a substitute for an architectural element which had previously existed, the southern ventilation shaft had no recognizable antecedent. It began in the burial-chamber, first running horizontally and then continuing upwards at a slope of about $45°$. Once every twenty-four hours the three stars in Orion's belt passed at culmination over the shaft. We learn from the Pyramid Texts that Orion and Sirius occupied almost as important positions in the king's plans for his after-life as the circumpolar stars. In Spell 821 the king is addressed in these words: 'Thou wilt regularly ascend with Orion from the eastern region of the sky, thou wilt regularly descend with Orion into the western region of the sky.' In Spell 882 the king is identified with Sirius: 'O king, thou art this great star, the companion of Orion, who traverses the sky with Orion.'

The Great Pyramid was unique in making provision for the king to associate himself with both the circumpolar stars and the constellation of Orion and Sirius. Ventilation shafts were begun in the pyramid of

Chephren, but they were soon abandoned, partly owing to technical difficulties and partly because the entrance corridor fulfilled the purpose of the northern shaft. Once the Pyramid Texts were inscribed in pyramids, the power of their magic would be enough and the king could dispense with material aids if they were difficult to provide. In the First Intermediate Period both the circumpolar stars and Orion and Sirius figured on the coffins as the representatives of the northern and the southern skies.

In the light of the foregoing explanations, it may be worth while to glance again at the Egyptian word for a pyramid; perhaps it may yet possess some significance. The Egyptians frequently designated the constituent parts of their temples and sacred enclosures by names which were indicative of their particular functions. In the temple of Heliopolis, for example, the building which housed the *benben* was named the 'House of the Benben'. The tomb, it has already been remarked, was called the 'Castle of Eternity'. Some of the elements within the pyramid complex also possessed descriptive names: the causeway was called 'place of the haul' or 'entrance of the haul' (*ra-seta*) because it was the way along which the sledges bearing the body of the dead king and his personal possessions would be hauled at his funeral; the stone false door in the sanctuary was named the 'entrance of the house' (*ra-per*).[24] *M(e)r*, a pyramid, could belong to the same class of name if it could be established that it was a compound consisting of the prefix *m*, found in Egyptian to convey the meaning 'instrument' or 'place', and the verb *ʿr*, 'to ascend', already mentioned: *m(e)r* would then mean either the 'place of ascension' or the 'object used for ascension'. Other examples of similarly formed words are *m(e)sw(e)r*, 'drinking place' or 'drinking bowl', *m(e)khat*, 'balance, scales' and *m(e)rkh(e)t*, 'indicator', literally 'instrument of knowing'. The disappearance of the ʿ (which corresponds with the *ayin* of the Semitic languages) thus postulated however constitutes a formidable objection to this derivation. In order to conform with known philological laws it would be necessary to suppose that the *ayin* had first been weakened into an *i* and then become assimilated with the *m*. No parallel to such a twofold development of one word has yet come to light and, in its absence,

24. Other names from the Abu Sir papyri are mentioned above, p. 164-5

the likelihood that it occurred in *m(e)r* must be open to justifiable doubt.

The Egyptians were not the only ancient people of the Middle East who believed that heaven and the gods might be reached by ascending a high building; a kindred trend of thought prevailed in Mesopotamia. At the centre of any city in Assyria or Babylonia lay a sacred area occupied by the temple complex and a royal palace. Within the temple complex was a high brick tower known as the Ziggurat. Describing the Ziggurat of Babylon – the supposed origin of the Biblical Tower of Babel – Herodotus states:

In the middle of the precinct there was a tower of solid masonry, a furlong in length and breadth, upon which was raised a second tower, and on that a third, and so on up to eight. The ascent to the upper towers is made on the outside, round all the towers ... On the topmost tower there is a spacious temple, and inside the temple stands a great bed covered with fine bedclothes, with a golden table by its side. There is no statue of any kind set up in the place, nor is the chamber occupied of nights by any one but a single native woman who, as the Chaldeans, the priests of this god, affirm, is chosen for himself by the deity out of all the women of the land. They also declare – but I for my part do not credit it – that the god comes down in person into this chamber, and sleeps upon the couch.[25]

Ziggurats, like the pyramids, were given individual names; the Ziggurat of Sippar, for example, was called the 'House of the Staircase of the Bright Heaven' – a name which itself emphasizes that the building was considered as a link between heaven and earth. The resemblance between the two edifices does not, however, extend to sepulchral realms, for the Ziggurat was certainly not a tomb, whereas every pyramid was intended for that purpose.

In contrast with the short chronological span of step pyramids, the history of the true pyramid extends over a thousand years, without taking into account its lineal successors in the Sudan. Only one king during the Old Kingdom, Shepseskaf of the IVth Dynasty, is known to have possessed a tomb of a different pattern, but doubtless the ephemeral kings, of whom there were many in the two Intermediate Periods, were seldom able to command the resources necessary for

25. *Herodotus*, I, 181-2 (Rawlinson's translation).

constructing pyramids, certainly not of monumental dimensions, even when their tenure of the throne might have allowed sufficient time. We now know that the kings of the XIth Dynasty at Thebes did not build pyramids, but their successors in the XIIth Dynasty resumed the practice.

It is difficult to believe that Shepseskaf, whose example was followed by Queen Khentkaues, whose position remains uncertain, was not trying to break away from the influence of Heliopolis and its powerful priesthood. Some suggestion of the same motive, or at least of incomplete confidence in the value of the true pyramid, may perhaps be detected in the pyramids of two other kings of the IVth Dynasty, Djedefrē and Nebka. Not only do they resemble the Step Pyramid of Zoser in the location of the burial-chamber at the base of a deep vertical shaft, but the name of one of these pyramids – Djedefrē is a *sehed*-star – and the name of a quarry-gang connected with the building of the other pyramid – Nebka is a star – clearly associate their owners with an astral after-life.

Apart from these apparent aberrations, the changes and developments follow a course which suggests at least the tacit acceptance of a well-established creed. Sceptics there may have been among the royal builders, but the prospect of achieving immortality – even though time has shown that this ambition could not have been realized without the services of the archaeologist – may itself have proved a sufficient inducement to maintain a custom long after confidence in its value had been lost. How little could these kings have imagined what opportunities for speculation they were providing for posterity! Centuries before John Taylor in 1859 had published his theory that the Great Pyramid had been built by a divinely chosen race of non-Egyptian invaders acting directly under God's guidance, Arab writers had associated the pyramids with the Biblical narrative of the Flood, claiming that they had been built as a result of a dream to serve as repositories for all the wisdom and scientific knowledge of the Egyptians which would otherwise have been lost. Julius Honorius (pre-fifth century A.D.) quoted a legend that the pyramids were Joseph's granaries which had been used for storing corn during the years of plenty, a legend which was still current in the Middle Ages and has been preserved in the decoration of a dome in the church of Saint Mark at Venice. Speculation only began to assume a more scientific appearance in 1864 when the Astronomer Royal of Scotland, Charles Piazzi Smyth, propounded his theories regarding the Great Pyramid based on a unit of measurement which he called the pyramid inch (equal to 1.001 inches). His prestige no doubt gave the movement in search of mystery a powerful impetus which, after a century of theory and counter-theory, shows no sign of reaching exhaustion.

MAJOR PYRAMIDS OF THE OLD
AND MIDDLE KINGDOMS

Name of King	Dynasty	Location	Approximate Dimensions of Base	Name of Pyramid
Zoser (Step Pyramid)	III (c. 2686 B.C.)	Saqqara	411 ft E.-W. by 358 ft N.-S.	–
Sekhemkhet	III	Saqqara	395 ft sq.	–
Khaba (?) (Layer Pyramid)	III	Zawiyet el-Aryan	276 ft sq.	–
Seneferu (?)	IV (c. 2600 B.C.)	Meidum	474 ft sq.	–
Seneferu (Bent Pyramid)	IV	Dahshur	620 ft sq.	The Southern Pyramid: 'Seneferu gleams' (?)
Seneferu (Northern stone pyramid)	IV	Dahshur	722 ft sq.	'Seneferu gleams'
Cheops (Great Pyramid)	IV	Giza	756 ft sq.	'Cheops is one belonging to the horizon'
Djedefrē	IV	Abu Roash	328 ft sq.	'Djedefrē is a sehed-star'
Chephren	IV	Giza	708 ft sq.	'Great is Chephren'
Mycerinus	IV	Giza	356 ft sq.	'Mycerinus is divine'
Nebka (?) (Unfinished Pyramid)	IV (?)	Zawiyet el-Aryan	–	–
Userkaf	V (c. 2490 B.C.)	Saqqara	247 ft sq.	'Pure are the places of Userkaf'
Sahurē	V	Abu Sir	258 ft sq.	'The ba of Sahurē gleams'
Neferirkarē	V	Abu Sir	360 ft sq.	'Neferirkarē has become a ba'
Neferefrē	V	Abu Sir (?)	–	'The bas of Neferefrē are divine'
Niuserrē	V	Abu Sir	259 ft sq.	'The places of Niuserrē are enduring'
Isesi	V	Saqqara	258 ft sq.	'Isesi is beautiful'
Unas	V	Saqqara	220 ft sq.	'Beautiful are the places of Unas'
Teti	VI (c. 2345 B.C.)	Saqqara	259 ft sq.	'Lasting are the places of Teti'
Pepi I	VI	Saqqara	259 ft sq.	'Pepi is established and beautiful'
Merenrē	VI	Saqqara	259 ft sq.	'Merenrē gleams and is beautiful'

Name of King	Dynasty	Location	Approximate Dimensions of Base	Name of Pyramid
Pepi II	VI	Saqqara	259 ft sq.	'Pepi is established and alive'
Ibi	VIII (c. 2170 B.C.)	Saqqara	109 ft sq.	–
Ammenemes I	XII (c. 1990 B.C.)	Lisht	296 ft sq.	'Ammenemes is high and beautiful'
Sesostris I	XII	Lisht	352 ft sq.	'The one who is associated with the places of Sesostris'
Ammenemes II	XII	Dahshur	263 ft sq.	'Ammenemes is strong'
Sesostris II	XII	Illahun	351 ft sq.	'Sesostris is strong'
Sesostris III	XII	Dahshur	350 ft sq.	–
Ammenemes III	XII	Dahshur	342 ft sq.	'Ammenemes is beautiful' (?)
Ammenemes III	XII	Hawara	334 ft sq.	'Ammenemes lives'
Queen Sebekneferu (?)	XII	Mazghuna	–	–
Ammenemes IV (?)	XII	Mazghuna	–	–
Khendjer	XIII (c. 1777 B.C.)	Saqqara	170 ft sq	–

BIBLIOGRAPHY

ABBREVIATIONS

A.J.A.	*American Journal of Archaeology.*
A.J.S.L.	*American Journal of Semitic Languages and Literatures.*
Anc. Egypt	*Ancient Egypt.*
Ann. Serv.	*Annales du Service des Antiquités de l'Égypte.*
Bull. F.A.C.	*Bulletin of the Faculty of Arts, University of Egypt, Cairo.*
Bull. Inst. d'Ég.	*Bulletin de l'Institut d'Égypte.*
Bull. Inst. fr.	*Bulletin de l'Institut français d'archéologie orientale.*
Bull. M.F.A.	*Bulletin of the Museum of Fine Arts, Boston.*
Bull. M.M.A.	*Bulletin of the Metropolitan Museum of Art, New York.*
Bull. Soc. fr. d'Ég.	*Bulletin de la Société française d'Égyptologie.*
Chron. d'Ég.	*Chronique d'Égypte.*
C.-R. Ac. Inscr. B.-L.	*Comptes-Rendus de l'Académie des Inscriptions et Belles-Lettres.*
J.E.A.	*Journal of Egyptian Archaeology.*
J.N.E.S.	*Journal of Near Eastern Studies.*
J.R.A.S.	*Journal of the Royal Asiatic Society.*
M.D.A.I.K.	*Mitteilungen des deutschen archäologischen Instituts, Abteilung, Kairo.*
P.R.S.H.S.	*Proceedings of the Royal Society of Historical Studies, Cairo.*
Rev. arch.	*Revue archéologique.*
Rev. d'Ég.	*Revue d'Égyptologie.*
W.Z.K.M.	*Wiener Zeitschrift für die Kunde des Morgenlandes.*
Z.Ä.S.	*Zeitschrift für ägyptische Sprache und Altertumskunde.*

When several works by one author appear they are listed chronologically.

GENERAL

Badawy, A. *A History of Egyptian Architecture*, Vols I–III. Cairo, Berkeley and Los Angeles, 1954–68.

Brinks, J. *Die Entwicklung der königlichen Grabanlagen des Alten Reiches.* (Hildesheimer Ägyptologische Beiträge, No. 10). Hildesheim, 1979.

Edwards, I.E.S. 'Pyramids: Building for Eternity', in Billard, J.B. *Ancient Egypt – Discovering its Splendors*, pp. 72–101. Washington, D.C., 1978.

Helck, W. 'Pyramiden', Pauly-Kroll-Ziegler, *Real-Encyclopädie der classischen Altertums-Wissenschaft*, XXIII, 2, cols. 2167–2282.

Korecký, M. *Objevy pod Pyramidami.* Prague, 1983.

Lauer, J.-P. *Observations sur les pyramides.* Cairo, 1960.

Lauer, J.-P. *Histoire monumentale des pyramides d'Égypte*, Vol. I. Cairo, 1962.

Lauer, J.-P. *Le Mystère des pyramides.* Paris, 1974.

Lauer, J.-P. *Saqqara – The Royal Cemetery of Memphis – Excavations and Discoveries since 1850.* London, 1976.

Lauer, J.-P. 'Architecture', in Leclant, J. *Les pharaons – le temps des pyramides*, pp. 58–113. Paris, 1978.

Maragioglio, V. and Rinaldi, C. A. *L'Architettura delle Piramidi Menfite*, Vols II–VIII. Turin and Rapallo, 1963–77.

Ricke, H. *Bemerkungen zur ägyptischen Baukunst des Alten Reichs*, 2 vols. *(Beiträge zur ägyptischen Bauforschung und Altertumskunde*, Vols 4 and 5). Zurich and Cairo, 1944–50.

Schott, S. *Bemerkungen zum ägyptischen Pyramidenkult. (Beiträge zur ägyptischen Bauforschung und Altertumskunde*, Vol. 5). Cairo, 1950.

Smith, W. S. *The Art and Architecture of Ancient Egypt (The Pelican History of Art).* London, 1958.

Spencer, A. J. *Death in Ancient Egypt.* Harmondsworth, 1982.

Stadelmann, R. 'Pyramiden, A.R.', in *Lexikon der Ägyptologie*, Vol. IV, pp. 1205–63.

Vandier, J. *Manuel d'archéologie égyptienne*, Vols I and II. Paris, 1952–5.

Vyse, H. *Operations carried out on the Pyramids of Gizeh*, 3 vols. London, 1840–42.

INTRODUCTION

Anthes, R. 'Egyptian Theology in the Third Millennium B.C.', in *J.N.E.S.*, XVIII (1959), pp. 169–212.

Breasted, J. H. *The Development of Religion and Thought in Ancient Egypt*. New York, 1912.

Černý, J. *Ancient Egyptian Religion*. London, 1952.

Drioton, É. and Vandier, J. *Les Peuples de l'orient Méditerranéen*, Vol. II, *L'Égypte* (4th edn). Paris, 1962.

Erman, A. *A Handbook of Egyptian Religion* (English translation by A. S. Griffith). London, 1907.

Erman, A. *Die Religion der Ägypter*. Berlin, 1934.

Gardiner, A. H. *The Contendings of Horus and Seth* (*The Chester Beatty Papyri*, No. 1). Oxford, 1931.

Gardiner, A. H. *The Attitude of the Ancient Egyptians to Death and the Dead*. Cambridge, 1935.

Griffiths, J. G. *Plutarch's De Iside et Osiride*. Cardiff, 1970.

Hayes, W. C. *The Scepter of Egypt*, 2 vols. New York and Cambridge, Massachusetts, 1953-9.

Junker, H. *Pyramidenzeit, Das Wesen der altägyptischen Religion*. Zurich, 1949.

Kees, H. *Der Götterglaube in alten Aegypten*. Leipzig, 1941.

Kees, H. *Totenglauben und Jenseits-Vorstellungen der alten Ägypter* (2nd edn). Berlin, 1956.

Sethe, K. *Übersetzung und Kommentar zu den altägyptischen Pyramidentexten*, 4 vols. Glückstadt.

Sethe, K. *Urgeschichte und älteste Religion der Ägypter*. Leipzig, 1930.

Steindorff, G. in Baedeker, K. *Guide to Egypt and the Sudan* (8th edn). Leipzig, 1929.

Vandier, J. *La Religion égyptienne* (2nd edn). Paris, 1949.

CHAPTER ONE

Davies, N. de G. *The Mastaba of Ptahhetep and Akhethetep*, 2 vols. London, 1900-1901.

Duell, P. *The Mastaba of Mereruka*, 2 vols. Chicago, 1938.

Edwards, I. E. S. *The Early Dynastic Period in Egypt*. Cambridge, 1964.

Emery, W. B. *The Tomb of Hemaka*. Cairo, 1938.

Emery, W. B. *The Tomb of Hor-Aha*. Cairo, 1939.

Emery, W. B. *Great Tombs of the First Dynasty*, 3 vols. Cairo and London, 1949-58.

Emery, W. B. *Archaic Egypt*. Harmondsworth, 1962.

Hassan, S. 'Excavations at Saqqara, 1937–38', in *Ann. Serv.*, XXXVIII (1938), pp. 503–21.

Junker, H. *Giza, Grabungen auf dem Friedhof des Alten Reiches bei den Pyramiden von Giza*, 12 vols. Vienna, 1929–55.

Lauer, J.-P. 'Évolution de la tombe royale égyptienne jusqu'à la pyramide à degrés', in *M.D.A.I.K.*, XV (1957), pp. 148–65.

Lauer, J.-P. 'La signification et le rôle des fausses-portes du palais dans les tombeaux du type de Negadeh', in *M.D.A.I.K.*, 37 (1981), pp. 281–7.

Millet, N. B. 'The Reserve Heads of the Old Kingdom', in W.K. Simpson and W.M. Davis *Studies in Ancient Egypt, the Aegean and the Sudan (Essays in honor of Dows Dunham on the occasion of his 90th birthday, June 1, 1980)*, pp. 129–31. Boston, 1981.

Petrie, W.M.F. *The Royal Tombs of the First Dynasty*, Part I. London, 1900.

Petrie, W.M.F. *The Royal Tombs of the Earliest Dynasties*, Part II. London, 1901.

Quibell, J.E. *The Tomb of Hesy*. Cairo, 1913.

Reisner, G.A. *The Development of the Egyptian Tomb down to the Accession of Cheops*. Cambridge, Massachusetts, 1935.

Ricke, H., *see under* General.

Smith, G.E. and Dawson, W.R. *Egyptian Mummies*. London, 1924.

Steindorff, G. *Das Grab des Ti*. Leipzig, 1913.

Vandier, J., *see under* General.

CHAPTER TWO

Altenmüller, H. 'Bemerkungen zur frühen und späten Bauphase des Djoserbezirkes in Saqqara', in *M.D.A.I.K.*, 28 (1972), pp. 1–12.

Barsanti, A. 'Ouverture de la pyramide de Zaouiét el-Aryān', in *Ann. Serv.*, II (1901), pp. 92–4.

Borchardt, L. 'Die Pyramide von Silah', in *Ann. Serv*., I (1900), pp. 211–14.

Dreyer, G. and Kaiser, W. 'Zu den kleinen Stufenpyramiden Ober- und Mittelägyptens', in *M.D.A.I.K.*, 36 (1980), pp. 43–59.

Dreyer, G. and Swelim, N. 'Die kleine Stufenpyramide von Abydos-Süd (Sinki) – Grabungsbericht', in *M.D.A.I.K.*, 38 (1982), pp. 83–91.

Drioton, É. and Lauer, J.-P. *Sakkarah, The Monuments of Zoser*. Cairo, 1939.

Firth, C.M., Quibell, J.E. and Lauer, J.-P. *The Step Pyramid*, 2 vols. Cairo, 1935–6.

Goneim, M.Z. *The Buried Pyramid*. London, 1956.

Goneim, M.Z. *Horus Sekhem-khet, The Unfinished Step Pyramid at Saqqara*, Vol. I. Cairo, 1957.

Helck, W., *see under* General.

Hurry, J.B. *Imhotep*. Oxford, 1926.

Kaiser, W. 'Zu den königlichen Talbezirken der 1. und 2. Dynastie in Abydos und zur Baugeschichte des Djoser-Grabmals', in *M.D.A.I.K.*, 25 (1969), pp. 1-22.

Lauer, J.-P. *La pyramide à degrés*, 3 vols. Cairo, 1936-9.

Lauer, J.-P. *Études complémentaires sur les monuments du roi Zoser à Saqqarah*. Cairo, 1948.

Lauer, J.-P. 'L'apport historique des récentes découvertes du Service des Antiquités de l'Égypte dans la nécropole memphite', in *C.-R. Ac. Inscr. B.-L.*, 1954, pp. 368-79.

Lauer, J.-P. 'À propos de la nouvelle pyramide à degrés de Saqqarah', in *Bull. Inst. d'Ég.*, XXXVI (1955), pp. 357-64.

Lauer, J.-P. 'Reclassement des rois des IIIᵉ et IVᵉ dynasties égyptiennes par l'archéologie monumentale', in *C.-R. Ac. Inscr. B.-L.*, 1962, pp. 290-310.

Lauer, J.-P. 'Les petites pyramides à degrés de la IIIᵉ dynastie', in *Rev. arch.*, 1962, pp. 5-15.

Lauer, J.-P. 'Nouvelles remarques sur les pyramides à degrés de la IIIᵉ dynastie', in *Orientalia*, 35 (1966), pp. 440-48.

Lauer, J.-P. 'Au complexe funéraire de l'Horus Sekhem-khet. Recherches et travaux menés dans la nécropole de Saqqarah au cours de la campagne 1966-67', in *C.-R. Ac. Inscr. B.-L.*, 1967 (Nov.-Dec.), pp. 493ff.

Lauer, J.-P. 'Recherche et découverte du tombeau sud de l'Horus Sekhem-khet dans son complexe funéraire à Saqqarah', in *Rev. d'Ég.*, 20 (1968), pp. 97-107.

Lauer, J.-P. 'Recherche et découverte du tombeau sud de l'Horus Sekhem-khet à Saqqarah', in *Bull. Inst. d'Ég.*, XLVIII and XLIX (1969), pp. 121-31.

Lauer, J.-P. 'Dix campagnes (1960 à 1970) de travaux d'anastylose, de reconstitution et de protection dans l'ensemble du "Heb-sed" au complexe monumental de la pyramide à degrés', in *Ann. Serv.*, LXI (1973), pp. 125-44.

Lauer, J.-P. *Saqqara, see under* General.

Maragioglio, V. and Rinaldi, C.A. Part II, *see under* General.

Petrie, W.M.F. and Quibell, J.E. *Nagada and Ballas*. London, 1896.

Stiénon, J. 'El-Kôlah, Mission de la Fondation Égyptologique Reine Élisabeth, 1949', in *Chron. d'Ég.*, 49 (1950), pp. 43-5.

Swelim, N.M.A. *Some Problems on the History of the Third Dynasty*. Alexandria, 1983.

Weill, R. 'Fouilles à Tounah et à Zaouiét el-Maietin', in *C.-R. Ac. Inscr. B.-L.*, 1912, pp. 484–90.

CHAPTER THREE

Abd es-Salam Mohammed Hussein. 'Pyramids' Study Project', in *P.R.S.H.S.*, I (1951), pp. 27–40.

Barsanti, A. 'Fouilles de Zaouiét el-Aryān (1904–6)', in *Ann. Serv.*, VIII (1907), pp. 201–10.

Batrawi, A. 'A Small Mummy from the Pyramid at Dahshur', in *Ann. Serv.*, XLVIII (1948), pp. 585–90.

Borchardt, L. 'Ein Königserlass aus Dahschur', in *Z.Ä.S.*, XLII (1905), pp. 1–11.

Borchardt, L. *Die Entstehung der Pyramide an der Baugeschichte der Pyramide bei Mejdum nachgewiesen.* Berlin, 1928.

Dunham, Dows. *Zawiyet el-Aryan. The Cemeteries Adjacent to the Layer Pyramid.* Boston, 1978.

Edwards, I.E.S. 'The Collapse of the Meidum Pyramid', in *J.E.A.*, 60 (1974), pp. 251–2.

Fakhry, A. 'The Southern Pyramid of Sneferu', in *Ann. Serv.*, LI (1951), pp. 509–22.

Fakhry, A. 'The Excavation of Sneferu's Monuments at Dahshur, Second Preliminary Report', in *Ann. Serv.*, LII (1954), pp. 563–94.

Fakhry, A. *The Monuments of Sneferu at Dahshur*, Vol. I, *The Bent Pyramid*, Vol. II, *The Valley Temple.* Cairo, 1959–61.

Goedicke, H. 'The Pharaoh Ny-Swth', in *Z.Ä.S.*, 81 (1956), pp. 18–24.

Griffith, F. Ll. 'The Inscriptions of the Pyramid of Medum', in Petrie, W.M.F. *Medum.* London, 1892.

Helck, W., *see under* General.

Jéquier, G. *Douze ans de fouilles dans la nécropole memphite.* Neuchâtel, 1940.

Lauer, J.-P. 'Sur la pyramide de Meïdoum et les deux pyramides du roi Snefrou à Dahchour', in *Orientalia*, 36 (1967), pp. 239–54.

Lauer, J.-P. 'À propos du prétendu désastre de la pyramide de Meïdoum', in *Chron. d'Ég.*, No. 101 (1976), pp. 72–89.

Maragioglio, V. and Rinaldi, C.A. Parts III and VI, *see under* General.

Maspero, G. and Barsanti, A. 'Fouilles de Zaouiét el-Aryān (1904–5)', in *Ann. Serv.*, VII (1906), pp. 257–86.

Maystre, Ch. 'Les dates des pyramides de Snefrou', in *Bull. Inst. fr.*, XXXV (1935), pp. 89–98.

Mustapha, H. 'The Surveying of the Bent Pyramid at Dahshur', in *Ann. Serv.*, LII (1954), pp. 595–601.

Petrie, W.M.F. *The Pyramids and Temples of Gizeh*. London, 1883.

Petrie, W.M.F. *A Season in Egypt, 1887*. London, 1888.

Petrie, W.M.F. *Medum*. London, 1892.

Petrie, W.M.F., Mackay, E., and Wainwright, G. A. *Meydum and Memphis (III)*. London, 1910.

Reisner, G.A. and Fisher, C.S. 'The Work of the Harvard University Museum', in *Bull. M.F.A.*, IX (1911), pp. 54–9.

Reisner, G.A., *see under* Chapter I.

Ricke, H. 'Baugeschichtlicher Vorbericht über die Kultanlagen der südlichen Pyramide des Snofru in Dahschur', in *Ann. Serv.*, LII (1954), pp. 603–23.

Ricke, H., *see under* General.

Rowe, A. 'Excavations of the Eckley B. Coxe, Jr. Expedition at Meydum, Egypt, 1929–30', in the *Museum Journal*. Pennsylvania, March 1931.

Smith, W.S. 'Inscriptional Evidence for the History of the Fourth Dynasty', in *J.N.E.S.*, XI (1952), pp. 113–28.

Stadelmann, R. 'Snofru und die Pyramiden von Meidum und Dahschur', in *M.D.A.I.K.*, 36 (1980), pp. 437–49.

Vandier, J., *see under* General.

Varille, A. *À propos des pyramides de Sneferu*. Cairo, 1947.

Vyse, H., *see under* General.

Wildung, D. 'Zur Deutung der Pyramide von Medûm', in *Rev. d'Ég.*, 21 (1969), pp. 135–45.

CHAPTER FOUR

Abubakr, Abdel Moneim and Ahmed Youssef Mustafa, 'The Funerary Boat of Khufu', in *Festschrift Ricke*, pp. 1–16. Wiesbaden, 1971.

Anthes, R. 'Was veranlasste Chefren zum Bau des Tempels vor der Sphinx', in *Festschrift Ricke*, pp. 47–58. Wiesbaden, 1971.

Badawi, A. 'The Stellar Destiny of Pharaoh and the So-called Air-shafts of Cheops' Pyramid', in *Mitt. deutschen Akad. Berlin*, Band X, Heft 2/3 (1964), pp. 189–206.

Baikie, J. 'The Sphinx', in J.H. Hastings, *Encyclopaedia of Religion and Ethics*, Vol. XI, pp. 767–8. Edinburgh, 1920.

Baly, T.J.C. 'Notes on the Ritual of Opening the Mouth', in *J.E.A.*, XVI (1930), pp. 173–86.

Bergmann, E. v. 'Die Sphinx', in Z.Ä.S., XVIII (1880), pp. 50-51.

Blackman, A.M. 'The Rite of Opening the Mouth in Ancient Egypt and Babylonia', in J.E.A., X (1924), pp. 47-59.

Borchardt, L. and Sethe, K. 'Zur Geschichte der Pyramiden', in Z.Ä.S., 30 (1892), pp. 83-106.

Borchardt, L. Gegen die Zahlenmystik an der grossen Pyramide bei Gise. Berlin, 1922.

Borchardt, L. Längen und Richtungen der vier Grundkanten der grossen Pyramide bei Gise. Berlin, 1926.

Borchardt, L. Einiges zur dritten Bauperiode der grossen Pyramide bei Gise. Berlin, 1932.

Brinks, J. 'Die Stufenhöhen der Cheops-Pyramide - System oder Zufall?', in Göttinger Miszellen, 48 (1981), pp. 17-23.

Černý, J. 'A Note on the Recently Discovered Boat of Cheops', in J.E.A., 41 (1955), pp. 75-9.

Černý, J. 'Name of the King of the Unfinished Pyramid at Zawiyet el-Aryan', in M.D.A.I.K., 16 (1958), pp. 25-9.

Clarke, S. and Engelbach, R. Ancient Egyptian Masonry. Oxford, 1930.

Cole, J.H. The Determination of the Exact Size and Orientation of the Great Pyramid of Giza (Survey of Egypt, Paper No. 39). Cairo, 1925.

Derry, D.E. 'Mummification', in Ann. Serv., XLI (1942), pp. 240-65.

Drioton, É. review of Grdseloff, B. 'Das Reinigungszelt', in Ann. Serv., XL (1940), pp. 1007-14.

Edwards, I.E.S. 'The Air-Channels of Chephren's Pyramid', in W.K. Simpson and W.M. Davis, Studies in Ancient Egypt, the Aegean and the Sudan (Essays in honor of Dows Dunham on the occasion of his 90th birthday, June 1, 1980), pp. 55-7. Boston, 1981.

Firchow, O. 'Königsschiff und Sonnenbarke', in W.Z.K.M., 54 (1957), pp. 34-42.

Goyon, G. 'Le mécanisme de fermeture de la pyramide de Khéops', in Rev. arch., 2 (1963), pp. 1-24.

Goyon, G. 'La chaussée monumentale et le temple de la vallée de la pyramide de Khéops', in Bull. Inst. fr., LXVII (1969), pp. 49-69.

Goyon, G. 'Quelques observations effectuées autour de la pyramide de Khéops', in Bull Inst. fr., LXVII (1969), pp. 71-86.

Grdseloff, B. Das ägyptische Reinigungszelt. Cairo, 1941.

Hassan, S. Excavations at Giza, 10 vols. Oxford and Cairo, 1932-60.

Hassan, S. The Sphinx. Its History in the Light of Recent Excavations. Cairo, 1949.

Helck, W. 'Zur Entstehung des Westfriedhofs an der Cheops-Pyramide', in Z.Ä.S., 81 (1956), pp. 62–5.

Helck, W., see under General.

Hölscher, U. Das Grabdenkmal des Königs Chephren. Leipzig, 1912.

Jenkins, Nancy. The Boat Beneath the Pyramid. London, 1980.

Jéquier, G. Manuel d'archéologie égyptienne. Paris, 1924.

Jéquier, G. Le Mastabat Faraoun. Cairo, 1928.

Junker, H. 'Von der ägyptischen Baukunst des Alten Reiches', in Z.Ä.S., 63 (1928), pp. 1–14.

Junker, H., see under Chapter 1.

Lauer, J.-P. 'Le temple funéraire de Khéops à la grande pyramide de Guizeh', in Ann. Serv., XLVI (1947), pp. 245–59.

Lauer, J.-P. 'Note complémentaire sur le temple funéraire de Khéops', in Ann. Serv., XLIX (1949), pp. 111–23.

Lauer, J.-P. 'Récentes découvertes dans la nécropole memphite', in C.-R. Ac. Inscr. B.-L., October 1954, pp. 368–79.

Lauer, J.-P. 'Sur l'âge et l'attribution possible de l'excavation monumentale de Zaouiêt el-Aryân', in Rev. d'Ég., 14 (1962), pp. 21–36.

Lauer, J.-P. 'Raison première et utilisation pratique de la "Grande Galerie" dans la pyramide de Khéops', in Festschrift Ricke, pp. 133–41. Wiesbaden, 1971.

Maragioglio, V. and Rinaldi, C.A. Parts IV, V and VI, see under General.

Mohammad Zaki Nour, Mohammad Salah Osman, Zaky Iskander and Ahmed Youssof Moustafa. The Cheops Boats, Part I. Cairo, 1960.

Perring, J.S. The Pyramids of Gizeh, 3 parts. London, 1839–42.

Petrie, W.M.F. The Pyramids and Temples of Gizeh. London, 1883.

Rawlinson, G. History of Herodotus (Everyman's Library, edited by E.H. Blakeney). London, 1912.

Reisner, G.A. 'The Tomb of Meresankh, a great-granddaughter of Queen Hetep-heres I and Sneferuw', in Bull. M.F.A., XXV (1927), pp. 64–79.

Reisner, G.A. Mycerinus, The Temples of the Third Pyramid at Giza. Cambridge, Massachusetts, 1931.

Reisner, G.A. A History of the Giza Necropolis, Vol. I. Cambridge, Massachusetts, 1942.

Reisner, G.A. and Smith, W.S. A History of the Giza Necropolis, Vol. II, The Tomb of Hetep-heres, the Mother of Cheops. Cambridge, Massachusetts, 1955.

Ricke, H. Der Harmachistempel des Chefren in Giseh (Beiträge zur ägyptischen Bauforschung und Altertumskunde, Vol. 10). Wiesbaden, 1970.

Rowe, A. 'Some Facts Concerning the Great Pyramids of el-Gîza and their

Royal Constructors', in *Bull. of the John Rylands Library*, 44, No. 1 (1961), pp. 100–118.

Smith, W. Stevenson. 'Old Kingdom Sculpture', in *A.J.A.*, XLV (1941), pp. 514–28.

Smith, W. Stevenson. *A History of Egyptian Sculpture and Painting in the Old Kingdom*. Oxford, 1946.

Thomas, E. 'Air Channels in the Great Pyramid', in *J.E.A.*, 39 (1953), p. 113.

Thomas, E. 'Solar Barks Prow to Prow', in *J.E.A.*, 42 (1956), pp. 65–79 and pp. 117–18.

Trimble, Virginia. 'Astronomical Investigation Concerning the So-called Air Shafts of Cheops' Pyramid', in *Mitt. deutschen Akad. Berlin*, 10 (1964), pp. 183–7.

Vyse, H., *see under* General.

Waddell, W.G. 'An Account of Egypt by Diodorus Siculus', in *Bull. F.A.C.*, I (1933), Parts 1 and 2.

Zivie, C.M. *Giza au deuxième millénaire*. Cairo, 1976.

CHAPTER FIVE

Allen, T.G. *Occurrences of Pyramid Texts with Cross Indexes of these and other Mortuary Texts*. Chicago, 1950.

Arnold, D. 'Rituale und Pyramidentempel', in *M.D.A.I.K.*, 33 (1977), pp. 1–14.

Baines, J.R. 'The Destruction of the Pyramid Temple of Sahure', in *Göttinger Miszellen*, 4 (1973), pp. 9–14.

Berlandini, J. 'La pyramide "ruinée" de Sakkara-Nord et Menkaouhor', in *Bull. Soc. fr. d'Ég.*, 83 (October, 1978), pp. 24–34.

Berlandini, J. 'La pyramide "ruinée" de Sakkara-Nord et le roi Ikaouhor-Menkaouhor', in *Rev. d'Ég.* 31 (1979), pp. 3–28.

Bissing, F.W. von. *Das Re-Heiligtum des Königs Ne-woser-Re*, 3 vols. Berlin and Leipzig, 1905–28.

Borchardt, L. *Das Grabdenkmal des Königs Ne-user-Re*. Leipzig, 1907.

Borchardt, L. *Das Grabdenkmal des Königs Nefer-ir-ke-Re*. Leipzig, 1909.

Borchardt, L. *Das Grabdenkmal des Königs Sahu-Re*, 2 vols. Leipzig, 1910–13.

Borchardt, L. *Die Pyramiden, ihre Entstehung und Entwicklung*. Berlin, 1911.

Drioton, É. 'Une Représentation de la famine sur un bas-relief égyptien de la Ve Dynastie', in *Bull. Inst. d'Ég.*, XXV (1942–3), pp. 45–54.

Erman, A. *The Literature of the Egyptians* (translated by A.M. Blackman). London, 1927.

Firth, C.M. and Gunn, B. *The Teti Pyramid Cemeteries*, 2 vols. Cairo, 1926.

Firth, C.M. 'Excavations of the Department of Antiquities at Sakkara (1928–9)', in *Ann. Serv.*, XXIX (1929), pp. 64–70.

Goyon, G. 'Les navires de transport de la chaussée monumentale d'Ounas', in *Bull. Inst. fr.*, LXIX (1971), pp. 11–41.

Hassan, S. 'The Causeway of Wnis at Sakkara', in *Z.Ä.S.*, 80 (1955), pp. 136–44.

Jéquier, G. *La pyramide d'Oudjebten*. Cairo, 1928.

Jéquier, G. *Les pyramides des reines Neit et Apouit*. Cairo, 1933.

Jéquier, G. *La pyramide d'Aba*. Cairo, 1935.

Jéquier, G. *Le monument funéraire de Pepi II*, 3 vols. Cairo, 1936–41.

Kaiser, W. 'Zu den Sonnenheiligtümern der 5. Dynastie', in *M.D.A.I.K.*, 14 (1956), pp. 69–81.

Labrousse, A., Lauer, J.-P. and Leclant, J. *Le temple haut du complexe funéraire du roi Ounas*. Cairo, 1977.

Lacau, P. 'Suppressions et modifications de signes dans les textes funéraires', in *Z.Ä.S.*, 51 (1914), pp. 1–64.

Lacau, P. 'Suppressions des noms divins dans les textes de la chambre funéraire', in *Ann. Serv.*, XXVI (1926), pp. 69–81.

Lauer, J.-P. 'Le temple haut de la pyramide du roi Ouserkaf à Saqqarah', in *Ann. Serv.*, LIII (1955), pp. 119–33.

Lauer, J.-P. 'Les statues de prisonniers du complexe funéraire de Pépi Ier', in *Bull. Inst. d'Ég.*, 51 (1971 ?), pp. 37–45.

Lauer, J.-P. and Leclant, J. *Le temple haut du complexe funéraire du roi Téti*. Cairo, 1972.

Leclant, J. 'La "famille libyenne" au temple haut de Pépi Ier', in J. Vercoutter, *Livre du centenaire*, 49–64. Cairo, 1980.

Maragioglio, V. and Rinaldi, C. Parts VI and VIII, *see under* General.

Martin, K. *Ein Garantsymbol des Lebens. Untersuchungen zu Ursprung und Geschichte des altägyptischen Obelisken bis zum Ende des Neuen Reiches (Hildesheimer Ägyptologische Beiträge, No. 3)*. Hildesheim, 1977.

Mercer, S.A.B. *The Pyramid Texts in Translation and Commentary*, 4 vols. New York, 1952.

Raslan, M.A.M. 'The Causeway of Ounas Pyramid', in *Ann. Serv.*, LXI (1973), pp. 151–69.

Ricke, H. 'Erster Grabungsbericht über das Sonnenheiligtum des Königs Userkaf bei Abusir', in *Ann. Serv.*, LIV (1956–7), pp. 75–82.

Ricke, H. 'Zweiter Grabungsbericht über das Sonnenheiligtum des Königs Userkaf bei Abusir', in *Ann. Serv.*, LIV (1956-7), pp. 305-16.

Ricke, H. 'Dritter Grabungsbericht über das Sonnenheiligtum des Königs Userkaf bei Abusir', in *Ann. Serv.*, LV (1958), pp. 73-7.

Ricke, H. 'Das Sonnenheiligtum des Königs Userkaf', in *Beiträge zur ägyptischen Bauforschung und Altertumskunde*, Heft 8, Band 11. Wiesbaden, 1969.

Schott, S., *see under* General.

Sethe, K. *Die altägyptischen Pyramidentexte*, 3 vols. Leipzig, 1908-22.

Sethe, K. *Übersetzung und Kommentar zu den altägyptischen Pyramidentexten*, 4 vols. Glückstadt.

Speleers, L. *Traduction, index et vocabulaire des textes des pyramides égyptiennes.* Brussels, 1935.

Verner, M. 'Excavations at Abusir – Season 1976 – Preliminary Report – The Pyramid Complex of the Queen Khentkaues ("A")', in *Z.Ä.S.*, 105 (1978), pp. 155-7.

Verner, M. 'Excavations at Abusir – Season 1978-1979 – Preliminary Report – The Pyramid of Queen Khentkaues ("A")', in *Z.Ä.S.*, 107 (1980), pp. 158-64.

Verner, M. 'Die Königsmutter Chentkaus von Abusir und einige Bemerkungen zur Geschichte der 5. Dynastie', in *Studien zur altägyptischen Kultur*, 8 (1980), pp. 243-68.

Verner, M. 'Les recherches archéologiques de l'Institut Tchécoslovaque d'Egyptologie à Abousir', in *Bull. Soc. Fr. d'Eg.*, 91 (July 1981), pp. 6-21.

Verner, M. 'Eine zweite unvollendete Pyramide in Abusir', in *Z.Ä.S.*, 109 (1982), pp. 75-8.

Winter, E. 'Zur Deutung der Sonnenheiligtümer der 5. Dynastie', in *W.Z.K.M.*, 54 (1957), pp. 222-33.

CHAPTER SIX

Arnold, D. 'Bemerkungen zu den Königsgräbern der frühen 11. Dynastie von El-Târif', in *M.D.A.I.K.*, 23 (1968), pp. 26-37.

Arnold, D. and Settgast, J. 'Der Aufweg des Königs *Mnṯw-ḥtp Nb-ḥpt-Rʿ*', in *Ann. Serv.*, LXI (1973), p. 182.

Arnold, D. *Der Tempel des Königs Mentuhotep von Deir el-Bahari*, 3 vols. Mainz am Rhein, 1974-81.

Arnold, D. *Gräber des alten und mittleren Reiches in El-Tarif*. Mainz am Rhein, 1976.

Arnold, D. 'Vom Pyramidenbezirk zum "Haus für Millionen Jahre"', in *M.D.A.I.K.*, 34 (1978), pp. 1-8.

Arnold, D., 'Das Labyrinth und seine Vorbilder', in *M.D.A.I.K.*, 35 (1979), pp. 1-9.

Arnold, D. *The Temple of Mentuhotep at Deir el-Bahari*. New York, 1979.

Arnold, D. 'Pyramiden, MR und später', in *Lexikon der Ägyptologie*, Vol. IV, cols. 1263 72. Wiesbaden, 1982.

Ayrton, E.R., Currelly, C.T. and Weigall, A.E.P. *Abydos III*. London, 1904.

Brunton, G. *Lahun I, The Treasure*. London, 1920.

Carter, H. 'Report on the tomb of Menthuhotep I', in *Ann. Serv.*, II (1901), pp. 201-5.

Farag, N. and Iskander, Z. *The Discovery of Neferwptah*. Cairo, 1971.

Firchow, O. *Studien zu den Pyramidenlagen der 12. Dynastie*. Göttingen, 1942.

Gardiner, A.H. and Bell, H.I. 'The Name of Lake Moeris', in *J.E.A.*, 29 (1943), pp. 37-50.

Gautier, J.E. and Jéquier, G. *Fouilles de Licht*. Cairo, 1902.

Goedicke, H. *Re-used Blocks from the Pyramid of Amenemhet I at Lisht*. New York, 1971.

Gunn, B. 'The Name of the Pyramid-Town of Sesostris II', in *J.E.A.*, 31 (1945), pp. 106-7.

Hayes, W.C. 'The Entrance Chapel of the Pyramid of Sen-Wosret I', in *Bull. M.M.A.*, XXIX (1934), Section 2, pp. 9-26.

Johnson, Sally B. 'Two Wooden Statues from Lisht: Do they represent Sesostris I?', in *Journal of the American Research Center in Egypt*, XVII (1980), pp. 11-20.

Lansing, A. 'The Museum's Excavations at Lisht', in *Bull. M.M.A.*, XV (1920), pp. 3-11; XXI (1926), Section 2, pp. 33-40; XXIX (1934), Section 2, pp. 4-9.

Lloyd, A.B. 'The Egyptian Labyrinth', in *J.E.A.*, 56 (1970), pp. 81-100.

Lythgoe, A.M. 'Excavations at the South Pyramid of Lisht in 1914', in *Anc. Egypt*, 1915, pp. 145-53.

Lythgoe, A.M. 'The Treasure of Lahun', in *Bull. M.M.A.*, December 1919, Part 2.

Mace, A.C. 'Excavations at Lisht', in *Bull. M.M.A.*, November 1921, Part 2, pp. 5-19 and December 1922, Part 2, pp. 4-18.

Morgan, J. de. *Fouilles à Dahchour*, 2 vols. Vienna, 1895-1903.

Naville, E. and Hall, H.R. *The XIth Dynasty Temple of Deir el-Bahari*, 3 vols. London, 1907-13.

Newberry, P.E. 'The Co-regencies of Ammenemes III, IV and Sebeknofru', in *J.E.A.*, 29 (1943), pp. 74-5.

Petrie, W.M.F. *Hawara, Biahmu and Arsinoe.* London, 1889.

Petrie, W.M.F. *Illahun, Kahun and Gurob.* London, 1890.

Petrie, W.M.F. *Kahun, Gurob and Hawara.* London, 1890.

Petrie, W.M.F., Wainwright, G.A. and Mackay, E. *The Labyrinth, Gerzeh and Mazghuneh.* London, 1912.

Petrie, W.M.F., Brunton, G. and Murray, M.A. *Lahun II.* London, 1923.

Randall-MacIver, D. and Mace, A.C. *El-Amrah and Abydos.* London, 1902.

Raphael, M. 'Nouveau nom d'une pyramide d'un Amenemhēt', in *Ann. Serv.*, XXXVII (1937), pp. 79–80.

Vandier, J., *see under* General.

Winlock, H.E. 'The Theban Necropolis in the Middle Kingdom', in *A.J.S.L.*, XXXII (1915), pp. 1–37.

Winlock, H.E. *The Treasure of El-Lahun.* New York, 1934.

Winlock, H.E. 'Neb-ḥepet-Rē' Mentu-ḥotpe of the Eleventh Dynasty', in *J.E.A.*, 26 (1940), pp. 116–19.

CHAPTER SEVEN

Ayrton, E.R., Currelly, C.T. and Weigall, A.E.P. *Abydos III.* London, 1904.

Bruyère, B. *Fouilles de l'institut français du Caire*, Vol. VIII. Cairo, 1933.

Davies, Nina M. 'Some Representations of Tombs from the Theban Necropolis', in *J.E.A.*, 24 (1938), pp. 25–40.

Dunham, D. *The Royal Cemeteries of Kush*, Vol. I, *El-Kurru*; Vol. II, *Nuri*; Vol. III, *Decorated Chapels of the Meroitic Pyramids at Meroe and Barkal*; Vol. IV, *Royal Tombs at Meroe and Barkal.* Boston, Massachusetts, 1950–57.

Eigner, D. *Die monumentalen Grabbauten der Spätzeit in der Thebanischen Nekropole.* Vienna, 1984.

Garnot, J.S.F. 'Les fouilles de la nécropole de Soleb (1957–8)', in *Bull. Inst. fr.*, LVIII (1959), pp. 165–73.

Gunn, B. and Gardiner, A.H. 'The Expulsion of the Hyksos', in *J.E.A.*, V (1918), pp. 35–56.

Hintze, F. 'Die Grössen der Meroitischen Pyramiden', in W.K. Simpson and W.M. Davis, *Studies in Ancient Egypt, the Aegean, and the Sudan (Essays in honor of Dows Dunham on the occasion of his 90th birthday, June 1, 1980)*, pp. 91–8. Boston, 1981.

Jéquier, G. *Deux pyramides du Moyen Empire.* Cairo, 1938.

Leclant, J. 'La nécropole de l'ouest à Sedeinga en Nubie Soudanaise', in *C.-R. Ae. Inscr. B.-L.*, *Avril-Juin*, 1970, pp. 246–76.

Maragioglio, V. and Rinaldi, C.A. 'Note sulla piramide di Ameny 'Aamu', in *Orientalia* 37 (1968), pp. 325–38.

Rammant-Peeters, A. *Les pyramidions égyptiens du nouvel empire (Orientalia Lovaniensia Analecta XI)*. Leuven, 1983.

Randall-MacIver, D. and Mace, A.C. *El-Amrah and Abydos*. London, 1902.

Reisner, G.A. 'Excavations at Napata, the Capital of Ethiopia', in *Bull. M.F.A.*, XV (1917), No. 89, pp. 25–34.

Reisner, G.A. 'Known and Unknown Kings of Ethiopia', in *Bull. M.F.A.*, XVI (1918), No. 97, pp. 67–81.

Reisner, G.A. 'The Royal Family of Ethiopia', in *Bull. M.F.A.*, XXI (1923), No. 124, pp. 12–27.

Vandier, J. *La tombe de Nefer-Abou*. Cairo, 1935.

Vandier, J., *see under* General.

Winlock, H.E. 'The Tombs of the Kings of the Seventeenth Dynasty at Thebes', in *J.E.A.*, X (1924), pp. 217–77.

Winlock, H.E. *Excavations at Deir el-Bahri, 1911–1931*. New York, 1942.

Winlock, H.E. 'The Eleventh Egyptian Dynasty', in *J.N.E.S.*, Vol. 2, No. 4 (1943), pp. 249–83.

Winlock, H.E. *The Rise and Fall of the Middle Kingdom in Thebes*. New York, 1947.

CHAPTER EIGHT

Ali Hassan. 'Waren die Aussenseiten der Pyramiden in Giza farbig?', in *M.D.A.I.K.*, 28 (1972), pp. 153–5.

Antoniadi, E.M. *L'Astronomie égyptienne depuis les temps les plus reculés jusqu'à la fin de l'époque alexandrine*. Paris, 1934.

Arnold, D. 'Überlegungen zum Problem des Pyramidenbaues', in *M.D.A.I.K.*, Vol. 37 (1981), pp. 15–28.

Badawy, A. 'The Periodic System of Building a Pyramid', in *J.E.A.*, 63 (1977), pp. 52–8.

Bennett, J. 'Pyramid Names', in *J.E.A.*, 52 (1966), pp. 174–6.

Borchardt, L. 'Ein altägyptisches astronomisches Instrument', in *Z.Ä.S.*, 37 (1899), pp. 10–17.

Breasted, J.H., *see under* Introduction.

Clarke, S. and Engelbach, R., *see under* Chapter IV.

Cole, J.H., *see under* Chapter IV.

Dunham, D. 'Building an Egyptian Pyramid', in *Archaeology*, 9 (1956), No. 3, pp. 159–65.

Faulkner, R.O. 'The King and the Star-Religion in the Pyramid Texts', in *J.N.E.S.*, XXV (1966), pp. 153–61.

Goyon, G. 'Quelques observations effectuées autour de la pyramide de Khéops', in *Bull. Inst. fr.*, LXVII (1969), pp. 71–86.

Goyon, G. 'Nouvelles observations relatives à l'orientation de la pyramide de Khéops', in *Rev. d'Ég.*, 22 (1970), pp. 85–98.

Goyon, G. 'Les ports des pyramides et le grand canal de Memphis', in *Rev. d'Ég.*, 23 (1971), pp. 137–53.

Goyon, G. *Le secret des bâtisseurs des grandes pyramides 'Khéops'*. Paris, 1977.

Gunn, B. review of Peet, T.E. 'The Rhind Mathematical Papyrus', in *J.E.A.*, XII (1926), pp. 123–37.

Hinkel, F.W. 'Erstmals Bauplan einer Pyramide gefunden', in *Spectrum*, 1979, Heft 6, pp. 30–32.

Hinkel, F.W. 'Pyramide oder Pyramidenstumpf? Ein Beitrag zu Fragen der Plannung, konstructiven Baudurichführung und Architektur der Pyramiden von Meroe (Teil A)', in *Z.Ä.S.*, 108 (1981), pp. 105–23.

Kuhlmann, K.P. 'Die Pyramide als König? Verkannte elliptische Schreibweisen von Pyramidennamen des Alten Reiches', in *Ann. Serv.*, LXVIII (1932), pp. 223–35.

Lauer, J.-P. 'Les grandes pyramides étaient-elles peintes?', in *Bull. Inst. d'Ég.*, XXXV (1953), pp. 377–96.

Lauer, J.-P. 'Comment furent construites les pyramides', in *Historia*, 86 (1954), pp. 57–66.

Lauer, J.-P. 'Sur le choix de l'angle de pente dans les pyramides d'Égypte', in *Bull. Inst. d'Ég.*, XXXVII (1956), pp. 57–66.

Lauer, J.-P. 'À propos de l'orientation des grandes pyramides', in *Bull. Inst. d'Ég.*, 1960, pp. 7–15.

Lauer, J.-P., *see under* General.

Lucas, A. 'Were the Giza Pyramids Painted?', in *Antiquity*, XII (1938), pp. 26–30.

Lucas, A. *Ancient Egyptian Materials and Industries*. 4th edition revised by J.R. Harris. London, 1962.

Mace, A.C. 'Excavations at the North Pyramid of Lisht', in *Bull. M.M.A.*, IX (1914), p. 220.

Martin, G.T. 'The Tomb of Tia and Tia: Preliminary Report on the Saqqara Excavations, 1982', in *J.E.A.*, 69 (1983), pp. 25–9.

Maspero, G. 'Note sur le pyramidion d'Amenemhaît III à Dahchour', in *Ann. Serv.*, III (1902), pp. 206–8.

Neugebauer, O. 'On the Orientation of Pyramids', in *Centaurus*, 24 (1980), pp. 1–3.

Petrie, W.M.F. *The Pyramids and Temples of Gizeh*. London, 1883.

Petrie, W.M.F. 'The Building of a Pyramid', in *Anc. Egypt*, 1930, Part II, pp. 33–9.

Pochan, A. 'Observations relatives au revêtement des deux grandes pyramides de Giza', in *Bull. Inst. d'Ég.*, XVI (1934), pp. 214–20.

Rawlinson, G., *see under* Chapter IV.

Robins, G. and Shute, C.C.D. 'Determining the Slope of Pyramids', in *Göttinger Miszellen*, 57 (1982), pp. 49–54.

Rowe, A., *see under* Chapter IV.

Scharff, A. *Das Grab als Wohnhaus in der ägyptischen Frühzeit*. Munich, 1947.

Smith, S. 'A Babylonian Fertility Cult', in *J.R.A.S.*, October 1938, pp. 849–75.

Thausing, G. 'Zum Sinn der Pyramiden', in *Anzeiger der phil-hist. Klasse der Österreichischen Akademie der Wissenschaften*, No. 7 (1948), pp. 121–30.

Waddell, W.G. *Herodotus*, Book II. London, 1939.

Wheeler, N.F. 'Pyramids and their Purpose', in *Antiquity*, IX (1935), pp. 172–85.

Žába, Z. *L'orientation astronomique dans l'ancienne Égypte, et la précession de l'axe du monde*. Prague, 1953.

INDEX

Aat, Queen, 213
Abbott Papyrus, 192, 196, 230
Abdel Hafiz, 130
Abdessalam Hussein, 169, 171; *v.*
Bent Pyramid
Abu Gurab, 151
Abu Roash, 2, 241-2; pyramid, 142-
4; *v.* Djedefrē
Abu Sir, 241; *v.* Sahurē, Neferirkarē,
Shepseskarē, Neferefrē, Niuserrē
Abu Sir papyri, 148, 154, 164-5, 167,
275, 280 n.24
Abydos, 10, 11, 13-14, 191-2, 199,
222, 230; early dynastic royal
tombs, 23-4, 27-8, 273;
chamberless pyramid, 66-7; late
pyramidal tombs, 252
Accretion theory, 268-9
After-life, 12-16 *passim*, 20, 272, 275
Aha, mastaba dated to reign, 21
Ahmed Fakhry, 86
Ahmed Yusuf, 113-14
Altenmüller, H., 151
Amanikhabale, pyramid, 256
Amélineau, 27
Amenophis II, temple at Giza, 122;
relief at Karnak, 182-3; tomb, 232
Amenyaamu, 225; *v.* Amenyqemau
Amenyqemau, 225
Ammenemes I, 201-3, 258; pyramid,
202-3
Ammenemes II, pyramid, 207-8
Ammenemes III, 143; pyramid (at
Dahshur), 79, 209-14, 222;
pyramidion, 263; (at Hawara), 217-
20; model of Hawara pyramid,
256
Ammenemes IV, 223
Amosis I, 225, 230
Amun, 234, 236; Karnak temple, 252
Andjeti, 9

Aniba, 232
Ankhes-en-Pepi, Queen, 186
Antiquities Service, *v.* Service des
Antiquités
Anubis, 11, 263; fetish, 205-6
Aramaic papyri, 68
Arnold, D., 183, 195, 196-7, 199-200,
217, 256; explanation of
chamberless pyramids, 68; Dahshur
pyramid of Ammenemes III, 79,
211-14; El-Tarif, 192; Deir el-
Bahri, 193-200; pyramid
construction, 267-8, 271
Ashayet, Queen, 198
Ashurbanipal, 239
Asiatics, 129, 161, 162, 163, 191, 193,
224
Aswan, 4, 38, 122, 148, 191, 232, 248,
249-50, 251
Asyut, 5, 10, 224
Atum, 121, 150, 274
Austrian Academy, excavations at
Giza, 31; *v.* Junker, H.
Austrian Archaeological Institute,
excavations at Thebes, 232
Avaris, 225

Ba, 16
Bab el-Husan, 199-200
Baraize, E., 120, 121
Barsanti, A., 27, 64, 144, 171
Bastet, 5, 123
Bay-en-imy-unut, 245, 246
Belzoni, G., 133
Benben, 6, 276, 280
Bent Pyramid, 77, 130, 276;
construction, 77-82; cracks in
masonry, 77, 79; portcullises, 82;
subsidiary pyramid, 83-4, 88 n.1;
mortuary temple, 84-5; northern
chapel, 85, 203; causeway, 85-6,

A CHOICE OF PENGUINS

☐ *The Complete Penguin Stereo Record and Cassette Guide*
Greenfield, Layton and March £7.95

A new edition, now including information on compact discs. 'One of the few indispensables on the record collector's bookshelf' – *Gramophone*

☐ *Selected Letters of Malcolm Lowry*
Edited by Harvey Breit and Margerie Bonner Lowry £5.95

'Lowry emerges from these letters not only as an extremely interesting man, but also a lovable one' – Philip Toynbee

☐ *The First Day on the Somme*
Martin Middlebrook £3.95

1 July 1916 was the blackest day of slaughter in the history of the British Army. 'The soldiers receive the best service a historian can provide: their story told in their own words' – *Guardian*

☐ *A Better Class of Person* John Osborne £2.50

The playwright's autobiography, 1929–56. 'Splendidly enjoyable' – John Mortimer. 'One of the best, richest and most bitterly truthful autobiographies that I have ever read' – Melvyn Bragg

☐ *The Winning Streak* Goldsmith and Clutterbuck £2.95

Marks & Spencer, Saatchi & Saatchi, United Biscuits, GEC . . . The UK's top companies reveal their formulas for success, in an important and stimulating book that no British manager can afford to ignore.

☐ *The First World War* A. J. P. Taylor £4.95

'He manages in some 200 illustrated pages to say almost everything that is important . . . A special text . . . a remarkable collection of photographs' – *Observer*

A CHOICE OF PENGUINS

A CHOICE OF PENGUINS

☐ *The Diary of Virginia Woolf*
Edited by Quentin Bell and Anne Olivier Bell

'As an account of the intellectual and cultural life of our century, Virginia Woolf's diaries are invaluable; as the record of one bruised and unquiet mind, they are unique' – Peter Ackroyd in the *Sunday Times*

☐ Volume One	£4.50
☐ Volume Two	£4.95
☐ Volume Three	£4.95
☐ Volume Four	£5.50
☐ Volume Five	£5.95

These books should be available at all good bookshops or newsagents, but if you live in the UK or the Republic of Ireland and have difficulty in getting to a bookshop, they can be ordered by post. Please indicate the titles required and fill in the form below.

NAME _____ BLOCK CAPITALS

ADDRESS _____

_____

Enclose a cheque or postal order payable to The Penguin Bookshop to cover the total price of books ordered, plus 50p for postage. Readers in the Republic of Ireland should send £IR equivalent to the sterling prices, plus 67p for postage. Send to: The Penguin Bookshop, 54/56 Bridlesmith Gate, Nottingham, NG1 2GP.

You can also order by phoning (0602) 599295, and quoting your Barclaycard or Access number.

Every effort is made to ensure the accuracy of the price and availability of books at the time of going to press, but it is sometimes necessary to increase prices and in these circumstances retail prices may be shown on the covers of books which may differ from the prices shown in this list or elsewhere. This list is not an offer to supply any book.

This order service is only available to residents in the UK and the Republic of Ireland.